PRAIRIE ALBION

PRAIRIE ALBION

AN ENGLISH SETTLEMENT IN PIONEER ILLINOIS

CHARLES BOEWE

SOUTHERN ILLINOIS UNIVERSITY PRESS

CARBONDALE

First edition

To Edgar L. Dukes,
HIMSELF A PIONEER

PREFACE

THE ENGLISH SETTLEMENT, established in 1817 by Morris Birkbeck and George Flower in the Illinois Territory, was an unusual pioneering adventure that deserves to be better known. Such was the interest in it, and such was the articulate opinion that rapidly accumulated around it, that the whole exciting story can be reconstructed from contemporary printed accounts.

Including book reviews, which were usually lengthy and argumentative, and pamphlets of armchair travelers whose prescience about the prospects of the settlement made observation unnecessary, there appeared in print more than fifty items dealing with the settlement. Public interest was great enough that for a few years, from about 1818 to 1825, any traveler who approached the Wabash River felt he had to mention Birkbeck and Flower's experiment, whether he went to the prairies or not; and in default of other evidence he could always find someone who had been there or who knew someone else who had. English travelers in particular liked to see how their countrymen were faring in Illinois.

Portions of these reports are repetitive, and much contained in them is trivial. Even the writings of the protagonists of the drama —Birkbeck and Flower and a few of their followers—contain material of small interest today. Birkbeck, for instance, in keeping a diary of the trek from the Virginia coast to Illinois Territory interlarded his accounts of people and places with precise notes on the kinds of soils he encountered and the mortality rates of different regions so far as he could ascertain them. Such facts were important to him, since he knew that he might have to backtrack and settle in a more easterly locality. He rightly assumed that they would also interest other pioneers who passed the same way looking for land. All such information has been omitted in the texts here reprinted, however.

Throughout I have kept in mind the interests of the general reader who wishes to relive the drama of pioneering in the first-hand accounts of the participants without fighting his way through the underbrush of controversy or wading through the swamps of triviality. The various reporters were much concerned with prices of land, wages, costs of commodities, and the like. Most of this, too, has been omitted. Birkbeck and Flower, whose adventures began the moment they touched foreign soil, naturally recorded their observations on parts of the United States other than Illinois. While this material has interest in its own right, their claim to fame rests upon the colony they founded, and I have taken them out to the prairies as quickly as possible by drastic excision of their narratives, leaving only those portions that contributed to their understanding of American life and manners and helped to condition their experience once there. Birkbeck and Flower, like the other English travelers, had much to say by way of observation and conjecture about the "American character." I have included some of this, not only because as outsiders these people were acute observers, and saw things the Americans themselves have overlooked, but also because this kind of speculation has again become respectable, and it is worth comparing our impressions with those of an earlier generation. We are still a nation always on the move, as they saw; we are still adept at balancing on the back legs of our chairs; perhaps, as here suggested, we were born in a cabin and have not yet lost all of our cabin ways.

None of the books, pamphlets, and articles from which this story is drawn is so rare as to be difficult of access if one visits a half dozen major research libraries. There seems no need, therefore, to strive for a definitive text. Rather, I have let interest and readability take precedence over the stringent demands of scholarship. I have not hesitated to make silent corrections of obvious typographical errors, to modernize punctuation, or to make spelling consistent. British spelling preferences usually have been let stand, for after all these people were mostly Englishmen. Proper names vary greatly in spelling in the different accounts (the backwoodsman Birk appears as Burk and Burke, for instance—which is not surprising, since he himself was illiterate and probably did not know), and these have been made consistent.

In some instances I have shifted about parts of narratives without giving notice of the change. Most of the accounts, written hastily on the spot and rushed through the press as speedily, never received the care their authors themselves might have appreciated in the interest of good storytelling. Grammatical eccentricities, representing eccentricities of mind perhaps—these I have not tinkered with. Nor have I cluttered the pages with dots to indicate omissions, though I have kept all dates that might be significant to pace the story. Throughout I have provided enough commentary to place each excerpt and, I hope, to relate it to others. For anyone interested, the notes show the original sources where the texts in all their dappled purity can be found.

In the course of assembling these pages I have incurred obligations to a number of people who have generously put their time and knowledge at my disposal. I am particularly grateful to the late Vincent Eaton whose quietly efficient aid in that great mountain of print, the Library of Congress, saved me weeks of labor. I am also indebted to other persons connected with public institutions who, true to their tradition of service, stood ready to answer questions, search out books, and advise on pictures. I would mention especially Miss Margaret A. Flint, of the Illinois State Historical Library; Mrs. Stuart H. Danovitch and Joseph B. Zywicki, of the Chicago Historical Society; and Miss Virginia Daiker, of the Prints and Photographs Division, Library of Congress. I am also grateful to Dr. Kenny Jackson Williams for exploring materials inaccessible at the time to me.

To Professor Robert E. Spiller and members of the special committee of the University of Pennsylvania who awarded me a postdoctoral fellowship for 1956–58, I am indebted for the time and encouragement to begin the work of which this is a partial result. To my teacher, Professor Merle Curti of the University of Wisconsin, I am grateful for being made to see the significance of the frontier phase of the region of which I am myself a native. To Professor Sigmund Skard, director of the Amerikansk Institutt in Norway, I am indebted for many courtesies during the Fulbright year I spent there, where I finished this book. And to my wife, Mary Scurrah Boewe, I am grateful both for counsel and consolation.

C. B.

GRATEFUL ACKNOWLEDGMENT is made to the following copyright owners for permission to reprint material under their control.

Jonathan Cape Limited, for excerpts from *A Pioneer Family* by Gladys Scott Thomson.

The Arthur H. Clark Company, for material from *Personal Narrative of Travels in Virginia*, etc., by Elias Pym Fordham.

The Chicago Historical Society, for passages from *History of the English Settlement in Edwards County*, etc., by George Flower.

The Indiana Historical Society, for selections from "The Diaries of Donald Macdonald, 1824–1826," introduction by Caroline Dale Snedeker, and "Diary of William Owen, 1824–1825," edited by Joel W. Hiatt.

CONTENTS

LIST OF ILLUSTRATIONS
Follows page 160

PRAIRIE ALBION

1

―――――――

"Keep a wagon-track in your eye . . .
and you will find the prairie."

Y OU HAVE ASKED about the English Settlement in Illinois,
the peripatetic feminist Frances Wright said in a letter to an
English friend in 1819. Fanny had not managed to get there yet—
she would visit the settlement first in 1825, and several times afterward—but she promptly found "two American gentlemen" who
had been there and whose report, translated through Miss Wright's
brocaded prose, was exactly what many British and some American readers wanted to hear: here was a bit of the English countryside miraculously transported across the Atlantic and beyond the
Alleghenies and set down in the midst of the raw Illinois frontier.

The village of Albion, the centre of the settlement, contains
at present thirty habitations, in which are found a bricklayer,
a carpenter, a wheelwright, a cooper, and a blacksmith; a well-
supplied shop, a little library, an inn, a chapel, and a post-
office, where the mail regularly arrives twice a week. Being
situated on a ridge, between the greater and little Wabash, it
is, from its elevated position, and from its being some miles
removed from the rivers, peculiarly dry and healthy. The
prairie in which it stands is described as exquisitely beautiful;

lawns of unchanging verdure, spreading over hills and dales, scattered with islands of luxuriant trees, dropped by the hand of nature with a taste that art could not rival—all this spread beneath a sky of glowing and unspotted sapphires. "The most beautiful parks of England," my friend observes, "would afford a most imperfect comparison."

Adlard Welby, a Lincolnshire farmer who actually visited the settlement about this time, joined the Americans in praising the park-like beauty of the natural setting—whatever his later reservations about the people he met there. Approaching the prairie from Vincennes, Indiana, he wrote that

after having traversed several miles of woodland and prairie covered with long grass and brushwood, and having lost our way once or twice, we at length crossed a narrow forest track and rising an eminence entered upon the so much talked-of Boltinghouse Prairie, just as the sun in full front of us was setting majestically, tingeing with his golden rays what appeared to be a widely extended and beautiful park, belted in the distance with woodland over which the eye ranged afar. The ground was finely undulated, and here and there ornamented with interspersed clumps of the white oak and other timber in such forms that our picturesque planters of highest repute might fairly own themselves outdone. The effect was indeed striking, and we halted to enjoy it until the last rays of the beautiful luminary told the necessity of hurrying on to the settlement in search of quarters for the night, indulging by the way sanguine hopes of an English supper and comfort as a matter of course at an English settlement.

Remarkable as the English Settlement was, travelers, who increased in numbers in the twenties, usually felt the need to approach it by giving a geographical summary much as they might if exploring darkest Africa. W. N. Blane, writing in 1823, after the territory had become a state, sets the scene thus:

The Wabash flows through a rich and level country, which is well adapted to cultivation, and in which cotton has of late been raised successfully.

On the Wabash are the towns of Harmonie, Vincennes, and Terre Haute, besides several others, which, having only been lately erected, contain as yet few inhabitants.

This river forms, for a considerable distance, the boundary between Indiana and Illinois. During the spring of the year it is easily navigated by flatboats as far as 450 miles from its junction with the Ohio, and craft drawing only two or three feet water may ascend it as far as Vincennes at almost any season.

It is not till the traveller has crossed the Wabash, and advanced a considerable distance into the state of Illinois, that he can see any of the large "prairies," of which there are many fertile ones on the west bank of the river. These prairies, as their name denotes, are large open tracts of natural meadow, covered with luxuriant and rank grass, and destitute of trees or even shrubs. There are no hills in them, though some have a gently undulating surface.

All of which underscores Adam Hodgson's sensible remark that

of the more recent settlements (even of those less remote than Mr. Birkbeck's) little is known on the coast, and the accounts which you receive from casual visitors are usually as vague and inaccurate as those derived from persons interested are exaggerated and partial. *Opinions* respecting all the settlements, it is easy enough to collect; but *facts*, on which to found opinions entitled to any consideration, it is extremely difficult to obtain.

No doubt opinions far outweigh facts in the accounts which follow; yet even opinions are of interest in re-creating something of the excitement generated by this pioneering venture. They certainly dramatize the hardships overcome both by the settlers and even by the travelers intrepid enough to try to gain firsthand facts concerning the success of the settlement, and these accounts also throw a strong light on the problems encountered by all those who acted out their roles in the epic drama of the peopling of the West.

It is curious that despite the intense interest in the movement of

the frontier westward, the English Settlement in southern Illinois
has been so largely neglected by historians. Lacking the swash-
buckling colors of the hunters' frontier as represented in a Boone
or a Crockett, this was nevertheless the frontier movement that
stuck—the farmers' frontier—and the proprietors of this settlement, Morris Birkbeck and George Flower, successful large-scale
farmers in England, were almost uniquely qualified by their
knowledge of scientific agriculture to make a striking contribution to backwoods America.

ii

BOTH BIRKBECK AND FLOWER, markedly different in temperament,
were men of unusual ability whose influence went far beyond
their own small settlement, beyond the state of Illinois itself, and
reached to some extent the nation at large. "No man, since Columbus, has done so much towards peopling America as Mr. Birkbeck,
whose publications, and the authority of whose name, had effects
truly prodigious," wrote the volatile William Faux, one of the
early visitors to the settlement, and himself a harsh critic of all
Birkbeck and Flower stood for. Nor did this influence extend
merely to England and English-speaking peoples. For example, a
letter by George Flower describing the prairies which was published in the Lowell, Massachusetts, *Courier* in the 1830's was
translated into Norwegian and widely circulated in Norway and
Sweden. The later flood of emigration from those countries was
to trouble Flower for years, as Scandinavians looking for their
uncles somewhere in the Dakota Territory wrote to him in the
innocent belief that it must be in the vicinity of southern Illinois.
    Morris Birkbeck was the son of a Quaker preacher by the same
name who was well known among the Friends both in England
and America. The elder Morris Birkbeck, like so many preaching
Friends, had visited America in the eighteenth century, and had
even purchased land in North Carolina. His son, an only child, was
born in 1764 and grew to manhood in Surrey near Guildford,
where his father had moved after his return from America.
    Well educated for his time and position, the son had Latin at
his disposal and some Greek, and in later years taught himself to
read French. When little more than a boy he became Clerk of the

Friends' Meeting; as his friend Flower remarked, "the duties of
this office made him a ready writer, and a systematic arranger of
documents and papers of every kind." He married Prudence Bush,
who during their ten years of married life bore him four sons and
three daughters. As soon as his financial condition permitted he
took 1,500 acres called Wanborough Farm on a long lease from the
Earl of Onslow. Here, as the happy old expression has it, he acquired a competence. But by 1816, when his father died at the
age of eighty-two, Birkbeck, a widower since 1804, found himself
aged fifty-two, financially well off, but strangely discontented.
With few family ties to keep him in Surrey, a dissenter's discontent with the tithes imposed by the Established Church, and without a voice in his government because he held no land in fee-
simple, he was ready to move elsewhere.

For some years he had known young George Flower, born 1788,
son of a prosperous Hertford brewer, Richard Flower, who had
retired from business and settled on an estate near Hertford
called Marden. In 1814, Birkbeck and George Flower spent three
months traveling in France, inspecting the agricultural regions
especially, where they believed the English innovation of crop
rotation might work wonders in an agricultural economy still devoted to the crop-and-fallow system. And on their return Birkbeck
published his *Notes on a Tour in France*, his first book, a book
widely distributed, which not surprisingly Flower was soon to
find on Thomas Jefferson's shelves at Monticello.

Like-minded about the plight of the English farmer, Birkbeck
and Flower agreed that their best interests lay elsewhere. In
Flower's opinion, the expenses of the recent war with France had
induced an artificial financial state from which the country was
not likely to recover soon. Wages had plummeted, but tenant
farmers were bound to leases executed when prices and wages
were high; now with the poor-rolls growing longer and longer,
farmers already losing money because of depressed prices faced
ruin as they were called upon also to pay increased poor-rates.

Emigration to France was tempting; land was cheap and there
was a ready market. But if the language difference were not
enough of an impediment, "the number and influence of the mili-
tary and the clergy," Flower wrote, "were, to persons of our republican tendencies, decisive against a residence in France as ci-
vilians." Where could they turn? Recalling their decision many
years later, Flower said:

To persons of fastidious political tastes, the United States of North America seemed to be the only country left for emigration. What added much to the character of the United States in the eyes of the people of Europe was the judicious choice of her first ambassadors to the courts of Europe. What must not that nation be that could send such men as Franklin and Jefferson to France, Adams and King to Great Britain! These eminent men were taken as samples of the talent and integrity of Americans, giving to the mass of the Republic a higher standard than it deserved. Men of reading read all that was written about the country. The Declaration of Independence, the Constitutions of the United States and of each state were among their reading. In these the principles of liberty and man's political equality are so distinctly recognized that they really supposed them to exist. They did not reflect that a perfect theory on paper might be very imperfectly rendered in practice.

There were personal ties as well. In France Birkbeck and Flower had visited that staunch friend of America, Lafayette, who gladly supplied letters of introduction to Jefferson. William Cobbett, later to be one of the most bitter opponents of the settlement in Illinois, provided letters of introduction to prominent persons in New York, Cambridge, Philadelphia, and Baltimore. But such aid merely directed Birkbeck and Flower's interest in the general direction of America; the specific place of settlement had to be sought out by personal inspection. Accordingly, it was the younger man Flower who undertook the task of advance scout. While his mind was open to any likely spot—and indeed the decision to come to America at all was not settled—Flower had heard of the attractions of the western prairies, and it was these in particular that he wanted to see, though he was far from sure of their exact location, much less concerned about the Illinois Territory itself.

Having determined to visit America, I sailed from Liverpool in April, 1816, in the ship *Robert Burns*, Capt. Parsons of New York. The experience of the captain can not be doubted, for he had crossed the Atlantic seventy-five times without accident, saving the loss of a yardarm. We arrived in New York fifty days after leaving Liverpool.

My emigration, or rather my journey—for it had not at that time taken the decided form of emigration—was undertaken from mixed motives, among others the disturbed condition of the farming interest, and my predeliction in favor of America and its government.

There were no steamers and clippers in those days. In so long a passage as fifty days, our little cabin-party—only four of us, two Englishmen and two Frenchmen—at first strangers, soon became as a little band of brotherhood. At landing, this new bond was broken. Each individual hastening to his family or friends (for the other three had been in the United States before), the solitary stranger for a moment stands alone. The ocean behind, and a vast continent before him, a sense of solitude is then experienced that has never been before and never will again be felt. "Baggage, sir!" and "What hotel?" restores him to the world and all its busy doings.

From New York I wrote to the late President Jefferson, to whom I had a letter of introduction from his old friend General Lafayette. A kind and courteous reply invited me to Monticello, an invitation I could not at that time accept. At Philadelphia, where I spent about six weeks, I became intimately acquainted with that most kind-hearted of men and active philanthropist, John Vaughan. The business of his life was to relieve the distressed, whether native born or foreign, and to give untiring assistance to the stranger, to aid him in carrying out his plans. To me he opened the institutions of the city, and introduced me to its best society.

It was with him, at one of Dr. Wistar's evening parties, that I made the acquaintance of Mr. Lesueur, the French naturalist. We little thought then how soon we were destined to become neighbors in the distant West. He at Harmonie, on the Great Wabash, a place then but a few months old, and I at Albion, in Illinois, a spot neither discovered nor inhabited.

In the first week of August, 1816, I was mounted on horseback, pursuing my journey westward. The first point of interest was the settlement of Dr. Priestley, on the Susquehanna, now known as Sunbury. A more romantically beautiful situation can scarcely be imagined. At the time he made his settlement, that was the Far West. Far beyond, in the midst of wild forests, at a settlement forming by Dr. Dewese and a Mr. Phillips, an Englishman, I spent an agreeable week in exploring the heavy-wooded district of hemlock and oak that bordered on the Mushanon Creek. From thence I made my way to Pittsburgh, through the wildest and roughest country that I have ever seen on the American continent. I was lost all day in the wood, without road or path of any kind, and a most exciting though solitary day it was to me. I climbed the tallest pines, only to see an endless ocean of tree tops, without sign of human life. Toward night I was relieved by a happy incident. The distant tinkling of a small bell led me to the sight of a solitary black mare. Dismounting, and exercising all my horse knowledge to give her confidence, I at length induced her to come and smell of my hand. Seizing and holding her firmly by the foretop with one hand, with the other I shifted the saddle and bridle from my horse to her. With a light halter (which I always carried round the neck of my riding horse) in one hand, I mounted my estray and gave her the rein; in half an hour she brought me to a small cabin buried in the forest, no other cabin being within ten miles, and no road leading to it. So terminated my first day's experience in backwoods forest life. It was no small job to get out of this wild solitude.

It was noon the next day before I met a man. We greeted each other, we shook hands, we fraternized. Ah! poor man; I should have passed you in a street, or on a road, or, if to notice, only to shun. He was a poor Irishman, with a coat so darned, patched, and tattered as to be quite a curiosity. He was one of a new settlement a few miles off. How I cherished him! No angel's visit could have pleased me so well. He pointed me the course, and, what was more, shewed me into a path. I soon afterward passed the settlement of his poor countrymen. A more forlorn place could never be seen.

Leaving the then town (now city) of Pittsburgh and its smoke, I passed in a northwestern direction, to the almost de-

serted town of Harmonie, built by Rapp and his associates.
The large brick buildings to be found in no other young
American town, now almost uninhabited, looked very deso-
late. Rapp and his Society had removed, to form their new
settlement of Harmonie, on the Great Wabash.

I crossed the state of Ohio diagonally, in a southwest direction, passing through Coshocton and Chillicothe, to Cincinnati. This route led me through the then celebrated Pickaway Plains—so named from the Pickaway Indians, whose
town and chief settlement was placed thereon. A level prairie,
about seven miles long and three broad, bounded by lofty
timber, and covered with verdure, must have presented a
grateful prospect in Indian times. Occupied by the white
man, covered with a heavy crop of ripe corn, disfigured by
zigzag fences, it now gave no inviting appearance. A narrow
road, in some places deep in mud, ran the length of the
plain. The little town of Jefferson (so called) was nothing
more than half-a-dozen log cabins, interspersed with corn
cribs. Not a garden, nor a decent house, nor a sober man to
be found in the place. Although I had made my sixty miles
that day, and the sun was setting, I pushed on without dismounting six miles further, to Chillicothe, situated on the
opposite bank of the Scioto River. In crossing the river that
night, not being aware of its size, and not knowing the ford,
my journey had well-nigh found a watery termination. Sometimes swimming and sometimes wading, I was long in great
jeopardy. At length, arriving safely on the other shore, I was
well prepared by sixteen hours of almost continuous riding
for supper and a sound night's rest.

Cincinnati, then a town of five or six thousand inhabitants,
rapidly increasing and encumbered with materials for building, presented no very attractive appearance. In a small cabin,
on the bank of the Ohio about two miles above Cincinnati,
were living two young men, brothers, with an aged and attached female who had been their nurse, and now kept their
house. Mr. Donaldson, their father, had retired from the
English bar to a farm in Wales; his two sons and their
faithful nurse had emigrated to America. I was requested,

before leaving England, to see them if possible, and here I found them.

At this time I could learn nothing of the prairies; not a person that I saw knew anything about them. I had read of them in Imlay's work, and his vivid description had struck me forcibly. All the country that I had passed through was heavily timbered. I shrank from the idea of settling in the midst of a wood of heavy timber, to hack and hew my way to a little farm, ever bounded by a wall of gloomy forest.

From Cincinnati, Flower made his way to Lexington, Kentucky, already a thriving little metropolis with its own university, already glowing under its self-bestowed title The Athens of the West. From here he went as a matter of course out to Lincoln County to visit Governor Shelby, who had won fame in the War of 1812 for his blunt but skillful command of the Kentucky horse-volunteers, and from Governor Shelby's brother he got his first eye-witness account of the beckoning prairies of Illinois. "This was enough," he wrote. "I felt assured of where they were, and that, when sought for, they could be found."

It was late October; he knew that at this time of year the prairies would be only a mass of burnt-over stubble, and that soon the snows would make travel back East difficult. Accordingly, he went no farther at this time but turned his face eastward, passing through Nashville and hurrying over the mountains of eastern Tennessee to spend the greater part of the winter as Jefferson's guest at Monticello. In Virginia during the winter he was also the guest of Col. John Coles for a time, while the Colonel's youngest brother, Edward, was in England conferring with Birkbeck. This friendship proved especially fruitful and no doubt contributed to Birkbeck's partiality for Illinois. Later, when both were citizens of the new prairie state, Coles was elected governor and he appointed Birkbeck his secretary of state.

Virginia had many attractions for Flower—not the least being the cultivated society of Jefferson and his friends—and he might have settled there except for one overriding consideration: "the brand of slavery was upon the land." So repugnant was slavery to both him and Birkbeck that they played a major part in 1823–24 in preventing its spread to Illinois, thus incurring the lasting enmity of many of their American neighbors who, having migrated

from the South, had none of the Englishmen's passionate antipathy
to it.

In the spring of 1817 Flower himself met Edward Coles, now returned from England. Flower moved on to Philadelphia after attending the inauguration of President James Monroe, still in doubt
whether to see more of the United States or to return to Britain.
Meanwhile Birkbeck, without further consultation with Flower,
had packed up most of his family and announced by letter that
they had landed at the port of Richmond. Without further hesitation Flower turned south once more; as he put it, "my first solitary journey was now ended, and a new experience in travel about
to begin."

iii

FROM THIS POINT FORWARD we have both Flower's and Birkbeck's accounts of the trip to Illinois and of the founding of the
English Settlement—accounts complementary in nature, reflecting
the different personalities of the two men, which also were com-
plements to each other. Flower's *History of the English Settlement
in Edwards County*—his only work of book length—was set down
some forty years after the events it describes and revised several
times before his death in 1862. It did not achieve publication for
another twenty years. The younger man had the honor of searching out the rough locus of settlement, and to him also fell the
task of being its first historian. His book is reflective, sober, and
makes an honest effort to assess the achievement of the settlers so
far as it lies in the power of a participant to do so. Sometimes
marred by an old man's garrulity and occasionally falling into
special pleading for understanding that the author thought had
been denied his colleagues on the prairie, it is nevertheless the
best single account of the whole endeavor and is richest in details
of everyday life. Flower had a genuine appreciation for history,
and his book is an excellent though modest contribution to the
record of the history that he helped to make. Professing to write
"in plain style, and in simple language," he captivates attention
because he had a keen eye for significant human detail. And he
had thought long enough about his narrative to get it into some
historical perspective.

Birkbeck's writing is very different. Drowned in 1825, he never lived to attempt the kind of deliberative prose that Flower excelled in, though one doubts that he would have found it congenial to his temperament if he had. As Flower appears somewhat impassive and phlegmatic—at least the man revealed by his writing and in the absence of contrary evidence—Birkbeck, on Flower's own testimony, "was originally of an irascible temper, which was subdued by his Quaker breeding, and kept under control by watchfulness and care. But eye, voice, and action would occasionally betray the spirit-work within."

Flower was steady, and perhaps slow; Birkbeck was volatile, and perhaps sometimes wavering. Flower's was a historical mind; Birkbeck's a scientific—Flower synthesized, Birkbeck analyzed. Flower took the long view and summed up the experiment; Birkbeck provided until his death both the theory and the apologetics. Birkbeck's writing, much admired by his contemporaries (even his enemies contended that his honeyed pen had seduced honest Englishmen away from hearth and home), stands up less well today than Flower's, for it veers from the sketchy and inadequate to the flaccid and orotund. But the great virtue of Birkbeck's account, despite its repetition and skittishness, is that it gives us an eye-witness day-to-day narrative of the events as they occurred, though his *Notes on a Journey in America from the Coast of Virginia to the Territory of Illinois*, which forms the spine of the following story, is oddly abstract at times, by itself hardly making clear even that Flower was a partner in the venture. Hence, Flower pieces out the details, names the names, and pauses long enough to attempt to give the unique flavor of some of the leading events. But as Birkbeck rushes along, Flower drags his feet. With a singleness of purpose that seems to throw all aside which does not contribute to his own felt destiny, Birkbeck leaves holes which Flower all too generously fills up. Flower never forgot a kindness, and forty years later he peppered his book with acknowledgments for favors from people probably forgotten to all save him, certainly of little interest now. The two accounts judiciously blended and greatly abridged bring us to the actual land-taking in 1817.

iv

BIRKBECK OPENS HIS JOURNAL on April 26, 1817, aboard ship "five hundred miles east of Cape Henry, Virginia."

After twelve months spent in the arrangement of my affairs, I have embarked in comfort with the greatest part of my family in quest of a new settlement in the Western wilderness. We sailed on the 30th of March from Gravesend on board the good ship *America*, of 500 tons burthen, Capt. Heth, for Richmond, Virginia.

Our party occupies both the cabin and steerage, except two strangers in the latter who are well-behaved, unobtrusive persons. The captain is an agreeable and most friendly man, and our accommodations are excellent; we have had a variety of winds and weather, but mostly favourable; some of us have suffered from sea sickness, but we are now generally in good health and our spirits seem to partake of the buoyancy of the noble vessel which is conveying us so cheerfully towards the place of our voluntary exile.

Having had the advantage of communicating with many respectable and well-informed Americans during this year of preparation, I have acquired some knowledge of the United States, as well as a good store of introductory letters.

A kind friend also put into my hands, just before our departure, a series of geographical works lately published by Mr. Melish of Philadelphia. With the information derived from these and other sources, I feel qualified to enter with the more confidence on the task before me, and I am in hopes that a journal of my proceedings may prove useful to others under similar circumstances, by way of warning or encouragement as the event of my own experience may prove. And that my readers may accompany me with more satisfaction and advantage, I shall premise something about myself, my motives, and plans, which will enable them to form a just estimate of my opinions. I hope, however, in so doing I shall not merit the imputation of egotism.

In the first place, being neither well able nor well disposed to combat the extremes of heat and cold which prevail to the east of the Alleghany mountains, I have predetermined to pitch my tent to the westward of that ridge and to the southward of Lake Erie, under a climate recommended by all travellers, as temperate, salubrious, and delightful.

Again, slavery, "that broadest, foulest blot," which still prevails over so large a portion of the United States, will circumscribe my choice within still narrower limits; for if political liberty be so precious that to obtain it I can forego the well-earned comforts of an English home, it must not be to degrade myself and to corrupt my children by the practice of slave-keeping.

This curse has taken fast hold of Kentucky, Tennessee, and all the new states to the south; therefore my inquiries will be confined to the western part of Pennsylvania and the states of Ohio and Indiana, and the Territory of Illinois. Thus, in the immense field before us, the object of our search will be found, if found at all, within a comparatively narrow space.

To this main object I shall apply myself immediately, deferring to a future day the gratification of travelling through the Atlantic states. I intend on my arrival to repair westward with all convenient speed, in order to take a deliberate survey of those Western regions with the hope of fixing on the place of our final settlement before the ensuing winter.

Before I enter on these new cares and toils, I must take a parting glance at those I have left behind; and they are of a nature unhappily too familiar to a large proportion of my countrymen to require a description.

How many are there who having capitals in business which would be equal to their support at simple interest are submitting to privations under the name of economy, which are near akin to the sufferings of poverty, and denying themselves the comforts of life to escape taxation; and yet their difficulties increase, their capitals moulder away, and the resources fail on which they had relied for the future establishment of their families?

A nation with half its population supported by alms, or

poor-rates, and one-fourth of its income derived from taxes, many of which are dryed up in their sources or speedily becoming so, must teem with emigrants from one end to the other; and, for such as myself, who have had "nothing to do with the laws but to obey them," it is quite reasonable and just to secure a timely retreat from the approaching crisis, either of anarchy or despotism.

An English farmer, to which class I had the honour to belong, is in possession of the same rights and privileges as the *villeins* of old time, and exhibits for the most part a suitable political character. He has no voice in the appointment of the legislature unless he happen to possess a freehold of forty shillings a year, and he is then expected to vote in the interest of his landlord. He has no concern with public affairs, excepting as a tax-payer, a parish officer, or a militia man. He has no right to appear at a county meeting unless the word *inhabitant* should find its way into the sheriff's invitation; in this case he may show his face among the nobility, clergy, and freeholders—a felicity which once occurred to myself when the *inhabitants* of Surrey were invited to assist the gentry in crying down the income tax.

Thus, having no elective franchise, an English farmer can scarcely be said to have a political existence, and political *duties* he has none, except such as under existing circumstances would inevitably consign him to the special guardianship of the secretary of state for the home department.

In exchanging the condition of an English farmer for that of an American proprietor I expect to suffer many inconveniences. But I am willing to make a great sacrifice of present ease were it merely for the sake of obtaining in the decline of life an exemption from that wearisome solicitude about pecuniary affairs from which even the affluent find no refuge in England; and, for my children, a career of enterprise and wholesome family connections in a society whose institutions are favourable to virtue; and at last the consolation of leaving them efficient members of a flourishing public-spirited, energetic community, where the insolence of wealth and the servility of pauperism, between which in Eng-

land there is scarcely an interval remaining, are alike unknown.

May 2. After a series of baffling winds and boisterous
weather, we find ourselves on the western or inside of the
Gulf Stream and of course not far from our destination. Yesterday the temperature of the air was 65° and of the water
71°. Today the air remains at 65°, but the water has fallen to
50°. We have therefore crossed this warm ocean river, which
flows from the Gulf of Mexico with a north and north-
easterly course until it meets the melting ice south of the
great bank of Newfoundland.

May 3. Last night we lay at anchor in the Hampton
Roads, and this morning I accompanied the captain in the
pilot boat to Norfolk, 14 miles off, to make entry of the ship
at the custom house.

This is a large town of 10,000 inhabitants. The streets are
in right lines and sufficiently spacious, with wide paved
causeways before the houses, which are good looking and
cleanly. A large markethouse, in the centre of the principal
street, with Negroes selling for their masters fine vegetables
and bad meat, the worst I ever saw and dearer than the
best in England. Veal, such as was never exposed in an English market, 10½d. per pound; lamb of similar quality and
price. Most wretched horses waiting without food or shelter
to drag home the carts which had brought in their provisions.
But, worst of all, the multitudes of Negroes, many of them
miserable creatures, others cheerful enough. On the whole,
this first glimpse of a slave population is extremely depress-
ing. And is it, thought I, to be a member of such a society
that I have quitted England?

Norfolk is fourteen miles from our anchorage off Cape
Comfort; the pilot boat took us thither in sixty-five minutes,
and was about the same time in returning. After dinner, we
proceeded about twenty miles up James River towards City
Point, which is our destination, about one hundred from its
mouth and fifty below Richmond.

The river with its edging of pines and cedars of various
tints, which seem to grow out of the water so low is the

country, is grand and beautiful beyond all that I had conceived of American rivers. Although perfectly flat, the indentures of its course relieve the scenery from the dullness that a continuance of pines on a level surface would otherwise occasion.

May 4. Forty-three miles up from Cape Henry, where we passed the night, the river is still fourteen miles in breadth. This day we proceeded fifty-three miles. The improving character of the country, and the indescribable beauty of the river render our voyage extremely pleasant. I was employed with a telescope incessantly, exploring every cultivated spot and every habitation, so interesting is all that we behold on our first introduction to a foreign land!

May 8. This day the captain paid off the crew, who almost to a man immediately assembled around the grog store of the village. Having escaped from the restraints of discipline and taken in a copious supply of whiskey, they engaged in a general fight, and shewed themselves to be little better than a ferocious banditti, with whom we had been so long cooped up within the narrow limits of the vessel.

May 9. The steamboat which plies between Norfolk and Richmond received us about nine o'clock in the morning, and with some feelings of regret we took a final leave of the good ship *America;* but not of our captain, who was to rejoin us at Richmond.

The steamboat is a floating hotel, fitted up with much taste and neatness, with accommodations for both board and lodging. The ladies have their separate apartment and a female to attend them. Here we found ourselves at once in the society of about thirty persons who appeared to be as polite, well dressed, and well instructed as if they had been repairing to the capital of Great Britain instead of the capital of Virginia. We had a delightful passage, and reached Richmond about seven o'clock in the evening.

May 10. After delivering sundry letters of introduction, we were anxious to secure a retreat from the crowded tavern which received us from the steamboat last evening. The elegant and cool abodes of the agreeable people to whom we

had presented our recommendatory letters formed such a contrast with the heat and bustle of an inn that we were determined at all events to make an escape before the approach of
another night.

After searching the town through and through we made
our retreat most gladly into two rooms in a lodging house,
where we were the more comfortable from having learnt
on shipboard to find many conveniences in a narrow space.

May 10. I saw two female slaves and their children
sold by auction in the street, an incident of common occurrence here though horrifying to myself and to many other
strangers. I could hardly bear to see them handled and
examined like cattle, and when I heard their sobs and saw the
big tears roll down their cheeks at the thought of being
separated I could not refrain from weeping with them.

May 13. Here is a grand stir about a monument to the
memory of General Washington, and about transferring
his remains from their own appropriate abode to the city of
Richmond; as though Washington could be forgotten whilst
America retains her independence! Let republicans leave
bones and relics and costly monuments to monks and kings:
free America is the mausoleum of its deliverers, who may
say to posterity, "*Si quæris monumentum, circumspice.*"

v

FLOWER

At Richmond I joined Mr. Birkbeck and his family, composed
of nine individuals. Himself aged about fifty-four; his second
son Bradford, a youth of sixteen; his third son Charles, a lad
of fourteen; a little servant-boy "Gillard," who had lived with
Mr. Birkbeck all his life, about thirteen years old; and with the
party was a cousin of mine and of my age—twenty-nine—
Mr. Elias Pym Fordham. Of the females, Miss Eliza Birkbeck
was nineteen, Miss Prudence Birkbeck sixteen, and Miss
Eliza Julia Andrews twenty-five.

Miss Andrews (now Mrs. Flower) was the second daugh-

ter of Rev. Mordicah Andrews of Eigeshall, in the county
of Essex, England. There was great friendship between the
members of Mr. Birkbeck's family and Miss Andrews, and,
latterly, she stood almost in the relation of an elder daughter.
Being on a visit to Wanborough at the time Mr. Birkbeck
decided on emigrating to America she consented to accompany them, and under his protection to share the adventures
that awaited them in the new world. A little orphan girl,
Elizabeth Garton, completes the list of Mr. Birkbeck's family
in America, and with me added to them made up the party
that made their way into Illinois. These were the original
band of explorers.

BIRKBECK

Fredericksburg, May 19. In two hacks, which are light
coaches with two horses, a Jersey wagon, and one horse for
the baggage, we have had a pleasant journey of two days
to this place. The distance 69 miles.

From Fredericksburg we took the stage to the river
Potomac, where we were received by the Washington steamboat.

The Potomac, upwards from our entering the steamboat,
flows through a bold country, and its banks are adorned with
houses in fine situations, among which stands conspicuous
Mount Vernon, the residence of the illustrious Washington.

The federal city contains, including Georgetown, which is
only separated from it by the river, about 20,000 inhabitants,
scattered over a vast space like a number of petty hamlets
in a populous country. The intended streets, radiating from
the Capitol in right lines, are for the most part only distin-
guishable from the rugged waste by a slight trace like that of
a newly formed road, or in some instances by rows of Lom-
bardy poplars, affording neither ornament nor shade but
evincing the exotic taste of the designer.

The Capitol and the president's house are under repair
from the damage sustained in the war. Ninety marble capitals
have been imported at vast cost from Italy to crown the
columns of the Capitol and shew how *un*-American is the

whole plan. There is nothing in America to which I can liken this affectation of splendour except the painted face and gaudy headdress of a half-naked Indian.

This embryo metropolis with its foreign decorations would have set a better example to the young republic by surrounding itself first with good roads and substantial bridges in lieu of those inconvenient wooden structures and dangerous roads over which the legislators must now pass to their duty. I think, too, that good taste would have preferred native decorations for the seat of the legislature.

M'Connel's Town, May 23. The road we have been travelling terminates at this place, where it strikes the great turnpike from Philadelphia to Pittsburgh; and with the road ends the line of stages by which we have been travelling, a circumstance of which we knew nothing until our arrival here, having entered ourselves as passengers at Georgetown, for Pittsburgh, by the Pittsburgh stage, as it professed to be.

So here we are, nine in number, one hundred and thirty miles of mountainous country between us and Pittsburgh. We learn that the stages which pass daily from Philadelphia and Baltimore are generally full, and that there are now many persons waiting at Baltimore for places; no vehicles of any kind are to be hired, and here we must either stay or walk off. The latter we prefer; and separating, each our bundle from the little that we had of travelling stores, we are to undertake our mountain pilgrimage, accepting the alternative most cheerfully after the dreadful shaking of the last hundred miles by stage.

We have now fairly turned our backs on the old world, and find ourselves in the very stream of emigration. Old America seems to be breaking up and moving westward. We are seldom out of sight, as we travel on this grand track towards the Ohio, of family groups behind and before us, some with a view to a particular spot, close to a brother perhaps or a friend who has gone before and reported well of the country; many like ourselves when they arrive in the wilderness will find no lodge prepared for them.

A small wagon so light that you might almost carry it

yet strong enough to bear a good load of bedding and utensils and provisions, and a swarm of young citizens—and to
sustain marvellous shocks in its passage over these rocky
heights—with two small horses and sometimes a cow or two
comprises their all, excepting a little store of hard-earned
cash for the land office of the district, where they may obtain
a title for as many acres as they possess half dollars, being
one-fourth of the purchase money. The wagon has a tilt or
cover made of a sheet or perhaps a blanket. The family are
seen before, behind, or within the vehicle, according to the
road or the weather, or perhaps the spirits of the party.
The New Englanders, they say, may be known by the cheerful air of the women advancing in front of the vehicle; the Jersey people by their being fixed steadily within it; whilst the
Pennsylvanians creep lingering behind, as though regretting
the homes they have left. A cart and single horse frequently
afford the means of transfer; sometimes a horse and pack
saddle. Often the back of the poor pilgrim bears all his
effects, and his wife follows barefooted, bending under the
hopes of the family.

May 26. We have completed our third day's march to
general satisfaction. We proceed nearly as fast as our fellow
travellers in carriages, and much more pleasantly, so that
we have almost forgotten our indignation against the pitiful
and fraudulent stage master of Georgetown, so apt are we to
measure the conduct of other people by the standard of our
own convenience rather than by its own merit.

May 28. The condition of the people of America is so
different from aught that we, in Europe, have an opportunity
of observing that it would be difficult to convey an adequate notion of their character. They are great travellers and
in general better acquainted with the vast expanse of country
spreading over their eighteen states, of which Virginia
alone nearly equals Great Britain in extent, than the English
with their little island.

They are also a migrating people, and even when in
prosperous circumstances can contemplate a change of situations which, under our old establishments and fixed habits,

none but the most enterprising would venture upon when urged by adversity.

To give an idea of the internal movements of this vast hive, about 12,000 wagons passed between Baltimore and Philadelphia and this place in the last year. Add to these the numerous stages loaded to the utmost and the innumerable travellers on horseback, on foot, and in light wagons and you have before you a scene of bustle and business, extending over a space of three hundred miles, which is truly wonderful.

But what is most at variance with English notions of the American people is the urbanity and civilization that prevails in situations remote from large cities. In our journey from Norfolk, on the coast of Virginia, to this place, in the heart of the Alleghany Mountains, we have not for a moment lost sight of the manners of polished life. Refinement is unquestionably far more rare than in our mature and highly cultivated state of society, but so is extreme vulgarity. In every department of common life, we here see employed persons superior in habits and education to the same class in England.

The taverns in the great towns east of the mountains which lay in our route afford nothing in the least corresponding with our habits and notions of convenient accommodation; the only similarity is in the expense.

At these places all is performed on the gregarious plan; everything is public by day and by night, for even night, in an American inn, affords no privacy. Whatever may be the number of guests, they must receive their entertainment *en masse* and they must sleep *en masse*. Three times a day the great bell rings, and a hundred persons collect from all quarters to eat a hurried meal, composed of almost as many dishes. At breakfast you have fish, flesh, and fowl; bread of every shape and kind; butter, eggs, coffee, tea; everything, and more than you can think of. Dinner is much like the breakfast, omitting the tea and coffee; and supper is the breakfast repeated. Soon after this last meal you assemble once more in rooms crowded with beds, something like the wards of an hospital, where, after undressing in public, you are fortunate if you escape a partner in your bed, in addition to the myriads of bugs which you need not hope to escape.

But the horrors of the kitchen from whence issue these shoals of dishes, how shall I describe though I have witnessed them? It is a dark, sooty hole, where the idea of cleanliness never entered, swarming with Negroes of both sexes and all ages, who seem as though they were bred there; without floor, except the rude stones that support a raging fire of pine logs extending across the entire place, which forbids your approach and no being but a Negro could face.

In your reception at a western Pennsylvanian tavern there is a something of hospitality combined with the mercantile feelings of your host. He is generally a man of property, the head man of the village, perhaps with the title of colonel, and feels that he confers rather than receives a favour by the accommodation he affords; and, rude as his establishment may be, he does not perceive that you have a right to complain. What he has you partake of, but he makes no apologies; and if you show symptoms of dissatisfaction or disgust, you will fare the worse, whilst a disposition to be pleased and satisfied will be met by a wish to make you so.

At the last stage our party of eight weary pilgrims, dropping in as the evening closed, alarmed the landlady, who asked the ladies if we were not English and said she had rather not wait upon us; "we should be difficult." However she admitted us and this morning at parting she said she liked to wait on "such" English, and begged we would write to our friends and recommend her house. We were often told that we were not "difficult" like the English; and I am sure our entertainment was the better because they found us easy to please.

May 29. Surrounded by all that is delightful in the combination of hilly woodlands and river scenery, at the junction of the Alleghany and Monongahela forming by their union the Ohio, stands the "city of Pittsburgh, the Birmingham of America." Here I expected to have been enveloped in clouds of smoke issuing from a thousand furnaces and stunned with the din of a thousand hammers.

There is a figure of rhetoric adopted by the Americans and much used in description. It simply consists in the use of the present indicative instead of the future subjunctive; it is called *anticipation*. By its aid, what *may be* is contemplated as though it were in actual existence. For want of being acquainted with the power and application of this figure, I confess I was much disappointed by Pittsburgh. A century and a half ago possibly the state of Birmingham might have admitted of a comparison with Pittsburgh.

June 4. We have purchased horses for our party at fifty to sixty dollars, and are making preparations for proceeding through the state of Ohio to Cincinnati.

It is more usual for a party, or even individuals who have no business on land, to pass down the Ohio. Arks, of which hundreds are on the river, are procured of a suitable size for the number. They are long floating rooms, built on a flat bottom with rough boards, and arranged within for sleeping and other accommodations. You hire boatmen and lay in provisions, and on your arrival at the destined port sell your vessel as well as you can, possibly at half cost. On the whole, when the navigation is good, this is pleasant and cheap travelling.

But we, putting health and information against ease and saving of expense, have unanimously given the preference to horseback. After a fortnight's confinement under the heats of the day and the dews of the night, the habit we think must be ill prepared for the effects of the new climate and country; but on our horses, taking the journey easily, we shall become gradually seasoned to it and fortified by the healthful exercise of both mind and body.

Maryland and Pennsylvania abound with horses of the good old English breed, with great bone, of beautiful form, and denoting a strain of high blood: the old English hunter, raised to a stout coach horse, but comprising all degrees of strength and size down to hackneys of fourteen hands. None of those wretched dog-horses which disgrace Virginia are to be seen here.

Pittsburgh is a cheap market for horses, generally rather more so than we found it. Travellers from the East often quit their horses here and take the river for New Orleans, &c. And, on the contrary, those from the West proceed eastward from this place in stages. Thus there are constantly a number of useful hackneys on sale. The mode of selling is by auction. The auctioneer rides the animal through the streets, proclaiming with a loud voice the biddings that are made as he passes along, and when they reach the desired point or when nobody bids more he closes the bargain.

FLOWER

It was from this point that our journey of exploration may be said to have begun. Each individual of our party of ten was to be furnished with a horse and its equipments. An under-blanket for the horse, a large blanket on the seat of the saddle for the rider, a pair of well-filled saddlebags, all secured by a surcingle, a greatcoat or cloak, with umbrella strapped be-hind, completed the appointments for each person. The purchase of the horses devolved upon me. In three days I had them all mounted.

BIRKBECK

June 5. Well mounted and well furnished with saddle-bags and blankets, we proceeded, nine in file, on our west-ward course to Washington, Pennsylvania.

FLOWER

The omens of our first day's journey were not auspicious. Crossing a bridge made of large logs over a creek emptying into the Ohio River one of the logs was missing, leaving a gap nearly two feet wide, showing the water twenty feet below. My horse, young and inexperienced, leaped high and fell, rolling over me, and falling into the Ohio River, twenty feet below. She went down out of sight. In a few seconds she rose again, and with some difficulty was saved from drowning and secured with no other loss than a broken umbrella and a soaking to the contents of the saddlebags. Farther on, Bradford Birkbeck's horse took fright and ran furiously with him through the woods, endangering life and limb of the rider. Luckily the girths broke and spilled everything, leaving the rider, fortunately, with whole bones but with some bruises.

BIRKBECK

June 7. Washington is a pretty thriving town of 2,500 inhabitants. It has a college with about a hundred students. From the dirty condition of the schools and the appearance of loitering habits among the young men, I should suspect it to be a coarsely conducted institution. It must, however, be an unfavourable period to judge of its character, as it has just undergone a contest about the change of presidents, and the session is only commencing. There is also a considerable concourse of free Negroes, a class of inhabitants peculiarly ill suited to the seat of education.

June 8. We were detained at Washington by the indisposition of one of our party, and today only proceeded twenty-two miles to Ninian Beal's tavern. We now consider ourselves, though east of the Ohio, to have made an inroad on the Western territory, a delightful region, healthy, fertile, romantic.

Our host has a small and simple establishment, which his civility renders truly comfortable. His little history may serve as an example of the natural growth of property in this young country.

He is about thirty, has a wife and three fine healthy children. His father is a farmer—that is to say, a proprietor—living five miles distant. From him he received five hundred dollars and "began the world" in the true style of American enterprise by taking a cargo of flour to New Orleans, about 2,000 miles, gaining a little more than his expenses and a stock of knowledge. Two years ago he had increased his property to nine hundred dollars; purchased this place, a house, stable, &c., 250 acres of land (sixty-five of which is cleared and laid down to grass) for 3,500 dollars, of which he has already paid 3,000 and will pay the remaining five hundred next year. He is now building a good stable, and going to improve his house. His property is at present worth 7,000 dollars, having gained or rather grown 3,500 dollars in two years, with prospects of future accumulation to his utmost wishes. Thus it is that the people here become wealthy without extraordinary exertion, and without any anxiety.

June 10. Having crossed the Ohio, we have now fairly set our foot on the land of promise. A heavy fall of rain has rendered the roads muddy and the numerous crossings of the two creeks between Beal's tavern and Wheeling rather troublesome.

Wheeling is a considerable but mean looking town of inns and stores on the banks of the Ohio. Here we baited our horses and took our noon's repast of bread and milk; but had we crossed the river and made our halt on the opposite side we should have escaped a drenching thunderstorm, which caught us as we were ferrying over the second channel. At this place the Ohio is divided into two channels of about five hundred yards each by an island of three hundred acres. We took shelter from the tail of the storm in a tavern at the landing place, and having dried our clothes by a good fire we cheerfully resumed our course in hopes of a fine evening for our ride of ten miles to St. Clairsville. But the storm soon came on again, and we rode nearly the whole of the way under torrents. We had sundry foaming creeks to ford, and sundry log bridges to pass, which are a sort of commutation of danger. We had a very muddy road over hills of clay, with thunder and rain during nearly the whole of this our first stage—such thunder and such rain as we hear of but seldom witness in England. And thus our party of nine cavaliers, five male and four female, made our gallant entré into the Western territory. To see the cheerful confidence which our young people opposed to difficulties so new to them was to me a more agreeable sight at that time than the fairest weather, the noblest bridges, and the best roads could have afforded. It was truly a gallant train making their way in Indian file through

the tempest, across those rocky creeks swelled with the fresh
torrents that were pouring in on every side.

FLOWER

The regular day's journey, steadily pursued, soon broke in
both horse and rider. In fine weather and hard roads it was
very pleasant; no remarkable fatigue felt, the party kept well
together, chatting agreeably by the way. At other times,
from excessive heat or some atmospheric change, a general
languor prevailed, and some dropped behind at a slower
pace. The party would be sometimes strung out, one behind
the other, for three or four miles. The horses, too, became
spiritless and dull, so as to require a touch of the whip or
spur. On such occasions, nothing brought us into order like a
loud clap of thunder and a drenching shower of rain. The
privations on the journey were many. The taverns, as they
were called but in reality often mere shanties, were sometimes
destitute of either door or window, affording only a place
on the floor to spread cloak or blanket. The hot sun, the
sudden storms accompanied by torrents of rain, thunder and
lightning, dangers imminent from crossing swollen and
rapid streams were incidents of travel, borne not only with
equanimity but cheerfulness by every member of the party.
So the journey wore along.

BIRKBECK

We were detained some days at St. Clairsville by the continued indisposition of our friend, a circumstance which
rendered the town more interesting to us than many others
of greater importance. An American town is however on the
whole a disagreeable thing to me; and so, indeed, is an
English one.

June 11.   In my stroll among the love-inclosures of this
neighbourhood, I called to enquire my way at a small farmhouse belonging to an old Hibernian who was glad to invite
me in for the sake of a little conversation. He had brought
his wife with him from his native island, and two children.
The wife was out at a neighbour's on a "wool-picking frolic,"

which is a merry meeting of gossips at each others' houses to pick the year's wool and prepare it for carding. The son and daughter were married and well settled, each having eight children. He came to this place fourteen years ago before an axe had been lifted except to make a "blaze road"— a track across the wilderness, marked by the hatchet—which passed over the spot where the town now stands. A free and independent American and a warm politician, he now discusses the interest of the state as one concerned in its prosperity; and so he is, for he owns one hundred and eighteen acres of excellent land and has twenty descendants. He has also a right to scrutinize the acts of the government, for he has a share in its appointment and pays eight dollars a year in taxes, five to the general treasury and three to his own county, in all about four pence per acre. He still inhabits a cabin, but it is not an Irish cabin.

The most perfect cordiality prevails between the Americans of German and those of English extraction in every part of the United States, if the assertions of all with whom I have conversed on this interesting topic are to be relied on. National antipathies are the result of bad political institutions, and not of human nature. Here, whatever their origin —whether English, Scottish, Irish, German, French—all are Americans. And of all the unfavourable imputations on the American character, jealousy of strangers is surely the most absurd and groundless. The Americans are sufficiently alive to their own interest, but they wish well to strangers, and are not always satisfied with wishing if they can promote their success by active services.

June 13. This morning we had the pleasure of meeting a group of nymphs with their attendant swains, ten in number, on horseback, for no American walks who can obtain a horse and there are few indeed who cannot. The young men were carrying umbrellas over the heads of their fair partners (fair by courtesy), and as there was no show of Sunday's best about them, we were the more pleased with their decent, respectable appearance.

June 16, Rushville. An American breakfast is in much

the same style on the eastern coast of Virginia and in the
centre of the Ohio state. A multifarious collection of discordant dishes, fatiguing to the mistress of the house in its preparation and occasioning much unpleasant delay to the traveller. A gentleman, myself, and three children sat down this
morning to a repast consisting of the following articles:
coffee, rolls, biscuits, dry toast, waffles (a soft hot cake
covered with butter, of German extraction), pickerel salted
(a fish from Lake Hudson), veal cutlets, broiled ham, goose-
berry pye, stewed currants, preserved cranberries, butter,
and cheese. And four gallons of oats and hay for four horses.
For all this, for myself and three children, we were charged
six shillings and nine pence sterling.

June 19. On my arrival at Chillicothe I repaired to the
land office to inspect the map of the district, and found a
large amount of unentered lands, comprehending several
entire townships of eight miles square, lying about twenty
miles south of the town, and in several parts abutting on the
Scioto.

Though it appeared morally certain that substantial ob-
jections have deterred purchasers from this extensive tract
in a country so much settled, the distance being moderate, I
determined to visit it, and am now with my son resting at the
cabin of a poor widow on the way.

As we sat at breakfast we heard a report like the discharge of cannon. It was a sycamore, one of the largest and
most ancient of the forest, which had just then arrived at its
term and fell under the weight of age. It formed one of a
venerable group about a quarter of a mile from our cabin,
and our hostess missed it instantly.

The unentered land we came in quest of is, as I supposed,
of inferior quality. That which abuts on the river consists of
sandstone hills without any portion of the rich alluvial bottom. The interior sections contain land which might be useful as an appendage to better.

Though we find no land fit for our purpose, we are repaid
by the pleasure of our ride through a fine portion of country,
and especially by the information we pick up as we pass along.

It is by multiplied observations that we must qualify ourselves to make a good final choice.

Greenfield, June 20. We are now again on our way towards Cincinnati. In leaving Chillicothe we pass through about seven miles of rich alluvial land, and then rise to fertile uplands. But as we proceed the country becomes level.

Before we entered on this flat country were some hills covered with the grandest white oak timber, I suppose, in America (should I meet with anything to compare with this hereafter, I shall not fail to note it). There are thousands, I think, of these magnificent trees within view of the road for miles, measuring fourteen or fifteen feet in circumference, their straight stems rising without a branch to the height of seventy or eighty feet, not tapering and slender but surmounted by full luxuriant heads.

For the space of a mile in breadth, a hurricane (which traversed the entire Western country in a northeast direction about seven years ago) has opened itself a passage through this region of giants and has left a scene of extraordinary desolation. We pass immediately after viewing those massive trunks, the emblems of strength and durability, to where they lie tumbled over each other like scattered stubble, some torn up by the roots, others broken off at different heights or splintered only and their tops bent over and touching the ground, such is the irresistible force of these impetuous airy torrents.

These hurricane tracks afford strongholds for game, and all animals of savage kind. There is a panther, the only one remaining, it is said, in this country which makes this spot its haunt and eludes the hunters.

June 27. Cincinnati. All is alive here as soon as the day breaks. The stores are opened, the markets thronged, and business is in full career by five o'clock in the morning; and nine o'clock is the common hour for retiring to rest.

Though I feel some temptation to linger here where society is attaining a maturity truly astonishing when we consider its early date, I cannot be satisfied without seeing that remoter country before we fix on this, still enquiring and observing as we proceed. If we leave behind us eligible situations it is like securing a retreat to which we may return with good prospects, if we think it advisable to return.

The probability is that in those more remote regions the accumulation of settlers will shortly render land as valuable as it is here at present, and, in the interim, this accession of inhabitants will create a demand for the produce of the new country equal to the supply. It is possible, too, that we may find ourselves in as good society there as here. Well-educated persons are not rare among the emigrants who are moving far west, for the spirit of emigration has reached a class somewhat higher on the scale of society than formerly. Some, too, may be aiming at the same point with ourselves, and others, if we prosper, will be likely to follow our example.

We are also less reluctant at extending our views westward on considering that the time is fast approaching when the grand intercourse with Europe will not be, as at present, through eastern America but through the great rivers which communicate by the Mississippi with the ocean at New Orleans. In this view, we approximate to Europe as we proceed to the West. The upward navigation of these streams is already coming under the control of steam, an invention which promises to be of incalculable importance to this new world.

Such is the reasoning which impels us still forward, and in a few days we propose setting out to explore the state of Indiana and probably the Illinois. With so long a journey before us we are not comfortable at the prospect of separation. Our plan had been to lodge our main party at Cincinnati until we had fixed on our final abode; but this was before our prospects had taken so wide a range. We now talk of Vincennes as we did before of this place, and I trust we shall shortly be again under way.

FLOWER

At Cincinnati we were entertained in the hospitable house of Mr. Jeremiah Neave. Before leaving the city we became acquainted with a Mr. Sloo, register of the newly opened land office at Shawneetown, in the Territory of Illinois. He gave us a more distinct account of the prairies in his land district. He was going to Illinois on horseback, and offered to accompany and conduct us there. By his advice, we added a pack horse to our already numerous train, for the journey through the wilderness of Indiana would be attended by more discomforts than the track through Ohio from Pittsburgh to Cincinnati. Our first halt after leaving the city was at the house of a friend of Mr. Sloo's, at North Bend—General Harrison. I thought it rather a cool proceeding to introduce such a strong party of strangers to the house and family of an absent friend. The pack horse was long in arriving. Bradford had his difficulties; the pack turned in the streets of Cincinnati, dropping a blanket here and a coffee pot there, the horse walking on with the greatest indifference with the pack swinging under his belly, strewing its contents from one end of the street to the other, to the mirth of the spectators and amid the jeers and jibes of all the urchins of the place. Perseverance conquers all things. Bradford gathered up his traps and joined us late at North Bend. We were very kindly received by Mrs. Harrison, and took our departure the next day. Cabins now became more distant to each other, roads deep in black mud, the forest more unbroken, dark, and gloomy.

BIRKBECK

July 7. I have good authority for contradicting a supposition that I have met with in England respecting the inhabitants of Indiana—that they are lawless, semi-barbarous vagabonds, dangerous to live among. On the contrary, the laws are respected and effectual, and the manners of the people are kind and gentle to each other and to strangers.

An unsettled country lying contiguous to one that is

settled is always a place of retreat for rude and even abandoned characters who find the regulations of society intolerable, and such no doubt had taken their unfixed abode
in Indiana. These people retire with the wolves from the
regular colonists, keeping always to the outside of civilized
settlements. They rely for their subsistence on their rifle
and a scanty cultivation of corn, and live in great poverty
and privation, a degree only short of the savage state of
Indians.

Of the present settlers, as I have passed along from house
to house I could not avoid receiving a most favourable impression. I would willingly remain among them, but pre-
occupation sends us still forward in the steps of the roaming
hunters I have just described, some of whom we shall probably dislodge when we make our settlement, which, like
theirs, will probably be in the confines of society.

As to the inhabitants of towns, the Americans are much
alike, as far as we have had an opportunity of judging. We
look in vain for any striking difference in the general deport-
ment and appearance of the great bulk of Americans from
Norfolk, on the eastern coast, to the town of Madison, in
Indiana. The same good looking, well-dressed (not what we
call gentlemanly) men appear everywhere. Nine out of ten
native Americans are tall and long-limbed, approaching
and even exceeding six feet; in pantaloons and Wellington
boots, either marching up and down with their hands in
their pockets, or seated in chairs poised on the hind feet and
the backs rested against the wall. If a hundred Americans of
any class were to seat themselves, ninety-nine would shuffle
their chairs to the true distance and then throw themselves
back against the nearest prop.

FLOWER

About two-thirds of the way across Indiana the road forked.
Mr. Sloo took the southern road, pointing to the lower ferry
on the Wabash, leading to Shawneetown. We continued due
west on the road to Vincennes.

One sultry evening, when in the deep forest with our line

extended for two or three miles, black clouds suddenly gathered up, extinguishing what light there was. Thunder, lightning, and rain descended and continued, accompanied by violent wind. The storm came so suddenly that the stragglers in the rear were driven into the woods, and there had to stay. Myself and three or four at the head of the line pushed on and reached a cabin.

BIRKBECK

Our rear party, consisting of one of the ladies, a servant boy, and myself, were benighted and without being well provided were compelled to make our first experiment of "camping out." A traveller in the woods should always carry flint, steel, tinder, and matches; a few biscuits, a half pint phial of spirits, and a tin cup; a large knife or tomahawk. Then with his two blankets and his greatcoat and umbrella he need not be uneasy should any unforeseen delay require his sleeping under a tree.

Our party having separated, the important articles of tinder and matches were in the baggage of the division which preceded; and as the night was rainy and excessively dark we were for some time under some anxiety, lest we should have been deprived of the comfort and security of a fire. Fortunately my powder flask was in my saddlebags, and we succeeded in supplying the place of tinder by moistening a piece of paper and rubbing it with gunpowder. We placed our touch paper on an old cambric handkerchief as the most readily combustible article in our stores. On this we scattered gunpowder pretty copiously, and our flint and steel soon enabled us to raise a flame; and collecting dry wood, we made a noble fire. There was a mattress for the lady, a bearskin for myself, and the load of the pack horse as a pallet for the boy. Thus, by means of greatcoats and blankets and our umbrellas spread over our heads, we made our quarters comfortable; and placing ourselves to the leeward of the fire, with our feet towards it, we lay more at our ease than in the generality of taverns. Our horses fared rather worse, but we took care to tie them where they could browse a little, and occasionally shifted their quarters. We had a few biscuits, a small bottle of spirits, and a phial of oil. With the latter we contrived, by twisting some twine very hard and dipping it in the oil, to make torches; and after several fruitless attempts we succeeded in finding water, and also collected plenty of dry wood. "Camping out," when the tents are pitched by daylight and the party is ready furnished with the articles which we were obliged to supply by expedients, is quite pleasant in fine weather. My companion was extremely ill, which was in fact the cause of our being benighted; and never was the night's charge of a sick friend undertaken with more dismal forebodings, especially during our ineffectual efforts to obtain fire, the first blaze of which was unspeakably delightful. After this the rain ceased, and the invalid passed the night in safety, so that the morning found us more comfortable than we could have anticipated.

FLOWER

Just before leaving the timber to enter the prairie on which the town of Vincennes stands we met an Indian on horseback. A new blanket wrapped around him, leggings and moccasins adorned with beads, a bandage round the head sustaining a bunch of feathers, his face and breast painted ochre red, with tomahawk and rifle, a stalwart savage was he. Others sat in groups among the bushes, cooling their legs in the lagoons of water or engaged in conversation with each other. Others lay scattered on the ground, some asleep and some dead drunk. As we proceeded their numbers increased. Painted warriors, bedecked squaws, bedizened papooses, all were there. They had come in to take their treaty stipend and traffic with the agents and traders that lived in Vincennes. They were a part of the valiant band that surprised Harrison on the battleground of Tippecanoe, and had nearly overpowered him. Though fighting hard and inflicting great loss upon Harrison's army, they lost the battle, and with it their prestige and their country! They came in now not as supplicants, but painted defiantly! Their look and manner plainly showed what was the feeling of their hearts. They only wanted the opportunity to tomahawk the inhabitants and burn the town. Unfortunate people! their courage broken, their country lost, their numbers diminishing, starvation their present doom, and utter extinction a speedy certainty.

At the well-known tavern of Colonel LaSalle, we quartered ourselves for some time, resting ourselves and horses, and looking at farms in the environs of the town. The Great Wabash seemed to be the terminus of emigration. The people from the Eastern states that were pouring in chiefly found locations on the east bank of the Wabash, toward Terre Haute. Even here, where the river Wabash is the dividing line between Indiana and Illinois, nothing seemed to be known of the prairies, excepting the "trace"—that is, the road or traveled way that crossed Illinois from Vincennes in Indiana, to St. Louis in Missouri. To ride that alone was then thought to be a perilous affair.

BIRKBECK

Vincennes exhibits a motley assemblage of inhabitants as well as visitors. The inhabitants are Americans, French, Canadians, Negroes. The visitors, among whom our party are conspicuous as English (who are seldom seen in these parts), Americans from various states, and Indians of various nations—Shawnees, Delawares, and Miamis, who live about a hundred miles to the northward, and who are come here to trade for their skins. The Indians are encamped in considerable numbers round the town, and are continually riding in to the stores and the whiskey shops.

Their horses and accoutrements are generally mean, and their persons disagreeable. Their faces are painted in various ways, which mostly gives a ferocity to their aspect. One of them, a Shawnee, whom we met with his family a few miles east of Vincennes, had his eyes, or rather eyelids, and surrounding parts daubed with vermilion, looking hideous enough at a distance. But, on a nearer view, he has good features, and is a fine, stout, fierce-looking man, well remembered at Vincennes for the trouble he gave during the last war. This man exhibits a respectable beard, enough for a

Germanized British officer of dragoons. Some of them are
well dressed and good looking people. One young man in
particular, of the Miami nation, had a clean light blue cotton
vest with sleeves, and his head ornamented with black
feathers. They all wear pantaloons, or rather long moccasins
of buckskin, covering the foot and leg and reaching halfway
up the thigh, which is bare, a covering of cloth passing
between the thighs and hanging behind like an apron of a
foot square. Their complexion is various, some dark, others
not so swarthy as myself; but I saw none of the copper colour
I had imagined to be their universal distinctive mark. They
are addicted to spirits and often intoxicated, but even then
generally civil and good humored. The Indians are said to be
partial to the French traders, thinking them fairer than the
English or Americans. They use much action in their discourse, and laugh immoderately. Their hair is straight and
black, and their eyes dark. The women are, many of them,
decently dressed and good looking; they ride sometimes like
the men, but sidesaddles are not uncommon among them.
Few of them of either sex speak English, but many of the
people here speak a variety of Indian languages.

  In the interior of the Illinois, the Indians are said sometimes to be troublesome by giving abusive language to travellers and stealing their horses when they encamp in the woods,
but they never commit personal outrage. Watchful dogs and a
rifle are the best security, but I believe we shall have no
reason to fear interruption in the quarter to which we are
going.

  Birkbeck makes no mention of Flower's marriage to his ward,
Eliza Julia Andrews, and Flower himself is sufficiently laconic
about the event which was to have great significance in the future
leadership of the settlement. Flower merely recalls that

I proposed for the hand of Miss Andrews, was accepted, and
was subsequently married to her at Vincennes in 1817, at the
house of Colonel LaSalle. The venerable Elihu Stout, a justice of the peace and editor of the only newspaper published
at that time, was the officiating magistrate. Present: Mr.

Birkbeck, as father to the bride, and Mr. Elias Pym Fordham and Judge Blake as invited guests and witnesses.

We immediately made arrangements for prosecuting the
final portion of our journey into that part of Illinois recommended by Mr. Sloo. We agreed to establish the family at
Princeton, the county town of Gibson County, thirty miles
south of Vincennes. For this purpose, Mr. Birkbeck and his
family immediately went there, and my wife and I were to
join him in a few days.

vi

BIRKBECK

July 19. We are at Princeton, in a log tavern where neatness
is as well observed as at many taverns in the city of Bath, or
any city. The town will soon be three years old. The people
belong to old America in dress and manners, and would not
disgrace old England in the general decorum of their deport-
ment.

But I lament here, as everywhere, the small account that is
had of time. Subsistence is secured so easily, and liberal pursuits being yet too rare to operate as a general stimulus to
exertion, life is whiled away in a painful state of yawning
lassitude.

July 20. The object of our pursuit, like the visions of
fancy, has hitherto seemed to recede from our approach; we
are, however, at length arrived at the point where reality is
likely to reward our labours.

Twenty or thirty miles west of this place, in the Illinois
Territory, is a large country where settlements are just now
beginning and where there is abundant choice of unentered
lands of a description which will satisfy our wishes, if the
statements of travellers and surveyors can be relied on after
great abatements.

Princeton affords a situation for a temporary abode more
encouraging than any place we have before visited in this
neighbourhood. It stands on an elevated spot, in an uneven

or rolling country, ten miles from the Wabash and two from
the navigable stream of the Patoka. But the country is very
rich, and the timber vast in bulk and height, so that, though
healthy at present to the inhabitants, they can hardly encourage us with the hope of escaping the seasoning to which
they say all newcomers are subject. There is a convenient
house to be let for nine months, for which we are in treaty.
This will accommodate us until our own be prepared for our
reception in the spring, and may be rented with a garden
well stocked for about £20. I think we shall engage it, and
should a sickly season come on recede for a time into the
high country about a hundred miles back, returning here
to winter when the danger is past.

July 25. Harmonie.   Yesterday we explored the country
from this place to the Ohio, about eighteen miles, and returned today by a different route.

There is a great breadth of valuable land vacant; not the
extremely rich river bottom land, but close cool sand of
excellent quality. It is not, however, so well watered nor so
much varied in surface as is desirable; and we are so taken
with the prairies we have seen, and with the accounts we
have heard of those before us in the Illinois, that no "timbered" land can satisfy our present views.

July 26.   Left Harmonie after breakfast, and crossing the
Wabash at the ferry three miles below we proceeded to the
"Big Prairie," where to our astonishment we beheld a fertile
plain of grass and arable, and some thousand acres covered
with corn more luxuriant than any we had before seen. The
scene reminded us of some open, well-cultivated vale in Europe
surrounded by wooded uplands; and forgetting that we were
in fact on the frontiers, beyond which few settlers had pene-
trated, we were transported in idea to the fully peopled regions
we had left so far behind us.

FLOWER

This was the first prairie in the southeastern part of Illinois,
and distant from the Ohio at Shawneetown about thirty miles
through woodland. It was being settled exclusively by small

corn farmers from the slave states. This prairie, not more than six miles long and two broad, was level, rather pondy, and agueish. Its verdure and open space was grateful to the eye, but it did not fulfil our expectations.

BIRKBECK

We had also an opportunity of seeing the youth of the neighbourhood, as the muster of the militia took place this day. The company amounts to about thirty, of whom about twenty attended with their rifles. In performing the exercise, which was confined to handling their arms, they were little adroit; but in the use of them against an invading foe, woe to their antagonists!

FLOWER

Following the directions given to us by Mr. Sloo, we inquired the way to the Boltinghouse Prairie, so-called from the name of a man who had built a small cabin on its edge, near the spot where his brother had been killed by the Indians the year before. By the side of the road we were following was a small log house, our last chance for information or direction. Our informant, stepping from his hut, indicated with his arm the direction we were to take across the forest without road or path of any kind.

"Keep a wagon-track in your eye if you can, and you will find the prairie." A wagon-track, or two ruts on the open ground made by wagon wheels, can be followed with some degree of certainty. But this was quite a different affair. A light-loaded wagon had passed a fortnight before through the woods and high underbrush, leaving no mark on the hard ground, and only here and there a bruised leaf or broken stem to indicate its passage. For seven mortal hours did we ride and toil in doubt and difficulty.

Bruised by the brushwood and exhausted by the extreme heat, we almost despaired, when a small cabin and a low fence greeted our eyes. A few steps more, and a beautiful prairie suddenly opened to our view. At first we only received the impressions of its general beauty. With longer gaze, all its distinctive features were revealed, lying in profound repose under the warm light of an afternoon's summer sun. Its indented and irregular outline of wood, its varied surface interspersed with clumps of oaks of centuries' growth, its tall grass, with seed stalks from six to ten feet high, like tall and slender reeds waving in a gentle breeze, the whole presenting a magnificence of park scenery, complete from the hand of Nature, and unrivalled by the same sort of scenery by European art. For once the reality came up to the picture of imagination. Our station was in the wood, on rising ground; from it, a descent of about a hundred yards to the valley of the prairie, about a quarter of a mile wide, extending to the base of a majestic slope, rising upward for a full half mile, crowned by groves of noble oaks. A little to the left, the eye wandered up a long stretch of prairie for three miles, into which projected hills and slopes, covered with rich grass and decorated with compact clumps of full-grown trees, from four to eight in each clump. From beneath the broken shade of the wood, with our arms raised above our brows, we gazed long and steadily, drinking in the beauties of the scene which had been so long the object of our search.

We had left Harmonie that morning soon after daylight, went south a few miles to Williams' Ferry, then, crossing over, came to the Big Prairie as before stated, and drank a cup of water from Mr. Williams' well. This was all the refreshment we had taken during the day. We must have traveled more than forty miles in that rough country in one of the hottest days of summer. Our clothing had for hours been wet through with profuse sweat, which trickled down our faces and dropped on our bodies. We felt wellnigh exhausted when we came in sight of our goal. There we stood. We felt no hunger, thirst, or fatigue. We determined to saddle up again, encounter the prairie and its flies, and finish our day's work by pushing into Birk's Prairie, which, by the route we took, must have been seven miles farther.

Immediately on entering the prairie, the quietude of our ride was interrupted by the restless and refractory actions of our horses. They stamped with their feet, started to a rough trot, and then broke into a gallop. It was from the sting of the prairie fly, a large insect, with brown body, green head, and transparent wings. These prairie flies have a peculiar liking for light and sunshine. They attack both horses and cattle, and sting them dreadfully in the open prairie, but will not follow them into the ordinary shade of a wood or forest. They rarely, if ever, attack men. This induces the grazing animals to feed in the prairies by night, and retire to the woods by day. This annoyance induces travelers, crossing the large prairies, to travel by night and rest by day.

Our first experiences in prairie life were not very comfortable. Camping for the night near a pool of stagnant water, we lay down to rest, turning our horses loose to graze. In the morning our horses were missing. We wandered all day in vain search. I had separated myself from my companions in my rovings. The second night found me in a small prairie, about three miles west of the one we first entered. I lay down in the open prairie without fire or supper; my umbrella, a walking stick by day, at night a house for my head. In the morning, somewhat stiff and cold, I again began my search, and soon became as wet as if I had walked through a river, from the dew on the tall grass. For once, I felt glad of the hot sun, to warm and dry me. As a resource in an emergency, I carried a small bag of ground parched cornmeal mixed with some sugar and a little ground ginger. A tablespoon of this, with water, in some shell or the hollow of your hand, is very grateful, prevents extreme hunger, and gives reasonable nutrition. On this I subsisted for a couple of days.

In my wanderings, the thought struck me of finding out a Captain Birk, mentioned to me by my old friend Sloo as living hereabout, the oldest settler in these parts; he had been here almost *a year*. Going in the direction in which I thought he lived, I espied a trail made by the dragging of a log. Following this, I came suddenly to a worm fence inclosing a small field of fine corn, but could see no dwelling. I wished to see Birk, but felt a little diffidence in appearing before the captain in my *deshabille*. After several days' travel, and two nights' camping out, my *toilette* was considerably compromised. Looking closely, I observed, between two rows of corn, a narrow path. This I followed until I came suddenly in sight of a small cabin, within twenty steps of me, a little lower than the surrounding corn. Looking in the direction of a voice calling back a savage dog that had rushed out to attack me, I saw a naked man, quietly fanning himself with a branch of a tree.

My first surprise over, finding his name was Birk I told him who I was and my errand, at which he did not seem at all pleased. These original backwoodsmen look upon all newcomers as obtruders on their especial manorial rights. The old hunters' rule is: when you hear the sound of a neighbor's gun it is time to move away.

What surprised me was the calm self-possession of the man. No surprise, no flutter, no hasty movements. He quietly said that he had just come from mill at Princeton, thirty miles distant, and was cooling himself a bit. Well, I thought he was cool. I afterward found all of this class of men, who live in solitude and commune so much with nature, relying on their own efforts to support themselves and their families, to be calm, deliberate, and self-possessed whenever they are sober. The best breeding in society could not impart to them more self-possession or give them greater ease of manner or more dignified and courteous bearing.

Birk's cabin, fourteen feet long, twelve broad, and seven high, with earth for a floor, contained a four-post bedstead; said posts, driven into the ground by an axe, were sprouting with buds, branches, and leaves. The rim of an old wire-sieve, furnished with a piece of deerskin punched with holes for sifting cornmeal, a skillet, and a coffee pot were all the culinary apparatus for a family of seven. A small three-legged stool and a rickety clapboard table the only furniture. An axe lay at the door, a rifle stood against the wall. Himself and boys were dressed in buckskin, his wife and three daughters in flimsy calico from the store, sufficiently soiled and not without rents. Mrs. Birk, a dame of some thirty years, was square built and squat, sallow, and smoke-dried, with bare legs and feet. Her pride was in her hair, which, in two long well-braided black and shining tails, hung far down her back.

Birk got his title as commander of a company of men like himself, employed as outlying scouts to the American army on the Canada frontier. The cabin door was made of two strong puncheons to withstand an Indian attack. You might always find in the behavior of the females of this class of people the degree of estimation or aversion in which you were held. Mrs. Birk was sour and silent—ominous indications. The British and Indians, having fought together against the Americans, were held by these people in the same category as natural enemies. To such an extent was this feeling exhibited, that, at a future time, quite a respectable farmer in the Big Prairie apologized to Mrs. Flower for the non-appearance of his wife by saying she had lost a brother at the battle of the River Raisin, and that she always went out of the house into the woods whenever an English person entered and remained there as long as he or she stayed. Besides, we came with the intention of settling and bringing other settlers. All this was distasteful to them. They came to enjoy the solitude of the forest and the prairie. They wished to be far from that species of civilization whose temptations could not be withstood by them, and which made the weaknesses of its victims augment its own gains. No wonder we were met by no cordial greetings. Our success would be their defeat, and the growth of our colony the signal for their removal. A few dollars liberally given for information and pilotage, and a dram of whisky whenever we had it to bestow, would modify the hostile feeling, and we soon became on friendly terms.

Two or three slices from a half-smoked haunch, a few pommes of coarse corn bread, seasoned by hunger, the best of sauce, gave us a relishing supper. How sleeping was to be managed, I felt at a loss. As night advanced, Birk reached his long arm up to a few clapboards over the joist and pulled down a dried hog's skin for my especial comfort and repose during the night.

Father, mother, sons, and daughters all lay on the one

bed. I, as in duty bound, lay my hog's skin on the floor and myself upon it. But I soon found that

> *Big fleas and little fleas,*
> *And less fleas to bite 'em,*
> *These again had lesser fleas,*
> *And so on* ad infinitum.

I removed my not over-luxurious couch outside the house, to a spot of earth free from vegetation, and there I lay until break of day, glad enough to run to the fire for a little warmth as soon as it was kindled.

Cold is never more felt than at daybreak, after lying on the ground without covering even in the summer season. Our horses which had strayed were brought back to us by John Anderson, one of those outlying hunters who for a liberal reward acted with efficiency on the occasion. Understanding the instinct of the horse, Anderson took a straight course toward Princeton until he reached the Great Wabash at La Vallett's Ferry. There he found the fugitives, arrested by the broad stream from immediately attempting a crossing.

Having again joined my companions, we once again mounted and proceeded to look at the prairies west of the Little Wabash. We were advised by Birk to call on a man named Harris who lived about twelve miles west of the Little Wabash. To find a little cabin through fifteen miles of forest and prairie, without road or even path, is no small job. But it is astonishing how necessity sharpens the wits, and how soon signs before unnoticed and unknown become recognized. We found him in a small cabin, sheltered by a little grove, but no field or cultivation of any kind about his humble dwelling. He lived in the same style as Birk and in the same destitution. One article of luxury only excepted. This was a fiddle with two strings.

BIRKBECK

This man and his family are remarkable instances of the effect on the complexion produced by the perpetual incar-

ceration of a thorough woodland life. Incarceration may seem
to be an epithet less applicable to the condition of a roving
backwoodsman than to any other, and especially unsuitable
to the habits of this individual and his family, for the cabin
in which he entertained us is the third dwelling he has built
within the last twelve months, and a very slender motive
would place him in a fourth before the ensuing winter.

The man, his pregnant wife, his eldest son, a tall, half-
naked youth just initiated in the hunter's art, and three
daughters growing up into great rude girls, and a squalling
tribe of dirty brats of both sexes are of one pale yellow without
the slightest tint of healthful bloom. In passing through a
vast expanse of the backwoods, I have been so much struck
with this effect that I fancy I could determine the colour of the
inhabitants if I was apprised of the depth of their immersion,
and, vice versa, I could judge of the extent of the clearing if
I saw the people.

Our stock of provisions being nearly exhausted, we were
anxious to provide ourselves a supper by means of our
guns but could meet with neither deer nor turkey; however,
in our utmost need we shot three raccoons, an old one to be
roasted for our dogs and the two young ones to be stewed
up daintily for ourselves. We soon lighted a fire and
cooked the old raccoon for the dogs, but famished as they
were they would not touch it, and their squeamishness so far
abated our relish for the promised stew that we did not press
our complaining landlady to prepare it. And thus our supper
consisted of the residue of our corn bread, and *no* raccoon.
However, we laid our bearskins on the filthy earth (floor
there was none), which they assured us was "too damp for
fleas," and, wrapt in our blankets, slept soundly enough,
though the collops of venison hanging in comely rows in the
smoky fireplace, and even the shoulders put by for the dogs
and which were suspended over our heads, would have been
an acceptable prelude to our night's rest had we been invited
to partake of them. But our hunter and our host were too
deeply engaged in conversation to think of supper. In the
morning the latter kindly invited us to cook some of the

collops, which we did by toasting them on a stick, and he also divided some shoulders among the dogs; so we all fared sumptuously.

The cabin, which may serve as a specimen of these rudiments of houses, was formed of round logs with apertures of three or four inches between. No chimney, but large intervals between the "clapboards" for the escape of the smoke. The roof was, however, a more effectual covering than we have generally experienced, as it protected us very tolerably from a drenching night. Two bedsteads of unhewn logs, and cleft boards laid across two chairs, one of them without a bottom, and a low stool, were all the furniture required by this numerous family. A string of buffalo hide stretched across the hovel was a wardrobe for their rags; and their utensils, consisting of a large iron pot, some baskets, the effective rifle and two that were superannuated stood in the corner; and the fiddle, which was only silent when we were asleep, hung by them.

Our raccoons, though lost to us and our hungry dogs, furnished a new set of strings for this favourite instrument. Early in the morning the youth had made good progress in their preparation, as they were cleaned and stretched on a tree to dry.

Many were the tales of dangerous adventures in their hunting expeditions which kept us from our pallets till a late hour; and the gloomy morning allowed our hunters to resume their discourse, which, no doubt, would have been protracted to the evening had not our impatience to depart caused us to interrupt it, which we effected with some difficulty by eleven in the forenoon.

FLOWER

Harris returned with us to Birk's, carrying the superannuated fiddle carefully along. It was kept in scream until a late hour, bringing to the inmates of the cabin happy recollections of Tennessee, the state from which they had emigrated. The people of which Birk and Harris were specimens were serviceable to us in our first settlement. Dexterous with the axe, they built all our first log cabins and supplied us with venison. In a year or two they moved into less-peopled regions, or to where there were no people at all, and were entirely lost to this part of the country. The people in this part of Illinois are mostly from the slave states, from the class of "poor whites" so-called. When they leave their homes and come into the little towns, on some real or pretended business, they are sober and quiet. They soon get to the whisky bottle, their bane and ruin. Getting into a state to desire more, they drink all they can, becoming disagreeable, fractious, and often dangerous men. One glass kindles the eye, the second loosens the tongue, the third makes them madmen. They own a horse, rifle, axe, and hoe. It is astonishing to see with what dexterity they use a good axe, and how well they shoot with even a bad rifle. They are not of industrious habits, but occasionally work with great vigor.

Solitude, watchfulness, and contemplation amidst the scenes of nature, from day to day, from week to week, and often from month to month, give them that calm and dignified behavior not to be found in the denizens of civilized life. Another portion of this class follow a different destiny. Their little corn patch increases to a field, their first shanty to a small log house, which, in turn, gives place to a double cabin, in which the loom and spinning wheel are installed. A well and a few fruit trees after a time complete the improvement. Moderate in their aspirations, they soon arrive at the summit of their desires. Does a more complicated mode of life and a larger amount of wealth add to human happiness? The only difference between these stationary settlers and the roving hunters appears to be in the sobriety of the one and the intemperance of the other.

BIRKBECK

The Little Wabash, which we crossed in search of some prairies which had been described to us in glowing colours, is a sluggish, scanty stream at this season; but for three months of the latter part of winter and spring it covers a great space by the overflow of waters collected in its long course. The Skillet Fork is also a river of similar character, and the country lying between them must labour under the inconvenience of seclusion for many months every year, until bridges and ferries are established. This would be a bar to our settling within the "fork," as it is called.

FLOWER

Before leaving Illinois, night overtook us. We halted by the side of a fallen log, at a point of timber that stretched into the prairie. A fire being kindled, we sat down on the grass, talked over and decided what was to be done. I remember the spot well; it was then called the Long Prairie, that runs west and east toward La Vallette's Ferry on the Great Wabash. This spot, so particularly fixed in my memory, I never passed in after years without a halt to allow the panorama of the past with all its vivid pictures to flit before me. Here our future destinies were fixed, and to the decisions made here the present English Settlement in Edwards County, Illinois, owes its existence.

BIRKBECK

We therefore separated this morning, without losing the time that it would require to explore this part thoroughly. I proceed to Shawneetown land office, to make some entries which we had determined on between the Little and the Big Wabash. Mr. Flower spends a day or two in looking about, and returns to our families at Princeton.

FLOWER

Our safe return to Princeton was hailed by our families with affectionate joy. Thankfully we enjoyed, for a few days, a home made comfortable by cheerful hearts and active hands. After needful rest from our harassing journey in the prairies, we thought of our own position. Our first measure was to secure as much land as our present means would allow in the Boltinghouse Prairie. By a journey to Shawneetown, seventy miles distant, this was done, and about three thousand acres secured by payment into the land office.

It was evident to Mr. Birkbeck and myself at the time we made our first entries of land in the Boltinghouse Prairie that we were exposed to the invasion of speculators. Having expended all the money we could then command, by securing but little more than half the land we intended for own families, we felt fearful, as the point of our settlement was designated, that speculators might buy the lands immediately around those we had purchased. We had not money enough with us to purchase the whole prairie. I was to return to England to remit him money as soon as possible; take with me and publish the manuscript of his book containing the record of our journey from Richmond to the prairies; bring out my father's family; and spread the information; point out the road to it; and facilitate emigration generally. He was on the home department to purchase more land and make the necessary preparations in building. I on the foreign mission, to bring in the people. As will be seen hereafter, he did his duty and I did mine.

2

"Many were discouraged . . .
but the mass of the settlers stayed."

CAPT. JEREMIAH BIRK was not the only squatter already on the land Birkbeck and Flower had come to purchase. Tradition has it that three brothers named Daston were the first white men to penetrate this particular section of wilderness, and though where they came from and where they went are equally vague, they were on the scene about 1800—a date that emphasizes the relative remoteness of this land despite the existence of the infant cities St. Louis, on the Mississippi, and Vincennes, on the Wabash. Other early settlers were the families of Jonathan Shelby, Thomas Carney, John Bell, Lot Sams, and Isaac Greathouse, all of whom had arrived before 1815. They were among the "Southerners" alluded to by Birkbeck and Flower, for all had passed through Tennessee or Kentucky on their long route north, and some of them had been born in the backwoods of the Carolinas. Of these, all but Carney, who moved on to Missouri in the 1840's, managed to get along with their English neighbors and lived out their lives in the settlement. Of particular interest is the backwoodsman Joseph Boltinghouse, whose name was attached to the prairie the English Settlement would occupy. Living alone in his remote cabin, he was murdered in 1816 by a marauding band of Shawnee Indians who left his severed head suspended on a pole. The outraged settlers dealt out stern justice when they captured the Indians near the Wabash River. Each had stones lashed to his body and was sunk, alive, in the river.

These were not all of the "Americans." After Boltinghouse's death his brothers, James and Daniel, took over his meager holdings—it was probably after them that the prairie was named—and among others early on the land were Walter Anderson, John Hunt, Hugh Collins, Rollin and Joseph Lane, William Ham, and Clem Martin, all Southerners, all useful to the struggling band of English for their skill with the axe and rifle. Even one native Irishman, Thomas Riley, had arrived before the English and had adopted the backwoods life of his American neighbors. Nor does this exhaust the list of backwoodsmen and squatters, many of whom are mentioned in contemporary accounts but are impossible to trace today.

Late in September, 1817, Birkbeck was in Shawneetown to make his purchase. Shawneetown, which had the land office for southeastern Illinois, was then enjoying the start of its spectacular but brief prosperity. The story current among the catfish fishermen who squat on their heels on the levee even today and rejoice about how a group of wild-eyed fellows came to "their" bank to borrow money to found the city of Chicago is probably apocryphal. Shawneetown turned down Chicago as a bad risk, so the story goes—which, if true, may speak volumes about Shawneetown business sagacity. But in the early nineteenth century, nevertheless, this was the financial capital of the whole region.

Then as now it took peculiar resistance to dampness to live there. W. T. Harris, passing this way the next year, wrote:

From the situation of Shawneetown its inhabitants might be supposed to partake of the nature of the wild duck, for every year they expect to be driven by the waters to their upper stories, as land high enough to avoid them is not to be found within a mile of the place. The consequent unhealthiness of such a spot is apparent in the sallow complexions of those who here deprive themselves of many comforts and risk both health and life for the sake of gain; considerable business being done here, as it is on the road from the southern states to St. Louis and the Missouri, and the land office is here.

Birkbeck stayed only long enough to enter his and Flower's land,
and then returned to Princeton via Harmonie, the Rappite colony
on the Wabash which was to figure largely in the early life of the
settlement as a source of supplies.

He continued his journal until he got back to Princeton, jotting
down at Shawneetown that

I have just constituted myself a land owner by paying
seven hundred and twenty dollars as one-fourth of the purchase money of 1,440 acres. This, with a similar purchase
made by Mr. Flower, is part of a beautiful and rich prairie,
about six miles distant from the Big and the same from the
Little Wabash.

In one of his last dated notes (August 10), he summed up the
situation they found themselves in and projected a typically op-
timistic glance into the future.

We are on the confines of society, among the true backwoodsmen. We have been much among them, have lodged in
their cabins, and partaken of their wretched and scanty fare.
They have been our pilots to explore situations still more remote and which only hunters visit.

From a nearer view of these people, something must be
withdrawn from the picture which was given of their moral
character. It is rather an ill-chosen or unfortunate attachment
to the hunter's life than an unprincipled aversion to the regulations of society which keeps them aloof from the abodes of
more civilized men.

They must live where there is plenty of "bears, and deer,
and wild honey." Bear hunting is their supreme delight; to
enjoy this they are content to live in all manner of wretchedness and poverty. Yet they are not savage in disposition, but
honest and kind, ready to forward our wishes and even to
labour for us, though our coming will compel them to remove
to the "outside" again.

Not a settlement in this country is of a year's standing; no
harvest has yet rewarded their toil. But our approach, as I
anticipated, will dislodge many of them, unless they should be

tempted by our dollars to try the effect of labour instead of the precarious supply derived from their beloved rifle. Half a dozen of these people who had placed themselves round a beautiful prairie have in fact come forward to sell us their all —cabin, cattle, hogs, and this their first crop of corn now just maturing. If we purchase, they will go to some deeper recess and build other cabins, and prepare cattle and corn, to be again quitted at the approach of some succeeding adventurers like ourselves, who may be considered in this view as the next grade in society.

But, that our friends in England who may read these notes may have an idea of our real position, let them consider our two families, viz. that of my friend Mr. George Flower, late of Marden, in England, and my own, about to be fixed upon eligible sites on our two adjoining estates of fifteen hundred acres each, which we have carved for ourselves from a beautiful prairie and the adjoining woods.

Here we are preparing to raise buildings. Carpenters and builders have offered themselves; estimates are made, and materials are at hand. We are also providing for gardens and orchards, that we may literally "sit under our own vines, and our own fig-trees." We might now mow many hundred acres of valuable grass if we had a stock of cattle to require it.

The fee-simple of these two estates amounts in the whole to three thousand dollars, £1,350 sterling. They are liable to a land tax of thirty dollars a year to the general government, and about the same to the county; together something more than one penny per acre.

We shall have a certain and good market for produce, from the growing population, or by export down the Ohio.

Cattle and hogs thrive well and even fatten, especially the latter, to a great size on the food they find; and there is no bounds to the number that may be raised but in the ability of the breeder. They require but little care, except to protect them from bears and wolves; keeping them tame by giving them salt frequently.

On these estates we hope to live much as we have been accustomed to live in England. But this is not the country for fine gentlemen, or fine ladies of any class or description, especially for those who love state or require abundance of attendants.

To be easy and comfortable here a man should know how to wait upon himself, and practise it, much more indeed than is common among the Americans themselves on whom the accursed practice of slave keeping has, I think, entailed habits of indolence even where it has been abolished.

Adding a postscript addressed "to my English friends," which he dated September 1, 1817, Birkbeck gave two copies of his manuscript to George Flower to deliver to the printers. In the postscript his cheerful optimism rose to new heights. Among other things he wrote:

It may be collected from the tenor of these notes that I am as well satisfied with this country as I had anticipated. And our friends will have sympathized with us on the success of our enterprise, having found a good country and secured for ourselves a situation in it so well adapted to our wishes.

There are advantages before us greater than I had in contemplation, and apparently attainable with less difficulty and fewer sacrifices. I have therefore nothing to regret in the step I have taken, and in my present knowledge I should find stronger motives for it.

The report of our intended establishment in the Illinois spreads far and wide; and such is the attraction of population to capital that many entries are already made by new settlers in our intended neighbourhood, and various applications occur daily from mechanics and others who are desirous of moving to us as we may be in a condition to provide them with employment. We see our way clear as to obtaining workmen, and even farming labourers.

Our design is to commence operations by building a number of cabins, with inclosures of two acres and a half each, along the sides of a section, which is to be reserved as their cow pasture. These cottages and inclosures, with a well between two, may be rented by persons who will resort to us for the sake of good earnings. If they were ready, I think they would be occupied by handicraftsmen immediately; that is, as soon as the transport of their families could be effected.

The proposals which have already been made anticipating our views warrant this conclusion. Here then is a town about to rise before us, of no equivocal origin but the necessary result of capital applied to cultivation under these favourable circumstances.

It is the intention of my friend, Mr. Flower, and myself to purchase, on terms as favourable as can be obtained from the government, one or more entire townships in the Illinois territory, where the country is partly prairie and partly woodland. A township comprises thirty-six square miles, or sections of 640 acres each; in all 23,040 acres. These lands we propose to offer (on terms proportionally favourable) to a number of our countrymen whose views may so far accord with our own as to render proximity of settlement desirable.

In the sale of public lands there is a regulation which I have before mentioned, that the sixteenth section, which is nearly the centre of every township, shall not be sold. It is called the reserve section, and is accordingly reserved for public uses in that township for the support of the poor and for purposes of education. This section, being of course at the disposal of the purchasers of the entire township, we shall, by judicious arrangements, provide out of it not only for the objects which the wisdom of the legislature had in view, but for the present accommodation of the more indigent but not the least valued members of our proposed community. To obviate the sufferings to which emigrants of this class are exposed on their arrival, it is a material part of our plan to have in readiness for every poor family a cabin, an inclosed garden, a cow, and a hog, with an appropriation of land for summer and winter food for cows, proportioned to their number.

With regard to the disposal of the lands in general, we shall probably offer them in sections, half sections, quarters and eighths; that is, in allotments of 640, 320, 160, and 80 acres, making other reservations of portions for public uses as circumstances may require.

We wish it to be clearly understood that we have no design
of forming a society of English, to be governed by any laws
or regulations of our own framing. We would not bind others,
nor be ourselves bound by any ties but those of mutual interest
and good neighbourhood, nor be subject to any law but the
law of the land.

Yet, as concentration of capital as well as of population will
be essential to the rapid prosperity of our colony, we shall
make a stipulation with regard to capital which we hope will
be generally approved.

That no person may be tempted by the low price at which
our lands shall be offered to possess more than he can fairly
manage, a statement or declaration will be required from
purchasers that they are in possession of capital (their own or
borrowed), which may and is intended to be applied to the
cultivation of the lands he proposes to purchase, equal, including the purchase money, to five pounds sterling per acre,
over and above the expense of his voyage.

I repeat that we have not fallen on this scheme from a wish
to form a society exclusively English or, indeed, *any* society
as distinct from the people at large. We would most willingly
extend our proposals to Americans, or emigrants of any nation with the requisite capital, could our plan embrace them.

Having proceeded thus far in the development of our plan,
it may materially forward its completion to take one step further. That is, to open a channel of communication with those
who may be so well pleased with it as to wish to join in its
execution.

Such persons will please to direct their letters, postage
paid, to the care of Richard Flower, Esq., Marden, near Hertford, or, if in America, to myself at Princeton, Indiana.

Now George Flower was to begin his long trip back to the coast,
and his longer trip across the Atlantic. Flower, always more cau-
tious than Birkbeck, was less sanguine about his likelihood of raising so much money to complete their purchase. Before he left for
England he took the precaution of writing to his friend Jefferson
to sound out the elder statesman on the possibility of Congress
making them a grant of a whole township. Jefferson carefully

weighed the pros and cons of the proposal but had to acknowledge
that in 1817 he was somewhat out of touch with the actual administration of land policy.

Poplar Forest, 12th July, 1817

Dear Sir:

Your favor of August 12th was yesterday received at this
place, and I learn from it with pleasure that you have found a
tract of country which will suit you for settlement. To us, your
first choice would have been gratifying, by adding yourself
and friends to our society, but the overruling consideration
with us, as with you, is your own advantage, and it would
doubtless be a greater comfort to you to have your ancient
friends and neighbors settled around you. I sincerely wish
that your proposition to purchase a tract of land in Illinois on
favorable terms, for introducing a colony of English farmers,
may encounter no difficulties from the established rules of our
land department.

The general law prescribes an open sale, where all citizens
may compete on an equal footing for any lot of land which attracts their choice. To dispense with this in any particular
case requires a special law of Congress, and to special legisla-
tion we are generally averse, lest a principle of favoritism
should creep in and prevent that of equal rights. It has, however, been done on some occasions, when special national advantages has been expected to outweigh that of adherence to
the general rule. The promised introduction of the culture of
the vine procured a special law in favor of the Swiss Settlement on the Ohio. That of the culture of oil, wine, and other
Southern productions did the same lately for the French Settlement on the Tombigbee. It remains to be tried whether that
of an improved system of farming, interesting to so great a
proportion of our citizens, may not also be worth a dispensa-
tion of the general rule. This, I suppose, is the principal
ground on which your proposition will be questioned, for although, as to other foreigners, it is thought better to discourage their settling together in large masses, wherein, as in
our German settlements, they preserve for a long time their

own language, habits, and principles of government, and that
they should distribute themselves sparsely among the natives,
for quicker amalgamation, yet English emigrants are without
this inconvenience, they differ from us but little in their principles of government, and most of those (merchants excepted)
who come here are sufficiently disposed to adopt ours. What
the issue, therefore, of your proposition may probably be, I
am less able to advise you than many others, for, during the
last eight or ten years, I have no knowledge of the administration of the land office, or the principles of its government; even the persons on whom it will depend are all
changed within that interval, so as to leave me small means of
being useful to you. Whatever they may be, however, they
shall be fully exercised for your advantage; and that not on
the selfish principle of increasing our population at the expense of other nations, for the additions are but as a drop in a
bucket to those by natural procreation, but to consecrate a
sanctuary for those whom the misrule of Europe may compel
to seek happiness in other climes. This refuge, once known,
will produce reaction, even of those there, by warning their
taskmasters that when the evils of Egyptian oppression become heavier than those of abandonment of country, another's
Canaan is opened, where their subjects will be received as
brothers and secured from like oppression by a participation
in the rights of self-government.

If additional motives could be wanting into the maintenance
of this right, they would be found in the animating consideration that a single good government becomes thus a blessing to
the whole earth; its welcome to the oppressed restraining
within certain limits the measure of their oppressions, but
should ever this be counteracted by violence on the right of
expatriation, the other branch of our example then presents
itself to their imitation, to use on their rulers, and do as we
have done.

You have set your country a good example, by showing
them a practicable mode of reducing their rulers to the necessity of becoming more wise, more moderate, and more honest,
and I sincerely pray that the example may work for the bene-

fit of those who can not follow it, as it will for your own.

With Mr. Birkbeck, the associate of your extraordinary journeyings, I have not the happiness of personal acquaintance, but I know him through his narrative of your journeyings together through France. The impressions received from that give me confidence that a participation with yourself in the assurances of the esteem and respect of a stranger will not be unacceptable to him, and the less when given through you and associated with those to yourself.

Th: Jefferson

To George Flower, Esq.

Leaving further political maneuvering to the capable Birkbeck, Flower got ready for his return to England. Already trouble was brewing between the two families, trouble which the separation of time and distance would magnify.

We had been two months at Princeton. The family always there; our two selves, almost always away, had completed our work of exploration. The time now approached for my return to England to carry out the next step. To make publication, bring people to the land, and place ourselves in funds. Our first plan was that Mrs. Flower should remain with Mr. Birkbeck's family and that I should proceed on my journey eastward and my voyage alone.

To make a will and dispose of our effects in a secure and desirable manner is always proper, yet how often deferred. I therefore, before leaving Princeton, made my will. Mr. Birkbeck, Miss Birkbeck, and Bradford Birkbeck were witnesses to that instrument. How little did we think that this was to be our last united act! That we were never more to meet again or speak a friendly word to each other! Before leaving Princeton, we agreed on the division of our land and the building of our houses. On the latter point we differed a little in opinion. He proposed that the north-and-south line which divided our land should run through one house. I living in the apartments on my land, and his family occupying the apartments on his land, both families, in fact, living in one house. Mrs. Flower

and myself thought it better to live in our own house, and that
Mr. Birkbeck's family should live in their house however near
those houses might be. This was the first difference in our
plan of operations that had ever occurred between us, and,
trivial as it may seem, perhaps we may ascribe to it that diver-
gence which carried the lasting separation that followed; as
the ridge-tile of a house separates two raindrops that fall
within an inch of each other in the same shower, casting one
eastwardly to mingle ultimately with the Atlantic Ocean, the
other westward, destined to add its atom to the Pacific.

Although our residence at Princeton was one of united effort and cordial friendship, our feelings did not exhibit that
even and warm glow which shone upon the party as it journeyed to the West. They partook now more of the character of
an April day, when the clouds fly high and rapidly cast shad-
ows on the bright sunshine as they pass.

We were now in changed circumstances; our plans required
the division and subdivision of our little party. Some to turn
back, encountering long journeys by land and voyages by sea
before they could be united again. And the part that remained, often to be divided through winter and succeeding
spring, some remaining in Indiana and some wandering in
Illinois. This naturally cast a shade of thought upon us all.

The time arrived for my return to England. All circumstances being considered, Mrs. Flower and myself thought it
better to take the journey East together. We should enjoy
each other's company three weeks longer, and, at my return
in the following spring, we should again meet months earlier
than we otherwise could. The last day at Princeton was spent
by Mr. Birkbeck and myself in talking over the business that
each was to do separately. He, in the further purchase of land
as soon as funds could be procured, and in the erection of
cabins and other necessary preparations for the settlement in
spring. He handed to me his two manuscripts. One to be published in Philadelphia and one in England.

Let it be remembered, in these days of convenience and
fast travel, that then horseback was the only mode of traveling, and the space contained in a pair of saddlebags all that

was allowed for papers, wardrobe, and often provisions for the traveler.

The little horse that had carried me on my solitary journey of over two thousand miles was a high-bred animal of mettle and of perfect but of rather slight frame; not of sufficient bone and substance to carry my weight with the baggage with which I was encumbered, and pressed, as I knew he must be, to a forty-mile daily travel. I gave him to my little friend Prudence Birkbeck. She loved a gallop on a mettlesome nag. Her light weight he would carry as a feather, and I was well pleased to place my faithful little horse, to whom I was much attached, with a friend that would take care of him.

Selecting two of the most suitable animals from our stud of ten for myself and wife, behold them caparisoned and both of us mounted. On the back of each horse was evenly laid a soft and rather thin blanket, which received the saddle kept steady in its place by girths and crupper. Over the saddle, folded double and sometimes triple, was laid a large and soft Whitney blanket kept in place by a broad circingle. The pad behind the saddle received the cloak and umbrella, tightly folded in one large roll and bound with two leathern thongs. The saddlebags, stuffed to their utmost capacity, were laid on the saddle, under the blanket, kept in place by two loops through which the stirrup leathers passed. On the top of all sat the rider. It is rather a skilful job to pack saddlebags well. As you put in their contents, you must poise them frequently to see that each side is equally weighted. If you fail in this, you are plagued the whole ride by the bags slipping to one side or the other, to the danger of their striking against the horse's legs, starting him off in a furious kicking gallop. A riding appendage peculiar to horsemen in America is the legging. It is a piece of blue or drab cloth, about a yard square, folded round the leg from knee to ankle, pinned with three pins to keep the edges in place, and tied by two bands of tape or galloon, one below the knee, the other above the ankle. It catches all the splash and mud, and, when cast off, the pantaloon is dry. The women, instead of the full cloth riding habit worn in England, draw over their usual dress a long skirt

made of bombazine or some dark-colored stuff, and over their
heads they cast a large handkerchief which they tie under
their chin. This keeps the bonnet and veil in place, and pro-
tects the face and ears from sun, wind, and rain. Our horses
and ourselves thus accoutred, we mounted; and this is done
by the horses being led to a block—in Western America,
generally the stump of a tree—and even then it takes a pretty
wide stride and fling of the leg for a man to clear saddlebags,
greatcoat, and umbrella. But when once mounted, with a high
pommel in front, cloak and umbrella behind, you are not easily
dismounted. In these long journeys there is very little mounting and dismounting; rarely more than once or twice in a day.
Accoutred and mounted, our friends came around us with
full hearts and tearful eyes, with hopes and, perhaps, some
regrets and forebodings. We turned our horses toward their
long and toilsome journey, and thus we parted with friends
we were destined never more to meet. There is little to re-
count in this journey excepting its daily toil.

ii

BACK IN ENGLAND Flower was surprised to find the intense interest
that existed about the new settlement, but was sometimes at a loss
to make his former countrymen understand the very different conditions that prevailed in backwoods America.

During the winter I was constantly applied to in person
and by letter for information and advice on the subject of
emigration, by persons in every rank but chiefly from those in
moderate circumstances.

In describing Western America, and the mode of living
there, I found some difficulty in giving a truthful picture to
the Englishman who had never been out of England. In
speaking of a field, the only field he had ever seen was a plot
of ground from five to fifty acres in extent, surrounded by a
ditch, a bank, and a live hawthorn fence; it has two or more
well-made gates that swing freely on their hinges and clasp

firmly when shut. The word field brings this picture to his eye. A zig-zag fence it is difficult for him to understand, but why gates should swing freely on their hinges in England and drag on the ground in America is incomprehensible.

You tell of a log house. The only houses he has seen are buildings with plastered or papered walls, with ceilings and floors, with halls, passages, cellars, and attics, and each room furnished with a good chimney and hearth. The simple log house he can scarcely realize. But few can comprehend the difficulties arising from an absence of population. To try and carry them from the conveniences of civilized life, ever present to their minds, I have said: suppose you and your family placed under a clump of oak trees such as stand in an extensive and beautiful English park, with the sky above, the earth below, no fence, no house, and perhaps no person within twenty miles, and you may have some conception of your situation in a new and unpeopled country. The gloomily disposed would shake their heads in despondency. The sanguine would make light of the difficulties, and be charmed with the picture. So people would reflect the color of their own minds upon the sketch you gave them.

The publication in England of our travels, my return, and personal communication with a host of individuals had given a widespread knowledge of what we had done and what we intended to do. Our call had received a response from the farmers of England, the miners of Cornwall, the drovers of Wales, the mechanics of Scotland, the West India planter, the inhabitants of the Channel Isles, and the "gentleman of no particular business" of the Emerald Isle. All were moving or preparing to move to join us in another hemisphere. The cockneys of London had decided on the reversal of their city habits, to breathe the fresh air of the prairies. Parties were moving, or preparing to move, in all directions. At one time, the movement appeared as if it would be national.

Much of the personal communication Flower speaks of was carried on by Birkbeck from the front lines when he was not engaged in supervising the construction of log buildings. The manuscript of his *Notes* on the journey had hardly left his hand before he began a series of letters to friends in England, copies of which he published in 1818 as *Letters from Illinois*. The facility of his pen did not escape censure by the conservative *Quarterly Review*, which concluded a scathing review of the *Notes* by remarking that

We had proceeded thus far, and were about to close our remarks, when another production of Morris Birkbeck reached us. For a farmer, he seems unusually fond of the pen, and, in justice to his taste, we may observe that he is likely to find it more productive than his plough. The date of his "Notes," which we have reviewed, is September, 1817, when, as he expresses it, he had just "*settled down*" in his wilderness; and only two months after (namely, in November), we find him busily at work on a second volume! A third, and a fourth, we doubt not, are already on the way to his publisher.

In his letter of January 17, 1818, Birkbeck describes some of the activity taking place in Flower's absence.

I am now going to take you to the prairies, to show you the very beginning of our settlement. Having fixed on the northwestern portion of our prairie for our future residence and farm, the first act was building a cabin about two hundred yards from the spot where the house is to stand. This cabin is built of round straight logs, about a foot in diameter, lying upon each other and notched in at the corners, forming a room eighteen feet long by sixteen; the intervals between the logs "chuncked," that is, filled in with slips of wood; and "mudded," that is, daubed with a plaster of mud; a spacious chimney, built also of logs, stands like a bastion at one end; the roof is well covered with four hundred "clapboards" of cleft oak, very much like the pales used in England for fencing parks. A hole is cut through the side, called, very properly, the "door (the through)," for which there is a "shutter" made also of cleft oak and hung on wooden hinges. All this has been executed by contract, and well executed, for twenty dollars.

I have since added ten dollars to the cost for the luxury of a floor and ceiling of sawn boards, and it is now a comfortable habitation.

To this cabin you must accompany me, a young English friend, and my boy Gillard, whom you may recollect at Wanborough. We arrived in the evening, our horses heavily laden with our guns and provisions and cooking utensils and blankets, not forgetting the all-important axe. This was immediately put in requisition, and we soon kindled a famous fire before which we spread our pallets, and, after a hearty supper, soon forgot that beside ourselves, our horses, and our dogs, the wild animals of the forest were the only inhabitants of our wide domain. Our cabin stands at the edge of the prairie, just within the wood, so as to be concealed from the view until you are at the very door. Thirty paces to the east the prospect opens from a commanding eminence over the prairie, which extends four miles to the south and southeast, and over the woods beyond to a great distance; whilst the high timber behind, and on each side to the west, north, and east, forms a sheltered cove about five hundred yards in width. It is about the middle of this cove, two hundred and fifty yards from the wood each way but open to the south, that we propose building our house.

Well, having thus established myself as a resident proprietor, in the morning my boy and I (our friend having left us) sallied forth in quest of neighbours, having heard of two new settlements at no great distance. Our first visit was to Mr. Emmerson, who had just established himself in a cabin similar to our own at the edge of a small prairie two miles northwest of us. We found him a respectable young man, more farmer than hunter, surrounded by a numerous family, and making the most of a rainy day by mending the shoes of his household. We then proceeded to Mr. Woodland's, about the same distance southwest. He is an inhabitant of longer standing, for he arrived in April; Mr. Emmerson in August. He has since built for us a second cabin connected with the first by a covered roof or porch, which is very convenient, forming together a commodious dwelling.

In our walk we saw no game but partridges and a squirrel.
We found plenty of grapes, which I thought delicious. The
soil seemed to improve in fertility on closer inspection, and
the country appeared more pleasant; in fact, my mind was at
ease, and this spreads a charm over external objects. Our
township is a square of six miles each side, or thirty-six square
miles; and what may properly be called our neighbourhood
extends about six miles round this township in every direction.
Six miles to the north is the boundary of surveyed lands. Six
miles to the east is the Bonpas, a stream which joins the Big
Wabash about six miles south of us where the latter river
makes a bold bend to the west, approaching within six miles
of the Little Wabash; this river forms our western boundary,
at about the same distance up to the northern line of survey
above mentioned. The centre of this tract is our prairie, containing about 4,000 acres.

There are many other prairies, or natural meadows, of
various dimensions and qualities, scattered over this surface, which consists of about two hundred square miles, containing perhaps twelve human habitations, all erected, I believe, within one year of our first visit—most of them within
three months. At or near the mouth of the Bonpas, where it
falls into the Big Wabash, we project a shipping port; a ridge
of high land without any intervening creek will afford an easy
communication with the river at that place.

There are no very good mill-seats on the streams in our
neighbourhood; but our prairie affords a most eligible site for
a windmill; we are, therefore, going to erect one immediately;
the materials are in great forwardness, and we hope to have it
in order to grind the fruits of the ensuing harvest.

Two brothers and the wife of one of them started from the
village of Puttenham, close to our old Wanborough, and have
made their way out to us. They are carpenters, and are now
very usefully employed in preparing the scantlings for the
mill and other purposes. You may suppose how cordially we
received these good people. They landed at Philadelphia, not
knowing where on this vast continent they should find us.
From thence they were directed to Pittsburgh, a wearisome

journey over the mountains of more than 300 miles. At Pittsburgh they bought a little boat for six or seven dollars and came gently down the Ohio, 1,200 miles, to Shawneetown. From thence they proceeded on foot till they found us. On their way they had many flattering offers; but true to their purpose, though uninvited and unlooked for, they held out to the end, and I believe they are well satisfied with their reception and prospects.

By the first of March I hope to have two ploughs at work, and may possibly put in 100 acres of corn this spring. Early in May, I think, we shall be all settled in a convenient temporary dwelling, formed of a range of cabins of ten rooms, until we can accomplish our purpose of building a more substantial house.

Nor had Birkbeck's pen been idle in the attempt to gain more land through Congressional aid, his hope being that Congress would set aside a tract of land as yet unsurveyed, and unavailable for purchase at the land office, which his group might have the exclusive right to buy. He had fired off a petition to Congress which he knew by the time of his letter of March 24 was likely to be ignored, as indeed it proved to be. Nevertheless, he copied it out for his English correspondent, no doubt proud of its high-minded sentiments and equally high-flown language.

To the Representatives of the United States in Congress assembled, the Memorial of Morris Birkbeck, an English farmer, lately settled in the Territory of the Illinois, respectfully states—

That a number of his countrymen, chiefly yeomen farmers, farming labourers, and rural mechanics, are desirous of removing with their families and their capital into this country, provided that, by having situations prepared for them, they might escape the wearisome and expensive travel in quest of a settlement, which has broken the spirits and drained the purses of many of their emigrant brethren, terminating too frequently in disappointment.

Many estimable persons of the classes above mentioned

have reposed such a degree of confidence in the experience
of your memorialist, as would attract them to the spot which
he has chosen for himself. Their attention has accordingly
been directed with some anxiety to his movements; and when,
after a laborious journey through the states of Ohio and Indiana, he has at length fixed on a situation in the Illinois
adapted to his private views, settlements are multiplying so
rapidly around it, that it does not afford a scope of eligible
unappropriated land, to which he could invite any considerable number of his friends.

There are, however, lands as yet unsurveyed lying about
twenty miles north of this place, on which sufficient room
might be obtained; and the object of this memorial is to solicit
the grant by purchase of a tract of this land, for the purpose
of introducing a colony of English farmers, labourers, and
mechanics.

Feeling, as does your memorialist, that the people of England and the people of America are of one family, notwithstanding the unhappy political disputes which have divided
the two countries, he believes that this recollection will be sufficient to insure, from the representatives of a free people, a
favourable issue to his application in behalf of their suffering
brethren.

(Signed)   *Morris Birkbeck*
Nov. 20, 1817.

My proposal in the above memorial was indefinite, design-
edly, that if acceded to it might be on a general principle to be
extended as far as would be found beneficial, and might be
guarded from abuse by provisions arising out of the principle
itself. I entertained a hope that it would be referred to a committee, who would have permitted me to explain my views,
and, possibly, I may yet have an opportunity of doing so, as I
have not yet learned that it has been absolutely rejected.
Other petitions for grants of lands in favour of particular
descriptions of emigrants have been rejected during this session for reasons which my friends give me to understand will
be fatal to mine.

Yet, as he said, a good number of his "suffering countrymen" might yet be "benefited by the arrangements we are making for their reception on a contracted scale."

As arrangements progressed and plans matured, Birkbeck also worked out a land policy to guide the settlement. Though he had emphasized strongly in his peroration to *Notes on a Journey* that he had no intention of forming a society exclusively English and that Americans were welcome, his thoughts, by the pressure of events, and his sympathies, by the fact of his origin, brought the English increasingly to the fore. There was an insistent demand in England for what he could offer. The *Monthly Review*, always kindly disposed to his books, editorialized in 1822 that

Every month brings forth a book of travels through Canada or the Western States of America, holding out the most flattering hopes of prosperity to those who will establish themselves on the other side of the Atlantic. Yet it is neither political nor religious persecution which now drives a healthy and a hardy race, in the prime of life, from our shores: it is distress of mind—impending poverty—the stagnation of trade, commerce, and agriculture—the intolerable weight of public burdens—and the hopelessness of any effectual relief, which have broken the spirit of so many thousands of wretched fugitives.

But there were also those who, like Frances Wright the previous year, spoke out against the practice of national groups huddling together, much as Jefferson had advised Flower. Wrote Miss Wright:

The settlement must undoubtedly possess some peculiar attractions for an English emigrant, promising him as it does the society of his own countrymen, an actual or ideal advantage to which he is seldom insensible. Generally speaking, however, it may ultimately be as well for him as for the community to which he attaches himself that he should become speedily incorporated with the people of the soil. It is not every man who is gifted with the vigorous intellect and liberal sentiments of Mr. Birkbeck; many emigrants bring with them

prejudices and predilections which can only be rubbed away
by a free intercourse with the natives of the country. By sitting down at once among them they will more readily acquire
an accurate knowledge of their political institutions and learn
to estimate the high privileges which these impart to them;
and thus, attaching themselves to their adopted country not
from mere sordid motives of interest but also from feeling and
principle, become not only *naturalized* but *nationalized*.

It was in this glare of publicity and under the burden of this
gratuitous advice that Birkbeck shaped his policy. He gave his
most mature expression of it in terms of a concrete case that he
posed to an English inquirer.

In this country they build "cob houses"; a "cob" is the interior
part of a head of Indian corn after the grains are stripped off.
With these cobs, which are lying about everywhere, structures are raised by the little half-Indian brats very much like
our "houses of cards," whose chief merit lies in their tumbling
down before they are finished—or like castles in the air, which
are built by most people in every country under the age of
fifty.

But my anticipations regarding our English Prairie are
neither cob houses nor card houses, nor, I think, castles in the
air, for the last weighty reason, the age of the architect. And
for a reason still more substantial, viz. our social building is
begun on a firm and good foundation, and with good materials.

And now I come (quitting all metaphor) to your commis-
sion. I will purchase for you a section of land, 640 acres, for
which I shall give, by paying the whole amount down, only
$1,036, or 1 dollar 62 cents per acre; and the remainder of
your remittance I shall hold at your disposal, to purchase
land, if you please, where we do not desire to see inhabitants.
This section I shall reserve for you in the full belief that you
will come and settle amongst us. If I were to lay out the whole
six hundred pounds in the usual way of entering land, by
paying the first instalment of half a dollar per acre, it would

cover more than *eight square miles;* and on your arrival a few
years hence to take possession of your estate, instead of finding yourself in a circle of perhaps thirty prosperous families
you would have to settle in a desert of your own creating. Had
I executed half the commissions of this kind which have been
proposed to me, I must have contented myself with "cob
houses" instead of those delightful and reasonable hopes of a
happy society round our English Prairie, in which I believe no
one can sympathize more fully than yourself.

I don't want an agrarian law to define the limit of every
man's estate; but it is plain that if we preoccupy the land we
must live by ourselves. Our colony must, to be prosperous, or
indeed to have an existence worthy the name, be composed of
persons who own the land they cultivate and cultivate the
lands they own. If any of us have funds to spare, and choose
to invest them in land, it must not be on our own settlement.
I have taken up far more than I have an intention of retaining,
merely to exclude speculations which would frustrate our
views.

Our application to Congress has not succeeded, which
renders it more desirable to make room for our countrymen,
many of whom are directing their steps to this place.

iii

ALL THIS WHILE Flower had been busy in England. By messenger
he sent back £3,000 from Birkbeck's farm interests at Wanborough, with the expectation that another £8,700 would soon
be forthcoming, making, as he says, about $55,000 as the share
Birkbeck contributed to the founding of the English Settlement.
And he had established himself in the counting-house of James
Lawrence, a merchant tailor in London, where he conducted a
kind of informal emigration office to supply information to en-
thusiasts who had read Birkbeck's book. Rapidly shaping up were
two groups of emigrants: forty-four men and one woman, under
the leadership of Charles Trimmer, a former neighbor of Birkbeck in Surrey; and another party of about the same size under
the leadership of Lawrence. The first was composed mostly of

farmers, many of whom had worked for Birkbeck; the second of
London mechanics and tradesmen. Both groups sailed from Bristol
in March, 1818, in the ship *Achilles*.

The Lawrence and Trimmer party landed safely at Philadelphia early in June. They made their way, some in wagons
some on horseback, over the mountains to Pittsburgh, then
descending the Ohio in flatboats to Shawneetown in August
proceeded without delay on foot, in wagons and on horseback,
to Mr. Birkbeck's cabin on the Boltinghouse Prairie. Of this
first party Mr. Birkbeck had long notice, and he had made
for them the best preparation he could. He had erected a
square of rough log cabins, with two doors in each, and a
small sash window in every door. This rendezvous, afterward
called the barracks, was for all comers. Into this the first
ship's company—eighty-eight in number—went, all men, excepting three women. I must leave to imagination the various feelings of its motly inmates, some used to the refinements
of civilized life, all to the comfort of a home however humble;
some without money, all for a time without occupation; without vegetables, corn bread and salt pork their only diet,
whisky their sole luxury and consolation, and some not able to
get that. It was for a time a fermenting mass. Strange and
conflicting emotions exhibited themselves in ludicrous succession. Some laughed and joked; some moped and sulked; some
cursed and swore. Things worked right in time. The activity and energy of the national character were soon displayed.
     The next ship with emigrants for the prairies, which sailed
from Liverpool in the following month of April, was chartered
by myself for the party that came with me. My own immediate family and friends occupied the cabin; my domestic servants and other emigrants going out to join us filled the steerage; and my livestock of cows, hogs, and sheep, of the choicest
breeds of England, took up all the spare room on deck. My
father and mother, in easy circumstances, and aged sixty-
three, accompanied me, with my two sisters, young women
grown, one brother, William, a young man, the other, Ed-

ward, a lad, Miss Fordham, my cousin, going to join her
brother in Illinois, with three attached female- and one man-
servant. The family of these most respectable people had
lived with our family for three generations, and a distant
removal could not now separate us. These, with myself and
my two sons, young boys, were my immediate family party.
But going to our settlement in this ship were also Mr. Francis
Rotch and brother, friends of Mr. Birkbeck, and Mr. Filder,
a gentleman rather advanced in years, a man of considerable
property. Dr. C. Pugsley and wife, and small family, from
London, and Mr. Adam Corrie, I think, from the county of
Nottingham, were also passengers. Besides these was Mr.
John Woods, then a young man; also, Mr. John Ingle, and his
family, from Cambridgeshire. Mr. David Bennett, and family; Mr. White, and family, carpenter and builder, from London; Captain (baptismal name) Stone, wife, and family, were
also of the company. Mr. Stone was steward on my farm in
England. He now had the care of my cattle, sheep, and swine.
These, and some other names not recollected, made a party of
three score and more bound to our settlement. It was the same
ship, the *Ann Maria*, and the same captain that brought me
over so safely and rapidly in the previous fall. We arrived
without accident at New York, after a passage of fifty days,
and but one week after the Bristol ship that sailed a month before us. To remove all these people and their luggage, and the
animals that I had brought, to our settlement nearly a thousand miles inland was no small undertaking at a time when
there was neither turnpike nor railroad, and steamboats
few and in the infancy of their management. Patience, toil,
time, and money were all required and all were freely bestowed.

Flower's mention of his two young sons comes as something of a
surprise, for he gives no hint anywhere of a marriage previous to
his with Miss Andrews. Since his book is the only reliable source of
information about his life, one must assume that his previous marriage was painful to recall—an assumption somewhat substanti-
ated by the gossip of William Faux which appears later and sug-

gests that Miss Andrews herself was the agent of a wrecked former marriage.

At any rate, the bulk of the original settlers had now reached American shores and were to begin their arduous trek westward.

On reaching land, the ship's party was broken up and smaller parties were formed of people of similar habits and tastes clubbing together for mutual assistance on the way. Those of small means proceeded on without loss of time. Those of more means lingered a little in the cities, and with their new friends, before taking their departure for what was then the Far West.

Mr. John Woods, Mr. Ingle, Mr. White, and Mr. Bennett formed a party for travel; on their arrival at Pittsburgh purchased a covered flatboat and descended the Ohio River together. Mr. Filder, I think, bought a horse and rode the whole distance to Vincennes, on the Wabash. The Rotches, brothers, came, I think, with my father's party as far as Cincinnati, from thence on horseback. My father's family spent the first winter in Lexington, Kentucky, whilst I was preparing their residence in Illinois. In this manner the various individuals and parties made the best way they could. Some of them were joined by individuals and families of English that were lingering on the seaboard without any specific reference to our settlement, but seeing the emigration, and having read the publications, joined and went on. I think every accession from the East was English. Not an American joined us, excepting one, a Captain Kenyon of a merchant vessel formerly trading to India. He came in my boat down the Ohio. He was not a man suited to the settlement by previous habits. An unavailable member, he did not stay long in the settlement.

I had traveled much before this trip. First, my journey alone, two thousand miles; then with Mr. Birkbeck's party westward; and the return with my wife, another one thousand miles; but always on horseback. Now I was to enter on a new experience of travel. With a covered traveling carriage, strongly built but light, and a capital pair of horses, I drove

from Philadelphia to Chambersburg. I had often driven on
English roads, but never before on American. The roads were
then for the most part in their natural state, pretty good when
dry, almost impassable for mud if the weather was wet, and,
in both cases, plentifully set with stumps. In many parts of the
Alleghany Mountains, the road was merely a track made by
the wagons from Philadelphia, going up the easiest water-
course on the mountainside, with all the large boulders unbroken, giving us severe bumps and sudden and dangerous
descents. The charge for carriage from Philadelphia to Pittsburgh was *reduced* then to $7 per hundred pounds. With me,
in my carriage, I took my two sons and Miss Maria Fordham.
My father and mother and sisters, resting longer at Philadelphia, traveling more deliberately, and proposing to pass
the winter at Lexington, Kentucky, Miss Fordham took a seat
in my carriage to accompany me and my wife to Illinois. The
roads were good to Chambersburg, and I rapidly drove
along.

My wife and I were once more together, and with us a little
daughter but a few weeks old. We stayed awhile at Chambersburg, to make acknowledgment to our newly found
friends there who had been so kind to Mrs. Flower during
her long and anxious solitude.

My carriage was soon filled, my horses were strong, and we
were proceeding onward to a given point in the pleasing hope
of meeting again, in the prairies, the friends we had left at
Princeton and of carrying out together the scheme of emigration and settlement that we had begun and thus far carried on
to a successful point. The various objects we had in view, for
which I was sent to England, were all accomplished with
singular success. My voyage across the Atlantic was of unusual speed. The funds for Mr. Birkbeck were safely sent, exceeding somewhat in amount his own expectations. The publications made by book, pamphlet, and newspaper had excited
general attention. By a singular coincidence, my father had
sold, a few days before my arrival in England, his dwelling
and lands in Marden for £23,000, thus giving to himself, my
mother, brothers, and sisters, an opportunity of returning

with me in the spring, which they willingly embraced, to take
up their abode in the prairies.

Both ships arrived in America without accident; most of the
people had crossed the mountains in health, and many of
these, by the time I got to Pittsburgh, were proceeding down
the Ohio River to their ultimate destination.

Many of us bound for Illinois met at Pittsburgh. Some were
ruffled in temper. All seemed to be more or less disturbed by
the roughness of the journey passed, and in anticipation of
the new experiences on the river to come. A week was often
lost at Pittsburgh in fitting up boats or chaffering for horses.
Some were buying flatboats; some purchased skiffs, fitted with
an awning, for one or two persons; some determined to take
it on horseback; but most of them went down the river. Here
my brother William joined me, and gave me great assistance
on the voyage and the first two months in Illinois. I purchased
a keelboat and a flatboat, and lashed them together, the
former for my family, the latter for my horses; carriage fastened on the top of the flat; four English farm laborers for
oarsmen. With difficulty I procured a pilot who engaged to go
a hundred and fifty miles with me down the river. But he left
me just before coming to a difficult part of the river called
Dead Man's Shoal. There was no other resource; I had to take
the steering oar, and was soon aground. With much labor
and difficulty we got off, poling and shoving up to our knees
in the river, trying to get the boat off. With a "Pittsburgh
Navigator" (a book with a map of the river in which all the
islands, shoals, and dangerous places are laid down) in one
hand and the steering oar in the other, I took my station at the
helm. With my total inexperience, I found my new position
both anxious and laborious. The labor and exposure I did not
mind, but the constant watching and state of doubt was trying. I got on pretty well, going along by day and tying up at
night. But it was not all smooth sailing. I got into one dangerous scrape, and out of it, too, as luck would have it. It was
this. The "Navigator" had described a certain island of great
length close to the north shore, with a narrow and dangerous
channel of rapid water, as especially dangerous and to be

avoided by every craft descending the river. I had been long
looking for this island, and presently it came in sight. I was
approaching it in the middle of the river, a very considerable
distance off. I was not sufficiently aware of the distance a
sand bar extended from a point of an island. When about to
steer for the Kentucky shore, my boats grounded. In pushing
off, we were swung round into the current leading into the
very channel we were warned to avoid. I felt as we approached the danger as a man may be supposed to feel when
he finds himself and craft drawing into the waters of Niagara.
I was, for a short time, uncertain, weak, and helpless through
sheer fright. Our two boats, lashed together, entered the dark
channel overhung by trees. The water was running at a rapid
rate, and the channel was full of black and dangerous snags.
I called to the oarsmen to give way with all their might. Seizing the steering oar myself, which felt in my hands as light as
a feather, giving it sudden twists and turns to port and lee,
going through the crooked channel with scarce room to pass
between the snags, we eventually came out safe. Passing a
flatboat tied up in the stream beyond, I was accosted by the
old man, as he sat smoking his pipe on the roof of his boat:
"I say, stranger, you must be a mighty favorite *summers* to
get through with your two boats from that devil's race-
course!"

At Cincinnati my crew deserted me, and it was some days
before I could muster another. As we were floating along one
warm summer day, my eldest son, Richard, walking on a narrow pathway between the body of the boat and the edge,
missed his foothold and fell into the river. Mr. Hayward, a
young gentleman from Oxfordshire whom we had taken into
our boat, heard the splash and plunged in; both child and man
disappeared. They came to the surface, Hayward holding the
child by the coat collar. They were on the lower side of the
boat. Hayward, who was a good swimmer, finding the boat
press against them, with great presence of mind dived with
the child in his arms under the boat and came up on the other
side, where I first lifted my son from the water and then assisted Hayward on board. Very fortunately, no other injuries

were experienced than a fright and a drenching. They were soon made comfortable by a change of clothing.

A few little incidents and we arrived at Shawneetown, a fortnight after Trimmer and Lawrence's party arrived at the same place.

Leaving my boats I again proceeded by land in my Philadelphia vehicle with two famous grays. Myself, my wife, my two sons, and Miss Fordham rode in the carriage, which was filled with articles of the first necessity. My brother William rode on horseback. Mr. Fordham, who had come to meet me, was also on horseback. He had remained with Mr. Birkbeck's family during the winter, making frequent excursions into the prairies to assist in the preparatory arrangements, as well as more distant journeys to Cincinnati and Louisville for a variety of articles with which he loaded a flatboat and descended the Ohio. From him we learned all the news of the settlement; the arrival of Lawrence and Trimmer's party, and various horsemen who had come overland from Cincinnati. All these were for the time occupants of the hollow-square of log cabins, afterward facetiously called the "barracks" from its limited space, offering unavoidably but limited accommodations to any, and this was becoming more and more crowded every day. Mr. Birkbeck's family occupied two cabins at some little distance from the general rendezvous.

Enquiring of the health and condition of everybody, he said they were generally well, but Mr. Birkbeck he thought had somewhat changed. He looked older, was rather testy, and occasionally gave short answers; and said some other things that rather surprised me. Mr. Fordham also told me that he had built two cabins on my land. Near to one he had dug a well. In this cabin he had placed a French Canadian family from Cattinet, that there might be some human beings on the place. The other he had built a quarter of a mile off on a more beautiful site, a situation which he thought I should like as my permanent residence. After hearing all this, I decided to drive to the last described cabin. After a drive of sixty miles in two days, we were at the prairies. I entered the prairie at the same spot from which we had first seen it; now with quite different feelings and other cares. On entering the prairie, my large horses were covered with the tall prairie grass, and laboriously dragged the heavy-laden vehicle. The cabin built for me was well sheltered by wood from the north and east, with an arm of the prairie lying south in a gently descending slope for a quarter of a mile; it was as pretty a situation as could be desired. The cabin could not boast of many comforts. With a clapboard roof held on by weight poles, and a rough puncheon floor, it had neither door nor window. Two doorways were cut out, and the rough logs were scutched down inside. All the chips and ends of logs left by the backwoods builders lay strewed upon the floor. We were now face to face with the privations and difficulties of a first settlement in the wilderness. But greater than all other inconveniences was the want of water. There was no water nearer than the cabin in which the French family lived, a quarter of a mile off.

It is impossible for any one living in old countries, where the common conveniences of life have been accumulating for centuries and ages, to understand the situation of an individual or small family when first alighting in the prairies without even that indirect aid from art and cultivation common to all in a civilized community.

The poorest man in an old country thinks nothing of a road or a path, or a drink of water from a well. He is the owner or occupier of some sort of a house, maybe a small cottage, but even he can shut his door against a storm and crouch in safety before a small fire, made in a fireplace, perhaps enjoying the luxuries of a three-legged stool and a small deal table, some shed outside to tie up a horse or cow. Not so here. A rough roof and a rough floor we had, and that was all. In three days the Frenchman, Jean Mummonie, brought us a turkey, for which we paid him a quarter dollar, but there were two days to live before the turkey came. The floor was cleared, and a fire kindled in a hole where a hearth was to be. One of us had a half-mile trip for the water. Then for the first time we knew the blessing of an iron teakettle. Our first meal on the floor from such provisions as the carriage afforded, crackers, cheese, and tea without milk, drunk alternately from one or two tin cups. Some sitting, some kneeling, some stretched at length, resting on an elbow ancient fashion. This may be called beginning at the beginning. Romantic certainly. Picturesque to be sure. The gypsies in England in their snug tents, sheltered by pleasant hawthorn hedges, camp kettles teeming with savory hare, partridge, and trout raised at other folks' expense—we were far before or behind them, as the case may be viewed. But then I was in my own house, on my own land, in a free and independent republic, might cast my vote into any hollow tree for coon or 'possum to be president of the United States. All this is very sustaining to a patriotic heart just from Europe, from the terribly oppressing kings, dukes, priests that we hear so much about. But for this how could we have stood it? The second day was only a little more embarrassing than the first. Our horses, untied from the carriage wheels, had to be led to grass, or grass cut for them by our pocket knives. The second night came. What, nobody from the settlement only two miles off; what did this mean?

I saw that I could receive no benefit or aid from any previous preparation and had only myself to rely upon. No water near, a well was of the first necessity. Two laborers, one English and one American, were set at work, and struck a solid sandstone rock three feet from the surface. The nearest forge was where the town of Carmi now stands, thirty miles distant. About every other day I sent to Carmi to have tools sharpened. Two sawyers set to work with a pit saw broke the iron handle of the saw. I sent a man on horseback to Harmonie, twenty-five miles, to get it mended. He left the saw, and then rode off with horse, saddle, and bridle. I never saw him more.

My old friend Birk gave me a call to say "howd'ye," bringing a haunch of venison, for which I paid him thirty-seven and a half cents, about eighteen pence sterling. Think of that, ye aldermen of London! Our money was not decimally divided then. It was the Spanish coin: dollar, half, quarter, twelve-and-a-half and six-and-a-fourth cents, all in separate silver coins, no copper passing.

"Birk, I want a smokehouse, well roofed, scutched inside, and well chinked. How much?" "Ten dollars," said he. "Find yourself (that is, feed yourself), haul your own logs. When?" "Tomorrow." The house was built; money paid; whisky given; man rode home, drunk and happy; all in a quiet friendly way.

For a moment let us glance at the situation of these settlers, a thousand miles inland, at the heels of the retreating Indians. A forest from the Atlantic shore behind them, but thinly settled with small villages far apart from each other. To the west, one vast uninhabited wilderness of prairie, interspersed with timber, extending two thousand miles to the Pacific Ocean. Excepting St. Louis, on the Mississippi, then a small place, and Kaskaskia, yet smaller, there were no inhabitants west of us. About the same time, one or two small American settlements were forming a few miles east of the Mississippi as we were planting ourselves a few miles west of the Wabash. The first member of Congress had to ride an intervening space of a hundred and fifty miles of wilderness between the little settlements of his constituents lying in the west and east of the state. There were no roads on land, no steamboats on the waters. The road, so-called, leading to Vandalia (then composed of about a dozen log houses) was made by one man on horseback following in the track of another, every rider making the way a little easier to find, until you came to some slush or swampy place, where all trace was lost, and you got through as others had done, by guessing at the direction, often riding at hazard for miles until you stumbled on the track again. And of these blind traces there were but three or four in the southern half of the state. No roads were worked, no watercourses bridged. Before getting to Vandalia, there was a low piece of timbered bottom land, wet and swampy and often covered with water, through which every traveler had to make his way as he best could, often at the risk of his life. Such was the state of the country. No man could feel sure that he was within the limits of the state but from knowing that he was west of the Wabash and east of the Mississippi.

We had some difficulties, peculiar to ourselves, as a foreign people. The Americans, by pushing onward and onward for almost two generations, had a training in handling the axe and opening farms, and, from experience, bestowing their labor in the most appropriate manner which we, from our inexperience, often did not. Fresh from an old country teeming with the conveniences of civilized life, at once in a wilderness with all our inexperience, our losses were large from misplaced labor. Many were discouraged, and some returned, but the mass of the settlers stayed, and, by gradual experience, corrected their first errors, thus overcoming difficulties which had wellnigh overcome them. The future success of the settlement was obtained by individual toil and industry.

Of the first inconveniences and sufferings, my family had its full share. The summer had been very hot and latterly wet. Thunder showers of daily occurrence sent mosquitoes in swarms. My cabin, recently built of course of green logs, unfurnished, with rank vegetation growing all around it and up to its very sides, was in its situation and in itself a sufficient cause of disease. My shepherd and his family came, bringing a few choice sheep and an English high-bred cow. His whole family, in a few days, all fell sick, lying in a small cabin just built about a hundred yards from my own. Mr. White, carpenter, from London, wife, and two children occupied a two-horse wagon and a soldier's tent. There was no house for him; they all fell sick. My two sons were speedily taken with fever and ague, to us then a new disease. Miss Fordham, who shared our cabin, was attacked with the same disease. My constitution, strong and good, yielding from exposure to heat and rain, took another form of disease. Boils and irritable sores broke out on both my legs, from knee to ankle, incapacitating me for a time from walking. Thus we were situated for two or three weeks, without the slightest assistance from any source or supplies other than from my own wagons, as they slowly arrived from Shawneetown, giving us sufficient bedding, with flour and bacon. All the other merchandise and furniture did but add to our present embarrassment, in attempts to protect them from the weather and in endeavoring to dry what was wet.

We were carried through this period of trial by the unremitting labor and self-sacrifice of my wife. She alone prepared all our food and bedding, and attended to the wants of the sick and the suffering by night and day. To all this was added a fatigue that a strong man might have shrunk from in bringing water from that distant well. Sustained in her unremitting labors by unbounded devotion to her family and a high sense of duty to all within her reach, her spirit and her power seemed to rise above the manifold trials by which she was surrounded. And thus we were saved from probable death or certain dispersion. The incessant labor of the mother told on the infant at the breast. It sickened and died.

The buildings necessary to secure our horses and our goods, now daily arriving, were built by the backwoodsmen of whom I have before spoken, among them my old friend Birk. These men worked well in the morning, slackened toward noon as the drams of whisky (which they would not work without) told upon them, and indulged in imprecations, brawls, and rough-and-tumble fights toward evening.

Emigrants were continually flowing in. They first visited Mr. Birkbeck, who had but small accommodations; then came to me, who, at that time, had still less. At this stage, we were experiencing many of the inconveniences of a population in the wilderness in advance of necessary food and shelter. Do as you will, if you are the very first in the wilderness, there are many inconveniences, privations, hardships, and sufferings that can not be avoided. My own family, one day, were so close run for provisions that a dish of the tenderest buds and shoots of the hazel was our only resort. Emigrants kept coming in, some on foot, some on horseback, and some in wagons. Some sought employment, and took up with such labor as they could find. Others struck out and made small beginnings for themselves. Some, with feelings of petulance, went further and fared worse; others dropped back into the towns and settlements in Indiana. At first, I had as much as I could do to build a few cabins for the workmen I then employed, and in erecting a large farmyard, a hundred feet square, enclosed by log buildings two stories high; also in building for my father's

family a house of considerable size and appointed with somewhat more of comforts than is generally found in new settlements, to be ready for their reception on the following summer.

iv

LIFE WAS MOVING FAST on the prairie; a number of important
things had happened before the new immigrants arrived in mid-
summer of 1818. Of lasting importance was the fact that they were
coming into a sovereign state of the Union now, no longer into a
territory. In a letter written to his brother-in-law in England in
April, 1818, and not intended for publication, Birkbeck expressed
the exaltation others must have felt.

We have this morning received official information that we,
the inhabitants of Illinois, are forthwith invited to assemble
by our deputies in convention to frame for ourselves and our
descendants a Constitution: To *make* the laws which hereafter we shall be bound in duty to respect and obey—and
defend. I am thus unexpectedly placed in a situation I little
thought of when I turned my back on English farming. A
mighty ridiculous position for a Surrey farmer, to be one of the
founders of a republic as extensive as Great Britain!

The English Settlement, thanks to Birkbeck's persuasive pen,
was already attracting the attention of travelers, many of whom
were willing to write it down as a failure even before it was well
under way; and these Birkbeck undertook to refute. At the moment the defense of the good name of the settlement was of even
greater importance than helping to frame a constitution.

Earliest among these critics was Henry Bradshaw Fearon, who
had been charged by thirty-nine English families in 1817 to search
out a place for settlement in the western wilds and report back to
them. He not only visited Illinois in his tour of five thousand
miles—though not the English Settlement—but had the chance of
delivering an appended critique of Birkbeck's *Notes* and *Letters*
before putting his book to press in 1818.

His *Narrative of a Journey* is remarkably slight in its firsthand treatment of the Illinois Territory. In brief, he didn't like it. The winters were too cold, the summers too hot. He divided the people into four groups: the old French settlers who lived in ease and comfort; the Indians who lived in savagery; the squatters who lived in misery; and "a medley of land jobbers, lawyers, doctors, and farmers who transverse this immense continent, founding settlements and engaging in all kinds of speculation." Birkbeck and his friends must obviously fall among the unsavory characters last mentioned. Then he posed four questions dripping with satiric candor which his patrons should ask themselves before they rushed off to Illinois. The answers were evident.

First—Is it essential to your prosperity and happiness that you should leave England?
Second—Do the habits and character of the American people afford you rational grounds for desiring to become their fellow citizens?
Third—Have all of you the dispositions requisite in order to become cultivators of a wilderness?
Fourth—Assuming that you have those dispositions, are you fitted for such an entire change of pursuits, and can you endure the difficulties and dangers necessarily attendant on such a situation?

If, after cool, deliberate, and rational consideration, with your minds as free from enthusiastic expectations connected with this continent as they well can be under the existence of the present order of things in England, you can answer in the affirmative, then I have little doubt of the propriety of recommending to your attention the Illinois Territory.

Even Elias Pym Fordham, Flower's cousin who had come out with Birkbeck, was writing letters home more than a little critical of Birkbeck's published views of the new Eden. Of *Notes on a Journey* he said

It is correct as far as it goes; but it is the sketch of a traveller who tells the truth when he finds it. But Truth, grotto-loving Goddess, is not often to be seen, except by glimpses, by a

traveller. Mr. Birkbeck could now write a better book if he
would; but, in describing this country, all he would say of
the manners of the people would be tinctured by his precon-
ceived notions. Sketches in general have hitherto been too
sunny.*

However, there were others more kindly disposed, one of whom,
Thomas Hulme, a bleacher from Manchester on an inspection tour
for William Cobbett, visited Birkbeck just before the arrival of
Flower's large party and left the most extensive account of the
settlement at this date.

June 28th. Left Princeton and set out to see Mr. Birkbeck's
settlement in Illinois about 35 miles from Princeton. Before
we got to the Wabash we had to cross a swamp of half a mile
wide; we were obliged to lead our horses, and walk up to the
knees in mud and water. Before we got half across we began
to think of going back; but, there is a sound bottom under it
all, and we waded through it as well as we could. It is, in
fact, nothing but a bed of very soft and rich land, and only
wants draining to be made productive. We soon after came
to the banks of the Great Wabash, which is here about half a
mile broad, and as the ferryboat was crossing over with us I
amused myself by washing my dirty boots. Before we
mounted again we happened to meet with a neighbour of Mr.
Birkbeck's who was returning home; we accompanied him,
and soon entered into the prairie lands, up to our horses'
bellies in fine grass. Our horses were very much tormented
with flies, some as large as the English horsefly and some as
large as the wasp. These flies infest the prairies that are un-
improved about three months in the year, but go away altogether as soon as cultivation begins.

Mr. Birkbeck's settlement is situated between the two Wa-
bashes, and is about ten miles from the nearest navigable
water. We arrived there about sunset, and met with a welcome which amply repaid us for our day's toil. We found

* Reprinted by permission of the publishers, The Arthur H. Clark Company, from Fordham's *Personal Narrative of Travels in Virginia*, etc.

that gentleman with his two sons perfectly healthy and in high spirits; his daughters were at Henderson (a town in Kentucky, on the Ohio) on a visit. At present his habitation is a cabin, the building of which cost only 20 dollars; this little hutch is near the spot where he is about to build his house, which he intends to have in the most eligible situation in the prairie for convenience to fuel and for shelter in winter, as well as for breezes in summer, and will, when that is completed, make one of its appurtenances. I like this plan of keeping the old log house; it reminds the grandchildren and their children's children of what their ancestor has done for their sake.

Few settlers had as yet joined Mr. Birkbeck; that is to say, settlers likely to become "society." He has labourers enough near him, either in his own houses or on land of their own joining his estate. He was in daily expectation of his friends, Mr. Flower's family, however, with a large party besides; they had just landed at Shawneetown, about 20 miles distant. Mr. Birkbeck informs me he has made entry of a large tract of land, lying, part of it, all the way from his residence to the Great Wabash; this he will re-sell again in lots to any of his friends, they taking as much of it and wherever they choose (provided it be no more than they can cultivate), at an advance which I think very fair and liberal.

The whole of his operations had been directed hitherto (and wisely in my opinion) to building, fencing, and other important preparations. He had done nothing in the cultivating way but make a good garden, which supplies him with the only things that he cannot purchase and at present perhaps with more economy than he could grow them. He is within twenty miles of Harmonie, in Indiana, where he gets his flour and all other necessaries (the produce of the country), and therefore employs himself much better in making barns and houses and mills for the reception and disposal of his crops, and fences to preserve them while growing, before he grows them, than to get the crops first. I have heard it observed that any American settler, even without a dollar in his pocket, would have had something growing by this time. Very true! I do not

question that at all; for, the very first care of a settler without
a dollar in his pocket is to get something to eat, and he
would consequently set to work scratching up the earth,
fully confident that after a long summering upon wild flesh
(without salt, perhaps) his own belly would stand him for
barn if his jaws would not for mill. But the case is very
different with Mr. Birkbeck, and at present he has need for
no other provision for winter but about a three-hundredth
part of his fine grass turned into hay, which will keep his
necessary horses and cows; besides which he has nothing
that eats but such pigs as live upon the waste, and a couple
of fine young deer (which would weigh, they say when full
grown, 200 pounds dead weight) that his youngest son is
rearing up as pets.

I was rather disappointed, or sorry, at any rate, not to
find near Mr. Birkbeck's any of the means for machinery
or of the materials for manufactures, such as the water falls
and the minerals and mines which are possessed in such
abundance by the states of Ohio and Kentucky and by some
parts of Pennsylvania. Some of these, however, he may yet
find. Good water he has, at any rate. He showed me a well 25
feet deep, bored partly through hard substances near the bottom, that was nearly overflowing with water of excellent
quality.

July 1st.   Left Mr. Birkbeck's for Harmonie, Indiana.

But the worst criticism was yet to come—attacks brought on in
part by Hulme's relatively sanguine view, which his employer, the
irascible Cobbett, could not accept, and in large measure by Birkbeck's own indiscreet pen. In the first place, Birkbeck was surely
guilty of the rhetoric of anticipation that he blamed the Americans for: contemplating that which might be someday as though
it were already in existence. All too often, as Flower remarked of
an English acquaintance, he raised pigs on paper; visitors were
ever ready to point out the discrepancies between his expectations and his actual results. Then, too, both by his Englishman's
blunt outspokenness and his open, rational cast of mind which
had already dispensed with the restraints of his ancestral religion,
he made observations unlikely to please many Americans. As early

as his *Letters from Illinois* he had outraged the pious by writing on Christmas Day, 1817, from Princeton:

What think you of a community not only without an established religion but of whom a large proportion profess no particular religion, and think as little about the machinery of it as you know was the case with myself? What in some places is esteemed a decent conformity with practices which we despise is here altogether unnecessary. There are, however, some sectaries even here with more of enthusiasm than good temper; but their zeal finds sufficient vent in loud preaching and praying. The courthouse is used by all persuasions indifferently as a place of worship; any acknowledged preacher who announces himself for a Sunday or other day may always collect an audience, and rave or reason as he sees meet. When the weather is favourable, few Sundays pass without something of the sort. It is remarkable that they generally deliver themselves with that chaunting cadence you have heard among the Quakers.

This is Christmas Day, and seems to be kept as a pure holiday—merely a day of relaxation and amusement. Those that choose observe it religiously; but the public opinion does not lean that way, and the law is silent on the subject. After this deplorable account, you will not wonder when you hear of earthquakes and tornadoes amongst us. But the state of political feeling is, if possible, still more deplorable. Republican principles prevail universally. Those few zealous persons—who, like the ten faithful that were *not* found by Abraham, might have stood between their heathen neighbours and destruction—even these are among the most decided foes of all legitimacy, except that of a government appointed by the people. They are as fully armed with carnal weapons as with spiritual; and as determined in their animosity against royalty and its appurtenances as they are against the kingdom of Antichrist, holding it as lawful to use the sword of the flesh for the destruction of the one as that of the spirit for the other.

Children are not baptized or subjected to any superstitious

rite; the parents name them, and that is all. And the last act
of the drama is as simple as the first. There is no consecrated
burial place or funeral service. The body is enclosed in the
plainest coffin; the family of the deceased convey the corpse
into the woods; some of the party are provided with axes and
some with spades; a grave is prepared, and the body quietly
placed in it; then trees are felled and laid over the grave
to protect it from wild beasts. If the party belong to a religious
community, preaching sometimes follows; if not, a few natural
tears are shed in silence, and the scene is closed. These simple
monuments of mortality are not infrequent in the woods.
Marriages are as little concerned with superstitious observ-
ances as funerals; but they are observed as occasions of
festivity.

And from his own settlement in Illinois he wrote even more
strongly when he said:

It is a matter of curious speculation, collecting as we are
from the four winds of heaven as it were, what our society
is to be in regard to religious demonstrations. In the region
we are to inhabit, "the sun shineth" not "upon the just, and
upon the unjust" but upon the earth and the trees and the
wild animals, as it shone before man was created.

There is nothing in the spirit of the government, nor in
the institutions of this Western country, nor in the habits of
the people which gives preponderancy to any sentiment on this
subject of social religion but that of abhorrence of priestly
domination and of all assumption of authority in these matters.

Now, having this "upward road" thus clear before us,
when we shall have settled ourselves in our cabins and fixed
ourselves in our minds as to this world, what sort of a garb,
think you, shall we assume as candidates for the next? To my
very soul I wish that we might assume none but the character
of men who desire to keep their conscience void of offence towards God and towards man—*Nil conscire sibi, nulla palles-
cere culpa.* Another foolish wish! you will say. We shall have

people among us, I dare say, who will undertake to teach religion, the most arrogant of all pretensions I should be apt to call it had not frequent observation convinced me that it has no necessary connexion with arrogance of character. But however that may be, teachers no doubt will arise among us. This most sensitive nerve has been touched, and already I have had the pleasure of two communications on the subject of religious instruction—both from strangers.

One of them, who dates from New Jersey, writes as follows: "I have read your notes on a journey from the coast of Virginia to the Illinois territory; and I sincerely wish you success in every laudable undertaking. The religion of Jesus Christ, disentangled from the embarrassments of every sect and party, I hope you will encourage to the utmost of your power and abilities. In the genuine, uncorrupted, native, and pure spring of the Gospel you view the world as your country and every man as your brother. In that you will find the best security and guaranty of virtue and good morals, and the main spring of civil and religious liberty," &c., &c. As this gentleman's good counsel was not coupled with any tangible proposition, his letter did not call for a reply; in fact, the writer did not favour me with his address.

My other zealous though unknown friend, who dates still more to the north than New Jersey, informs me that many are coming West, and that he wants to come himself if he can "pave the way." "We must," he says, "have an Unitarian church in your settlement, wherever it may be, and I will, if I live, come and open it. I am using every means in my power to promote the principles in. . . . and ultimately to raise a congregation, and give, if possible, a mortal stab to infidelity and bigotry." To this gentleman I replied as follows: "As to your idea of coming out in the character of a minister, I have not a word to say, dissuasive or encouraging. For myself, I am of no sect; and generally in my view those points by which sects are distinguished are quite unimportant, and might be discarded without affecting the essence of true religion. I am, as yourself, a foe to bigotry; but it is a disease for which I think no remedy is so effectual as letting it alone, especially in this happy country where it appears under its mildest character, without the excitements of avarice and ambition." So endeth the first chapter of the first book of our ecclesiastical history.

It would not, however, be the last.

3

"We were silent ever after."

On the arrival of emigrants in the summer of 1818 there were no cabins to shelter them from the heat of the sun by day, or from the dew by night; neither a cow or pig for food, and scarcely a sufficiency for human subsistence to be procured. Sickness to a considerable degree prevailed; but not more than three or four cases of death ensued. Since these inconveniences have been overcome, few places, I believe I may say in the world, have been healthier than the English Settlement in the Illinois.

THUS WROTE RICHARD FLOWER, father of George, in the little book he published soon after settling in America, *Letters from Lexington and the Illinois.* Brother of the celebrated pamphleteer Benjamin Flower, Richard was an articulate controversialist himself, and his voice would be needed in the public squabbles to come.

For now began a time of incessant troubles—between the Birkbeck and Flower families, within each family, and in the community at large. The central issue was the strained relations that mysteriously obtained between Morris Birkbeck and George Flower after Flower's return from England. Whatever occurred in these leading families was bound to be reflected in the entire colony. The break between Birkbeck and Flower resulted in a physical breach in the settlement, leading finally to the founding of two separate towns—Birkbeck's Wanborough and Flower's Albion—and thus to the weakening of both factions in an environment that demanded unity and strength.

Birkbeck says almost nothing about the establishment of his town, and Flower says little more, merely noting that

In August, 1818, the village of Wanborough sprang into existence for the accommodation of the first ship's party, on Mr. Birkbeck's property and under his immediate direction. In October of the same year, Albion was founded under my more immediate superintendence.

And in another place that

The village of Wanborough was laid off by Mr. Birkbeck in five-acre lots. On these were built cabins, rented by some, bought by others. A good ox mill and blacksmith's shop were soon after added to the village. So the settlement was planted in two parts, side by side, about two miles distant from each other.

Travelers were quick to begin playing one town off against the other, usually to Birkbeck's discredit, as Adlard Welby did in 1820.

Our tavern keeper, who was a very respectable farmer, left a good farm near Baldock in Hertfordshire, guided by Mr. Birkbeck's book, to find health, wealth, and freedom at Boltinghouse Prairie. Of the two first both himself and family were quickly getting rid, while they were absolutely working each day like horses without one comfort left. "How came you," said I, "to leave so good a farm as you had in England?" His answer was, "Mr. Birkbeck's book." "You would be glad now to return?" added I. "Sir," said he, "we must not think that way; we have buried our property in getting here, and must here remain!" Such facts as these are worth a thousand flattering theories on the other side; and another may be here added—perhaps a salutary caution to Mr. Birkbeck if this should be the first intimation—that the angry feelings of the poor people who had been entrapped by the deceptious colouring of his writings flashed out in true English threats of tossing him in a blanket! I abstain from comment upon this, my business being to state facts. I forbear too from respect for a man of good natural abilities, misled himself by a sanguine temper which has been the cause of his misleading others. I will be silent too upon the subject of private differences, conceiving that public acts alone are those in which the public are interested and ought to be inquisitive.

He has led people into this wilderness where, for anything he has done, they may in vain look around for the expected shelter; they will see only Mr. Birkbeck's house and garden and perhaps two or three log huts which at present constitute the whole of the new town of Wanborough; in short, he seems only to have thought of himself and to have falsified his public promises. I believe it to be a fact that the colony could not have outlived the winter of 1818, but that the whole must have been dispersed or starved, had it not been for the exertions of Mr. Flower, who perceived in time the coming want, and at considerable trouble and expense obtained a sufficient and timely supply.

Mr. Birkbeck, in his publication, inveighs strongly against land-jobbing; yet if I am correctly informed he has obtained and is now gaining great profits by it—he has entered as many as thirty thousand acres which he now disposes of in lots as high, where he can, as four dollars per acre; it seems indeed to be his only business, to carry on which with better success he has given to others, it is said, an interest in the concern to find out and bring in purchasers of more money than judgment. One of these jackals, reported to be so employed, I met with on the road.

Having said thus much of an individual who has become noted for promissory books, and who therefore deserves to be noted for non-performance, let us turn to the contemplation of that which has been accomplished by those who did not promise anything, but who have done much. Mr. Flower,

ably assisted by his father and in conjunction with a few
others, has formed the settlement of New Albion (an auspicious name); and notwithstanding the miserably unprovided
state in which I found it, much had certainly been done, and
more was rapidly doing towards rendering the place habitable. Among other well-judged resolutions, they had determined that in future all the houses should be substantially
built of bricks, for the manufacture of which they have, as I
understood, plenty of good clay in the neighbourhood.

Welby even goes so far as to blame Birkbeck for the odd characters he finds in Flower's Albion.

The strange heterogeneous mixture of characters which are
collected hither by the magic pen of Morris Birkbeck is truly
ludicrous. Among many others, a couple now attend to the
store at Albion who lately lived in a dashing style in London
not far from Bond Street; the lady brought over her white
satin shoes and gay dresses, rich carpets, and everything but
what in such a place she would require; yet I understand
that they have accommodated themselves to their new situations, hand out the plums, sugar, whiskey, &c., with tolerable
grace, and at least "do not seem to mind it." At Bonpas we
sat down to a wild turkey with a party among whom was an
exquisite so complete that had it been the age of genies I
should have thought *it* had been pounced upon while loung-
ing along Rotten Row, whirled through the air, and for sport
set down in this wilderness to astonish the natives. The whole
has truly a most pantomimic effect, and Momus might keep
his court at this anomalous scene and laugh to his full content.

Two years later, W. N. Blane, who doesn't stop to consider Wanborough as a possible place for settlement, gives Albion a black
mark because the contentions of the two families have spread to
the whole community. Reporting opinions he picked up in the
town, he places the blame on Flower, however.

What appeared to me to be one of the great drawbacks to settling at Albion was that there were two parties who were in open hostility with one another, and whose eternal prosecutions enabled two lawyers, even in this small settlement, to thrive upon the dissensions of the community. Mr. Flower was the person against whom the greatest indignation of the opposite party was pointed; but, although I was at the time informed of their mutual grievances, yet I have since so entirely forgotten them that I cannot take upon me to say which party was in the right. I must confess, however, I was greatly mortified at seeing these foolish people, after having left their country, crossed the Atlantic, and travelled 1,000 miles into the wilderness, quarrelling with one another and making each other's situation as disagreeable as possible. The hostile parties do not even speak; and thus the respectable inhabitants, who might constitute a very pleasant little society, are entirely kept apart from one another.

The long-standing foe of the settlement, William Cobbett, knew all along that something like this would happen, and he jubilantly pointed the moral of the tale.

As if the inevitable effects of disappointment and hardship were not sufficient, you had, too, a sort of partnership in the leaders. This is sure to produce feuds and bitterness in the long run. Partnership sovereignties have furnished the world with numerous instances of poisonings and banishments and rottings in prison. It is as much as merchants, who post their books every Sunday, can do to get along without quarrelling. Of man and wife, though they are flesh of flesh and bone of bone, the harmony is not always quite perfect, except in France, where the husband is the servant, and in Germany and Prussia, where the wife is the slave. But, as for a partnership sovereignty without disagreement, there is but one single instance upon record; that, I mean, was of the two kings of Brentford, whose cordiality was, you know, so perfect, that they both smelt to the same nosegay.

Though neither Welby nor Blane was willing to hazard an explanation for the misunderstanding, there are hints that it was so complex a matter that Cobbett was probably more right than wrong in emphasizing the cumbersome mechanics of partnerships. There were others, though, with ready explanations at hand.

In 1832, after Birkbeck's death but not long enough for the settlers to forget they had derisively called him "Emperor of the Prairies," Simon Ansley Ferrall on *A Ramble of Six Thousand Miles through the United States of America*, as he called his book, got, to his own satisfaction, the explanation in a few minutes' talk in Albion.

The whole secret and cause of this *guerre à mort* declared by the backwoodsmen against Messrs. Birkbeck and Flower was that when they first settled upon the prairies they attempted to act the *patron* and the *benefactor*, and considered themselves *entitled* to some respect. Now a west-country American would rather die like a cock on a dunghill than be patronized after the English fashion; he is not accustomed to receive benefactions, and cannot conceive that any man would voluntarily confer favours on him without expecting something in return, either in the shape of labour or goods—and as to respect, that has totally disappeared from his code since "the Declaration."

And earlier, in 1819, when it might have been possible to get at the facts, the sharp-tongued William Faux laid most of the troubles of the settlement squarely on the self-seeking of both Birkbeck and Flower, and especially on their improvidence.

The hope, it seemed, of preserving and increasing his property was amongst Mr. Birkbeck's ruling motives for emigration. To those to whom he is known he is very hearty and sociable. To J. Ingle he said, "There are so many thousand dollars in that drawer; they are of no use to me. Go, and take what you like." He is very careless and improvident, like the rest of his literary fraternity, and unconscious of what his powerful pen and high reputation were effecting by exciting a strong feeling in favour of emigration at a moment when the people of England were despairing; so strong, indeed, that what he did and wrote burst in upon them like a discovery. Unconscious of all this, he left undone all which he ought in common policy to have done. The weakest head could see that after purchasing land and alluring settlers, he ought to have guarded against a famine by providing for their accommodation, building a few log houses, storehouses, and a tavern, and cultivating corn so that the numerous callers in this inhospitable waste might have found food, and a shelter, and a person to shew the land which he had to resell. Whereas a stable, a covered wagon, and prairie grass formed their only shelter and bed; and not having food sufficient for himself, there was little or none for strangers, and no person to shew the land, nor did he know himself where it lay. He idly thought that if they wished land they would find it themselves; and being in expectation of many such families from England, he thought he had no land to spare, so that the real practical farmers of both worlds who called turned away disgusted to other and better neighbourhoods. He, therefore, as the rich families did not come, has no real farmers in his settlement. Trusting, too, to his own judgment, he has settled down on and entered indiscriminately good and bad land, much of which will never be worth anything, being wet, marshy, spongy, on a stratum of unporous clay, over which pestilential fogs rise and hang continually. A United States' surveyor would, for a few dollars, have prevented such a choice. Common policy and prudence, too, ought to have induced him to reduce his fine farming theory into practice, otherwise it seemed as if intended merely to deceive others. Even if he should (as he now says) lose by it, or could buy produce cheaper than he could raise it, he still ought not so to buy it but set an example of farming. For of what use is land if it is not worth cultivating?

As a proof of his improvident conduct and bad management, his thirteen horses were all miserably poor and unfit for use, and when any were wanted he would say to a hunter, "Here's five dollars for you if you find and drive up the horses"; for he had no inclosure. The man knew where they

were, and soon found them and received the fee; none then
were fit for use. "Oh! don't tease me about horses."

Amongst the inducements of the Flower family to emigrate
may be reckoned the probability of their wasting all their
property by farming their own estate, about 500 or 600 acres
at Marden. It was badly farmed, and the Merino trade failed,
which was Mr. Flower's hobbyhorse; and seeing his favourite
son was determined to live in America, emigration now
ceased to be a matter of choice.

Faux's testimony is questionable at best. Yet his account of the
settlement is the fullest we have at this time, and in the lack of
any better must be heeded. He tells, for instance, that

Mr. and Mrs. Doctor Pugsley, late of London, live in the
only house, which, if it had a servant, would boast of English
comforts, politeness, and hospitality. She sighs to revisit
England, where she might see her friends and rest her delicate hands, now destined to all kind of drudgery. He has purchased land largely, on speculation, without intending to cultivate any, and offers it at three dollars an acre, or at a corn
rent. Much of the land has been thus purchased by capitalists
here, and is offered again on these terms, because the Kentucky speculators, it is said, would otherwise have bought
all up and charged more for it, and because the profit demanded is thought to be reasonable. But what is the effect?
That of driving away good little practical farmers to other
neighbourhoods.

This is the same physician George Flower has in mind when he
writes:

Who can calculate the extent of mischief spread by an en-
vious temper, a false heart, and a loose tongue? There came
over in my ship, as I have before stated, a doctor from London, a man of some skill in his profession, with a pretty wife.
They assumed to be fashionable people, and were so, but of
that part of fashion which assumes something of its external

appearance without possessing any of its sterling qualities. I
had no particular knowledge of him, but wishing to come to
our settlement, and reputed of some skill, I gave him every
information and all facilities. Having made his neighborhood
in England too hot to hold him, he for some time disturbed
our settlement, until he went elsewhere to follow his unhappy
instincts. He made a point of coming out in my ship, and,
unfortunately for the peace of our neighborhood, bought a
town share, and so became a town proprietor. I note the unhappy propensities of this man as a prominent cause of the
troubles which for a time disturbed our settlement.

But just how Pugsley was a "prominent cause" of their troubles is
shrouded in silence.

Faux tells another anecdote indicating the general dissatisfaction, and suggesting quarrels inside other quarrels. One of the
"sprightly sons" of Hanks whom he mentions was named Francis.
It must have been a further blow to Birkbeck that in a few years
Francis would marry his second daughter, Prudence, the most
vivacious of his children.

After sleeping and breakfasting at Mr. Birkbeck's, I called
and dined with Joseph Hanks, Esq., and his fine Irish family
of sprightly sons and one little motherless daughter. They are
Protestants, and lived, as long as they could keep their comforts, in Ireland. He was a banker, and a correspondent of the
Right Hon. N. Vansittart and George Canning, Esq., while
the young sons were the dandies of Dublin. But here the
father is a storekeeper, and the sons are cooks, housemaids,
carpenters, and drudges for all work. He brought considerable property away. He has bought no land, and professes to
dislike the prairies and America generally. He would have
bought from Mr. Birkbeck but could get only a "cup," that is,
a swamp. He says his funds are yet entire, and he means to
leave the country and live in England, in a garret, in either
London or Dublin, rather than remain here if he should be
cast in a suit in which he is the plaintiff against the magistrates of Illinois, who, he thinks, have unjustly taken Birkbeck's part against him, he and his family having quarrelled

with Mr. Birkbeck and family about water, &c. Mr. Hanks
is a wild, hot-headed, sprightly Irishman, charging Mr. Birkbeck's writings with falsehood and deception, and him as a
deceiver, idly spending already 30,000 dollars; no farmer,
and now out of funds, and embarrassed. "I was caught," said
he, "by his fascinating writings; it was impossible to resist
them. Who could? Did ever man write like him? I admire
both him and his writings, and notwithstanding all I say
against him, I love him still. Whatever may be his opinions,
I hope and believe the Almighty will never let such a man
slip through his fingers. He must, however, fail in his enterprise. Never come here, Sir. Here is no money, no labourers. The English are the most dishonest." I returned to sup
and sleep at Birkbeck's, who, on hearing where we spent the
day, said, "You have heard much falsehood. Hanks is a bad
man, having quarrelled with me and nearly all around him."

ii

THE SIMPLEST EXPLANATION of the trouble between the families
is that given quite bluntly by William Owen in his diary in 1824.

We dined with Mr. G. Flower. His cottage or log house is
near Mr. R. Flower's and was the first cabin built in this
neighborhood. He contrived to make himself very comfortable
—comparatively—in it. Mrs. G. Flower is a very pretty, lively
woman. She has 3 children. She came out with Mr. Birkbeck,
who was to marry her, but Mr. F. won the day. This caused
a rupture between the families.

Despite the rather grim visage that stares out at us from the only
known portrait of Mrs. Flower, travelers were unanimous in
praising her beauty. William Owen, who had a sharp eye for
pulchritude and peppered his diary with comments about pretty
women, can be trusted. What better explanation, then, than the
romantic one? The beautiful Miss Andrews, Birkbeck's ward,
snatched from under the nose of the older man by the impetuous
young Flower—all this occurring during the trek westward, in the

heart of the trackless wilderness. Perhaps so. Faux supplies the details, not neglecting a scent of scandal, which he dearly loved sniffing out. Richard Flower, he says,

read to me a manuscript letter which he had recently written, addressed to Mr. Birkbeck respecting the conduct of the latter gentleman, the object of which is to put him on his defence in all matters public and private relating to their mysterious and unfortunate quarrel. As I have heard both sides from both parties, or at least as much of both sides as the parties voluntarily and unquestioned thought proper to give me, I shall endeavour to give a faithful account of what I heard. The Flowers charge Mr. Birkbeck with an intention of driving their family out of Illinois and of deceiving the public generally in the hope of monopolizing all the prairies to himself, so that he might sell, at what advanced price he pleased, to such of his countrymen as came hither, induced by his tempting publications. Wishing to visit America to relieve himself from domestic unhappiness, Mr. George Flower was the precursor of Mr. Birkbeck. Mr. Birkbeck now met the Flower family to persuade them to emigrate with him to their son George Flower, and make one property and share all things in common, a measure too utopian for Mr. Flower, senior, to approve. Mr. Birkbeck then reproached Mr. Flower with *croaking;* and the emigration of the Flower family was deferred while Mr. Birkbeck prepared for his departure.

The Miss Birkbecks seeing a young lady at Mr. Flower's, Miss Andrews, wished her to accompany them to America, a measure to which the father objected but soon afterwards consented, and away they sailed to Norfolk, in Virginia, where they were met by George Flower, who agreed to accompany them westward. Miss Andrews and George Flower, unknown to Birkbeck, were agreeing to marry; and on arriving at Vincennes, both parties made it known to Mr. Birkbeck, who, with considerable agitation and surprise, gave his consent and sanction to the marriage. This consent, however, was wildly given, and apparently with extreme reluctance, for he also was attached to this lovely female. Mr. George Flower had hoped that his strong emotions would subside. He offered to leave Mr. Birkbeck and his family forever, to which Mr. Birkbeck would not consent, but, on leaving the happy pair at Vincennes, went on to Princeton, where all, in a few days, met in friendship, and proceeding into Illinois, subsequently settled in the prairies as one family, until Birkbeck showed symptoms of violent attachment, which excited alarm as to consequences. It was then thought advisable, as Mr. George Flower was going to England, that Mrs. Flower should not continue there, but go eastward and remain there until her husband returned. She did so, and Mr. Birkbeck parted with them in friendship, promising to prepare houses and purchase land for them and the family before they returned. All seemed peace, and money was sent over express from England to Mr. Birkbeck for purchasing and building; but, when the Flower family arrived, he had done nothing, nor purchased anything for them.

The senior branches of the Flower family were now at Lexington, ignorant of these evils until a letter from Mr. Birkbeck reached them, wishing they should settle in the East (where he supposed them to be), telling his reasons for so advising them; namely, because he thought that they would all make common cause with their son, George Flower, and that he had not bought them any land but ordered the funds to be returned to their banker in Philadelphia. Mr. Flower answered with great bitterness and asperity, accusing Mr. Birkbeck of fraud, treachery, and cruelty, threatening summary justice, and expressing a determination to come and live there to protect his son and family against his malice. Mr. Birkbeck then offered peace, at least to Mr. Flower, senior. "But," said Mr. Flower, "I could not take him by the hand now; it would be loss of character. I had done nothing to offend him, and why was I thus made to suffer? I am bound up with my family; their lives are precious in my sight." This was a part of his letter to Birkbeck which he read to me, but when he came to that part, he burst into tears, and rushed out, putting it into my hands.

Neither Mr. Richard Flower nor Mr. George Flower have ever since met Mr. Birkbeck. "I avoid seeing him," says Mr. Richard Flower, "because, if I came near, I must lay violent hands on him; I must knock him down. I will never see him or speak to him more. A reconciliation is impossible; to me it would be a stain and loss of character."

All the evil to both families and to the settlement they impute to Birkbeck. They wonder why he should have so changed, when he had sanctioned the conduct of George Flower and given him the lady in marriage. They deem it hypocrisy of the first order, as well as the greatest impolicy; "but," say they, "he is now punished for it, being nearly in the situation of an embarrassed man." Mrs. George Flower, however, more charitably imputes nothing in Mr. Birkbeck's conduct to vile or corrupt motives, but all to love, and to that kind of revenge which such a disappointment was likely to generate when the mind was lonely and abandoned to its own feelings. They deem the event a great evil to themselves and to the settlement, because it happened at a time when the joint exertions of these two families were so necessary for its success. It deranged everything; and all connected with, or who came nigh the prairies, wondered and felt the evil because the secret was unknown. Mr. George Flower professes not to defend his departure from law and custom in this second marriage, but very ingenuously confesses that having missed his chance of happiness in his first he was determined to try a second marriage which promised better things; and as Mr. Birkbeck knew his situation intimately, he would not have censured him had he not wished to marry the lady himself. As this could not be, he and Mr. Birkbeck had, instead of consulting the good of the settlement, laid by to give each other mortal stabs, or rather to blast each other's good name. This ends one side of the case.

Mr. Birkbeck in reply takes a disinterested, high, moral stand, suffering nothing to escape him relating to his own disappointments, though in a letter to Mr. Melish he admits "that scandal is busy with his name and affairs." He states that soon after landing in this country and being joined by

Mr. George Flower, he began to suspect a connection was forming between Miss Andrews and George Flower. At length it became unequivocal, and he consented to and sanctioned their marriage as the least of two unavoidable evils; for the parties had determined either on marriage (if not impracticable), or at least on cohabitation; and, as he respected both as his children, he consented to the former as the least evil.

The grand cause of a change of conduct to them (so much wondered at by the Flowers), and of not fulfilling his promises of purchasing and building for the reception of the families, will be seen in the following circumstances. He had been deceived; while George Flower was gone to London, he became undeceived. He learnt, from the best authority, that Miss Andrews had been the cause of all the jealousy, unhappiness, and separation in George Flower's former marriage, and that the senior branches had placed this young lady in his family for the express purpose of effecting their purposes, namely of marrying her to their son, a circumstance calculated to injure the honour of himself and family in the eyes of an uncharitable world. Seeing himself, then, to have been made the innocent tool of such iniquitous measures, it no longer remained a matter of choice whether he should receive or abandon them; it was impossible for him to act otherwise than he had done if he intended to preserve his reputation. It was certainly not his wish to quarrel with Mr. Richard Flower; but as father and son were one, it was impossible to avoid it; he therefore declined purchasing the promised land or using their money in any way.

Mr. Birkbeck rids himself of the charge of fraud and breach of trust by saying, in reply to Mr. Flower's severe letter, that it was optional whether he purchased lands with the money sent; it was not binding upon him to do it. And, moreover, he thought it for the interest of both families, under such circumstances, to be more distantly situated.

Thus have I given both sides of the question as completely as they could be gathered from verbal statements.

The two villes of Albion and Wanborough, the abodes of

contention, party spirit, speculation, and feuds, arose out of this greatly to be regretted quarrel. If it had produced competition and extraordinary exertions in agriculture, and a desire to conciliate, accommodate, and invite settlers, it had been well; but the reverse was the consequence.

More than this we cannot learn, and much of this is open to doubt. Faux was credulous and gossipy. He didn't really like America, where "knavery damns the North, and slavery the South," he said. He came prepared to find fault with the English Settlement and with the country at large, and of course he had no trouble discovering evidence of shortcomings—not when he could believe that a cow brought from Yorkshire to America "gives but little milk, and pines for the sweet, green pastures of her dear native land."

George Flower, who might have verified Faux's story or denied it, remains strangely silent about the romantic implications and professes bewilderment over the ultimate cause of the quarrel, never even mentioning Faux's book by title or its author by name. He does, however, detail his last meeting with Birkbeck, and here as elsewhere speaks with respect for Birkbeck's ability and integrity. He tells us that on the third day after his arrival with the band of immigrants from England:

I took my horse and rode over to Mr. Birkbeck's cabin. When almost in the act of dismounting, I saw him rise from his seat, from under the shade of an oak that stood opposite to his cabin door. He passed before my horse's head into the cabin, pale, haggard, and agitated. With eyes cast down, and shaking his head, he said: "No, we can not meet, I can not see you." Sitting on my horse, and looking at him in wonder, I said: "We must meet, our property is undivided, business is urgent, heavy payments are to be provided for freight and charges." But what! "Stop, stop," said he, "let a third person arrange all." "So be it," said I, and rode on. These were the last words that ever passed between us.

When we take a cold, we are troubled to know how it happened, and think if we had taken an umbrella, or put on a greatcoat, or changed our shoes, or done something we had not done, we should not have got it. So it is in our moral diseases. We cannot help looking back to see how they came. Was it both of us leaving him at Princeton alone with his family on the frontier? We did not consider, perhaps, sufficiently at the time that the absence of both myself and wife would leave a dreary, void, and lonely winter for our aged friend. We, in the vigor of our years and affection for each other, perhaps overlooked this; and, possibly, he might feel somewhat aggrieved on that account in the solitary winter he had to pass, for a father with his children only is in some sort a solitary being. He might feel that he was deserted, and a thought may have crossed his mind that we might never return. I think he felt something of this sort from an expression in a letter to an intimate friend in England, where he said: "You will see Mr. George Flower, who intends to return in the spring, but we all know when time and distance intervene, they are great barriers to the execution of our intentions." I was struck with the sentence when I saw it, but the friend had no such doubt, for he put into my hands a considerable sum of money to be especially invested. Then again, instead of riding on with some feeling of injury at my reception, had I dismounted and insisted on an explanation, things might have been different.

Here let me pause in the narrative, to do justice to ourselves in our after unfortunate and unpleasant situation. We never quarrelled or descended to altercation, never spoke ill of each other, and never, as I believe, attempted to do each other any injury. We were silent ever after, as if we ignored each other's existence. The line of demarcation between our lands was about three miles long. Ever after, I worked on one side, he on the other. When strangers visited the settlement, they called on each of us. I say this in contradiction to the extraordinary falsehoods promulgated at the time. Regret and sorrow were, no doubt, the prevailing feelings in each breast.

But we were now parted forever, and in that situation were, with all our caution, very much at the mercy of go-betweens and tale-bearers, ever to be found on an errand of mischief. The void which our silence left was more than filled up by our intermeddling neighbors, and Mr. Birkbeck's annoyance from indiscreet partisanship was much greater than mine. The wildest reports, mostly ridiculous and some scandalous, were carried from one to the other, and were so often repeated as to obtain some credence with those that invented and circulated them; and some individuals were so indiscreet as to write to their distant friends these fabulous accounts. This brought to Mr. Birkbeck letters asking explanations of the strange things they had heard. From this annoyance he could scarcely free himself by silence or reply. It has been said that none but fools intermeddle with other people's dissensions. If judged by that rule, we had many *non compos* in our settlement at that time.

There was that sense of justice in Mr. Birkbeck that prompted him to repair an injury inflicted from erroneous impressions or heat of temper. Seven years after our short meeting and parting, Mr. Birkbeck went to Harmonie and solicited Mr. Robert Owen to use his influence for a reconciliation between us; but from that journey he never returned.

I should willingly have avoided these personal incidents, but our histories are so interwoven with the history of the settlement that I could not entirely omit them.

iii

CUT LOOSE from the association with Birkbeck, Flower now had to establish, in co-operation with new associates, his own town and marketplace.

I had as yet done nothing in erecting buildings for the public in general, as there had been no time. One evening, Mr. Lawrence, Mr. Ronalds, and, I think, Mr. Fordham called at my cabin, and, after their horses were cared for and supper over, we discussed the measures that should be taken to form some village or town as a centre for those useful arts necessary to agriculture. Every person wanted the services of a carpenter and blacksmith. But every farmer could not build workshops at his own door. Daylight ceased, darkness followed. We had no candles, nor any means of making artificial light. On a pallet, mattress, or blanket, each one took to his couch, and carried on the discussion. After much talk, we decided that what we did do should be done in order, and with a view to the future settlement, as well as our own present convenience. The tract of forest lying between Mr. Lawrence's settlement in the Village Prairie on its southern border and mine at the north of the Boltinghouse Prairie was about three and a half miles through. Somewhere in the centre of this tract of woodland seemed to be the place. To the right of this spot, eastward, lay, about a mile distant, several prairies running north and south for many miles, and others east and west to the Bonpas Creek, from three to five miles distant. Northeastward from Mr. Lawrence's cabin prairies of every form and size continued on indefinitely. About two miles west, and beyond Wanborough, were numerous small and fertile prairies extending to the Little Wabash, from six to ten miles distant. On the south was my own beautiful prairie. Thus the spot for our town in a central situation was decided upon. Now for a name. We were long at fault. At last we did what almost all emigrants do, pitched on a name that had its association with the land of our birth. Albion was then and there located, built, and peopled in imagination. We dropped off, one by one, to sleep, to confirm in dreams the wanderings of our waking fancies.

Albion would take more than dreams to bring it into existence, but whatever George Flower may have lacked in resolution to carry out his dreams was well made up by his determined father, who now took the place in his life that Birkbeck had filled. There was no shilly-shallying when Richard Flower was about. The first thing the elder Flower did was set the religious life of the community to rights. Recalling to mind his good work later, he wrote:

When I arrived at Albion, a more disorganized, demoralized state of society never existed. The experiment has been made, the abandonment of Christian institutes and Christian Sabbaths, and living without God in the world has been fairly tried. If those theologians in England who despise the

Sabbath and laugh at congregational worship had been sent to the English Settlement in the Illinois at the time I arrived, they would or they ought to have hid their faces for shame. Some of the English played at cricket; the backwoodsmen shot at marks, their favourite sport; and the Sunday revels ended in riot and savage fighting. This was too much even for infidel nerves. But when a few, a very few, better men met and read the Scriptures, and offered prayer at a poor contemptible log house, these revellers were awed into silence and the Sabbath at Albion became decently quiet. One of its inhabitants of an infidel cast said to me, "Sir! this is very extraordinary that what the law could not effect, so little an assembly meeting for worship should have effected."

Many people here openly express their gratitude to me as the saviour of this place, which they say must have dispersed if I had not arrived. This is encouraging to a heart wounded with affliction as mine has been, and is urging me on to plans of usefulness. A place for education, a Sunday school, and above all a Bible society, if we increase, shall be my aim and endeavour.

He also told his English correspondent that their prayers were of the "reformed Unitarian service," and that "amongst our congregation we often number a part of Mr. Birkbeck's children and servants"—Birkbeck himself, of course, staying away from Albion. But apparently Flower's one-man reformation reverberated through Wanborough as well, and unseated Birkbeck's freethought convictions. For soon Flower was writing:

Of the particular news of this place, there is one piece of intelligence that will surprise you; the author of "Letters from Illinois" (Mr. Birkbeck) has opened a place of worship at Wanborough; he officiates himself, and reads the Church of England service, so that Wanborough is the seat of orthodoxy and our place stands, as a matter of course, in the ranks of heresy!

Thus endeth a second chapter of their ecclesiastical history.

Orthodoxy could not save Wanborough, however. Albion, drawing from the combined vigor of the Flowers, father and son, soon

outstripped it in growth. Some indication of the relative vitality
of the two towns is given by the diarist William Hall, who conducted an informal census in 1822, and wrote:

We reckoned the population of Wanborough on Decr 1 to be
68 persons exclusive of Mr. Birkbecks, of Albion 170 excluding Mr. Flowers. Of the surrounding neighborhood, English,
Birks, Burnt, Village, & Long Prairies 522, total 760. We
had only our own knowledge to guide us & most likely
omitted several families.

For whatever reason—his age, his impracticality, perhaps his
despondency over the quarrel—Birkbeck never worked very hard
at building up his village. Some of his energy was drawn off by the
need to answer attacks on the settlement, for, with Richard
Flower, he continued to pamphleteer in defense of the whole
community. But Wanborough, so far as it grew at all, developed
haphazardly and at random, without the benefit of Birkbeck's
strong instinct for planning—giving some justification for the
criticism that he had lured settlers to the prairies and left them to
shift for themselves once there.

The controversy in Illinois about slavery was the kind of issue
that could still rouse the banked fires in Birkbeck's soul and, as
will be seen, this mounted the old champion on his white horse
again to enter the lists in defense of honor and justice. But more
and more he turned to private pursuits: the management of his
farm, the building of his house, his scientific studies. And as he did
so, Wanborough continued to dwindle. From a peak population of
perhaps 75 people in 1822, it shrank to fewer than a dozen families
by the time of Birkbeck's death, and shortly thereafter disappeared. Now there is only a historical marker to indicate its site,
while Albion's continuity remains unbroken to the present day.

4

"There stood Albion . . . a fixed fact."

ONE OF THE MANY VISITORS during the first year of settlement, W. T. Harris, found both families temporarily settled
and going about their business of raising a community.

From Mr. Flower and family I received a polite reception,
which was extended also to my companion; this, considering
their situation, is the more to be noticed as their house was
not completed and their supplies of grain, flour, and vegetables were drawn from Harmonie. They were building other
log houses for the people, were enclosing a garden, and had
cut two large stacks of hay from the prairie for their cattle
during the winter.

By Mr. Birkbeck I was treated with the same attention I
received from Mr. Flower. They reside about a mile and a
half from each other; and each of the parties appears to feel
as though it were the seat of his earliest associations. I asked
one of the ladies whether they had no desire to return to
England, after experiencing the loss of that society to which
they had been accustomed. Her answer proved that they had
not hastily or thoughtlessly put into practice a resolution
suggested by the unfortunate posture of affairs in that coun-

try. "As long as those causes exist which induced us to leave
England, we can have no desire to return; as for society,
even supposing no other could be obtained, our own families
afford it; and as for seeking it in what on your side of the
water is called 'the world,' experience has already convinced
us that all it can offer is vapid and unsatisfying."

Mr. Birkbeck is busily employed in making brick to re-
place his present log buildings. Three miles distant from him
is another settlement; and on the northern part of Mr.
Flower's tract a town plat was surveying, to be named New
Albion.

So far as Albion was concerned, Flower tells how he and his
friends set about immediately putting their plans into execution.

One day only was suffered to elapse between our decision
and the execution of our purpose. Before dispersing the next
morning, it was agreed that Mr. Fordham and myself should
start north from my dwelling. Mr. Lawrence and Mr. Ronalds
were to go south from the Village Prairie at a given hour on
the following morning. We met the next day in the woods,
according to appointment. The spot seemed suitable. The
woods were rather open, and the ground level. "Here shall
be the centre of our town," we said. The spot of our meeting
is now the public square in the centre of Albion. The surveying and laying of the town was entrusted to Mr. Fordham,
who forthwith went to work, and completed the survey and
the plat.

Fordham himself jotted down on October 30, 1818:

I am laying off a new town to be called Albion. It will consist
of 8 streets and a public square. Most likely it will be the
county town, and if so there will be a courthouse and a gaol,
as well as a markethouse and a chapel, which last will be
built whether it be the seat of justice or not. I have never
been more busily employed in my life than I am now.

The dreams of the town planners were spacious, to say the least.
Flower continues:

One of our number went to Shawneetown and entered the section of six hundred and forty acres, which was all laid off in town lots. The public square was in the middle. The blocks immediately around, and in the main street, were divided into quarter-acre lots. The blocks outside were divided into half-acres. As the distance increased from the centre the lots increased in size, until the outer belt of allotments were five and seven acres.

But a dozen years later, when the Rev. James Hoby passed through Albion, the large-scale expectations were still far from being realized. With some disappointment he wrote:

Judging from the names given to the roads around Albion, it might be supposed it was a city of no ordinary dimensions, but as we drove along Bond Street, I did not observe a single house.

Flower indicates other early accomplishments.

The first double cabin built was designated for a tavern, and a single one for its stable. This was occupied by Mr. John Pitcher, who, with his family, came out with Mr. Lawrence. He was an excellent mechanic and a man of more than ordinary intelligence. Unsuccessful in England, he came to the settlement almost without a dollar.

Another and second double and single cabin were occupied as dwelling and shop by a blacksmith. I had brought bellows, anvils, tools, and appliances for three or four blacksmith shops from the city of Birmingham, England. There were three brothers that came with Mr. Charles Trimmer, all excellent mechanics, Abraham, Isaac, and Jacob Penfold. Jacob, the blacksmith, was immediately installed, and went to work. There stood Albion, no longer a myth but a reality, a fixed fact.

A log tavern and a blacksmith shop; two germs of civilization were now planted—one of the useful arts, the other a necessary institution of present civilization. Any man could now get his horse shod and get drunk in Albion, privileges which were soon enjoyed, the latter especially.

The town proprietors—at first four, afterward increased to eight (each share five hundred dollars)—went to work vigorously. They put up cabin after cabin, which were occupied as soon as put up by emigrants coming in. The builders of these were the backwoodsmen, some from twenty to thirty miles distant. Attracted by our good money and good whisky, these men gathered in. The work was generally done by contract or piecework—the price twenty-five to thirty dollars for single cabins, 16 by 18; from forty to fifty for double cabins. The builders generally worked hard by day. In the evening they gathered around the whisky barrel as bees around a favorite flower. As the evening advanced, in succession were heard the sounds of mirth and jollity, threats, loud oaths, and imprecations. Rough-and-tumble fights succeeded, and silence was only restored by the exhaustion of the mutilated combatants. The birth of our infant town was heralded by all the scenes of riot and debauch incident to such occasions.

John Woods, whom Faux called "a real Nottinghamshire farmer, a plain, judicious, industrious man," lived in one of these log cabins in the midst of 400 acres of his own land. He left the most complete account of how cabins were built and of the kind of farm accommodations the early settlers had.

I will give the best description in my power of a log cabin, as I could form no idea of it till I saw one. They are of various widths, lengths, and heights, but generally only one story high. The usual shape a long square. Some are made of round, and others of hewn logs. In building a cabin— suppose 30 feet long and 20 wide—first, two logs 30 feet long are placed on the ground on a level, and about 18 feet from each other. These two logs are then notched in, near their ends, for a few inches; and then two more logs of 20 feet long, having their undersides also notched, are laid on the two first, forming a long square about 26 feet long and 16 feet wide on the inside. One square being thus formed, they next proceed to place on two more of the longest logs on the sides, notched as before, and then two of the shortest, as before. This they continue till the building is nine or ten logs high on each side, when the two last cross logs are laid on three or four feet longer than the other cross ones; this is to form a sort of eaves to drip the logs. Two more of the longest logs are then laid on, and this completes the upright of the building. Two cross logs cut slanting at the ends are next placed on, just the length of the width of the building; and then two more of the side logs on the cross logs, but not to the end of them by some distance. Then two more, cut slanting at the ends, are placed just to reach to the last side logs, thus drawing in the sides till the side logs meet in a point at the top of the building. A cleft piece of a tree is next placed on the outer end of the long cross logs and pegged on to prevent the cleft boards from sliding off. This is done on each side of the building. The whole is then covered with cleft boards (here called clapboards); they are about four feet long and six inches wide, laid on nearly double, so as to cover the joints. The boards at the top of the cabin on one side come a little over those on the other. When the roof is thus covered, some poles are laid along the building to keep the boards on; these poles are kept at about three feet distance from each other by some short pieces of wood placed on the boards to keep up the weight poles as they are called. When they have done thus far, they call the cabin "raised."

But no doorplace, window, fireplace, floor, or ceiling is yet made. Nor is the house very close on the sides, but looks something like a bird cage. Next a doorplace of the usual size is cut through the logs, and two pieces of wood are nailed or pegged up to the ends of the sawed logs to keep them in their places and to serve for doorposts. Frequently two doors are made opposite to each other. The windows are made in the same manner as the doorplaces. The chimney is generally placed at the end of the building, and is made as follows: first, four or five logs are cut out the same as for a doorplace, of what width people choose, and then some logs are cleft and placed on the outside so that the ends of them are let in between the ends of the end logs of the cabin that were sawed. The cleft logs are thus continued till they rise as high as the logs that were sawed out. The chimney is then carried up exactly in the form of the cabin, but of much smaller logs, till it rises above the roof of the building. It is drawn in and made smaller from the bottom to the top. It is then chunked; that is, cleft pieces of wood are driven in between the logs to fill up the open places.

The next thing to be done is to mud the cabin on the outside between the logs; that is, it is plastered with loam or clay. This is sometimes done on the inside also, but more frequently cleft boards are pegged on to cover the joints on the inside. A few pieces of timber are next laid to lay the floor on, which is most commonly made of cleft logs hewn smooth on one side and notched a little on the under side to lie level on the sleepers or joists. A ceiling is then made. Some small saplings are cut and put in between the side logs of the building, just under the roof about three feet apart; and these ceiling joists are then covered with cleft boards, beginning at one end of the cabin and laying a line across the end on the two joists, and then another row with their ends just resting on the first; and this is continued till the whole is covered.

Most times the chimney is walled up several feet on the inside. The stones are laid in loam or clay instead of mortar, and above the wall it is plastered on the inside, and sometimes on the outside to the top of the chimney. The hearth is made of stone or clay. The doors are generally made of cleft boards, nailed or pegged on some ledges, with wooden hinges, made in the following manner. A piece in the back part of the door is left longer than the door, and enters a hole in the sill; and at the top of the door a piece is also left to rest against the top of the doorplace, which is covered with a piece of wood, either nailed or pegged over it. The windows are always sash ones; the usual size of the glass is eight inches by ten. The windows are sometimes made to open with hinges, and others to slide backwards and forwards, while others take out and in. When the doors are made of sawed boards they have eight or ten panes of glass in them, and then it is seldom there is any other window in the cabin. A porch is often made before the cabin, the whole length of it, and covered with cleft boards, which cost seventy-five cents a hundred, cutting the trees and cleaving out. They are always made from large trees, mostly the black oak.

Cabins are frequently made double; that is, two are built from 10 to 20 feet apart, with a roof laid over the space between them. A shelter like this is very convenient, and in the summer it is more comfortable than a close room in so warm a country.

Many cabins belonging to the Americans have no ceiling or windows, and some of them have no floor, nothing but the bare earth; and some are not mudded, but open on all sides. Locks to doors are nearly unknown, but wooden bolts are common with the English. Many of the American houses have only a latch, and some have not even that.

A double cabin, with a 20-foot porch between, with floor and ceiling, finished as above described, may be built for the sum of 150 dollars, 33*l*. 15*s*., or something less. But with ceiling, floor, and doors made of sawed boards, will come, I suppose, to near 50*l*. Sawing comes very high, being 9*s*. per hundred feet; but the sawyers cut down the trees and go with the horses that draw them to the pit.

The cabin I inhabit first consisted of a double one with a porch 20 feet wide between them. This I have since converted into two rooms; the end rooms are of logs, the centre ones of frame and board, with a brick chimney. At the back of the cabin I have added a cellar, &c.

Smokehouses are very common, and built much as dwelling houses, only slighter, and not often mudded. Some cross pieces are put on the joists to hang the bacon on. I have built one; it cost 23 dollars; it is about eighteen feet square and nine feet high. We are obliged to cut our flitches asunder, as we have not sufficient height above the fire. Old wood, nearly rotten, is best for drying bacon, as it makes much smoke and but little strong fire. The fires are kept burning a considerable length of time, as bacon, in this warm climate, requires to be well dried to keep.

Farm buildings are not yet numerous. Corn cribs are built the same as cabins, except that they are placed on logs so as to stand hollow for some distance from the earth; the bottom is made of cleft pieces laid pretty close. They are built of different lengths and widths, but about six feet on the inside is deemed wide enough, as corn will dry in them better than if wider. The roof is only drawn in on one side, which two lengths of boards will cover. As they lay the top pretty flat, they most times take off the greater part, or the whole of the boards, when filling them with Indian corn ears, as they only gather the ears. When full, or the whole growth of the year is put in, the boards are put on and the weight poles again laid on. Should a heavy shower, or even a set rain, come on whilst the corn crib is filling, as the bottom and sides are not close, not being mudded, it will soon dry out again without damaging the corn. I had one built for 15 dollars that will hold upwards of 600 bushels of corn in the ear. I suppose it would hold near 1,000 bushels of cleared corn. The Americans never shell theirs till it is wanted for use or market, but most of what it sold is in the cob or ear. They measure it by barrels; that is, they fill an old flour barrel, then shell and measure it, and from the produce of it they calculate on the whole number of barrels sold.

Cow and pig pens, with cart and wagon lodges, are yet scarce. When pigs are shut up for fatting it is common to make a fence for them of rails, in the same manner as for fields; sometimes one corner is covered over for a lodging-place for them, but it is more common for them to be left to the mercy of the winds and weather. But as they are hardy animals, and accustomed to hard living and lodging, it does not appear to hurt them. There are but few cattleyards and sheds; and the cattle are mostly left abroad in winter with no shelter but what the leafless trees afford. I have seen no barn in any part of the English Settlement, although several of our American neighbours grew some wheat last year. A person at Birk's Prairie has built a threshingfloor, to which he purposes adding a barn. Mr. Birkbeck, Mr. Flower, and other wheat growers of this year have put up their wheat in the fields where it grew, in very small stacks, with little or no covering. This I think hazardous to the wheat, but the Americans say no. They do not stand on trifles; however, time will show.

I have seen barns at a distance from the English Settlement that would hold, perhaps, six loads of wheat (forty bushels to the load) in the straw, supposing it to yield tolerably well; with a large threshingfloor, for threshing or treading out the grain with horses. One similar to these might be built for a hundred dollars (twenty-two pounds ten shillings).

There are no granaries or storehouses except corn cribs, a few poultry houses, mostly built the same as the cabins; as are stables also, but they are sometimes carried higher to allow room for a hayloft. Some have a rack, but this is not common among the Americans. Generally they only have a manger, which is frequently made out of a hollow tree, the ends being stopped with wood or clay.

Some log cabins were astonishingly well furnished. Fordham, when not surveying, traveled about the backwoods searching out land for himself, and left this note:

Crossed the Piankeshaw Prairie at noon—Sun—burning hot. Reached Mr. Q———'s Cabin just at dinner time—it is floored and carpeted. It is made of hickory logs, and is ornamented with large mirrors in gilded frames, a handsome four-post bedstead, &c. It looked like a fairy bower in the wilderness.

And Faux said that

George Flower lives in the completest log cabin I have ever seen, near his father. It contains six or seven rooms, with other needful buildings, and as a log establishment, I will venture to say, possesses more comfort and elegance than any ever seen in America. It is a model for all future log builders.

ii

GEORGE FLOWER was especially busy. In addition to the erection of his own elaborate log cabin and to overseeing the other building going on in Albion, he had to lay the foundation for Park House, Albion's mansion, which his father and mother were to occupy.

During the winter, I rode on horseback to Lexington, Kentucky, to visit my father's family. On the road, I was shocked to hear of the sudden death of my brother William. This was a melancholy affair for us all, and a severe affliction to my aged parents.

I was busily engaged, during the winter and spring, in building a comfortable dwelling for my father, not far from my own cabins. The body of the house, 50 by 40 feet, covered by a hipped roof, consisted of four rooms in the lower and the upper story, divided by a hall passage from north to south. The south front was protected by a broad, well-floored porch that extended the length of the house. Every room was plastered or papered, and furnished with a good brick chimney and stone hearth. The north front was stuccoed to resemble stone; the south, weatherboarded and painted white. The house was well furnished. Its good proportion, large windows, and Venetian blinds gave it an appearance of the old country rather than the new. It had two wings, one of hewn stone, the other of brick, used as kitchen and offices. A well, a cellar, stables, cow house, and every other convenience of that sort was appended. A handsome garden to the south was fenced in by an English hawthorn hedge. Thirty acres of the northern woodland was preserved, the underbrush cleared and sowed with blue grass. It had the appearance of a park. Hence its name—Park House.

Old Park House, near Albion, will long be remembered by old settlers and distant visitors for its social reunions and open-handed hospitalities. Here the family party of children and grandchildren met at dinner on a Sunday. An English plum pudding was a standing dish that had graced my father's dinner table from time immemorial. Here all friends and neighbors that had any musical tastes or talent, whether vocal or instrumental, met once a fortnight for practice and social enjoyment. Strangers and visitors to the settlement received a hearty welcome, saw all that was to be seen, and received all the information they wished for, with necessary refreshment and repose. It may be truly said that for thirty years old Park House was never without its visitors, from every country in Europe, and every state in the Union. They were welcome, unless the family was absent, if their stay was for a week, a month, or a year.

By summer, in 1819, the elder Flowers were living in their fine new house, though it was not yet finished. Richard Flower tells something of the wonder excited by his style of life.

My house, which is nearly finished, is a comfortable one, and can boast a roof that neither Hertford nor Marden could. It stands the most drenching rains and drifting snows without letting in any wet. While I am satisfied with the comfort it affords, the Americans behold it with surprise. I had a visit from Captain Birk, a sensible and intelligent backwoodsman. He paid me a short visit; put off his business that he might fetch his wife, which he did. We thought we saw through the plan. He returned with her the next day, and we felt disposed to gratify their curiosity. "There, wife," said he, "did you ever see such fixings?" He felt the paper, looked in a mirror over our chimney piece which reflected the cattle grazing in the field before the house, and gazed with amazement. But turning from these sights to the library— "Now," said he to my wife, "does your old gentleman" (for that is my title here) "read those books?" "Yes," said she, "he has read most of them." "Why if I was to read half of them, I should drive all the little sense in my head out of it." I replied that we read to increase our sense and our knowledge; but this untutored son of nature could not conceive of this till I took down a volume of Shaw's Zoology. "You, Mr. Birk, are an old hunter, and have met with many snakes in your time. I never saw above one in my life. Now if I can tell you about your snakes and deer and bears and wolves as much or more than you know, you will see the use of books." I read to him a description of the rattlesnake, and then shewed him the plate, and so on. His attention was arrested, and his thirst for knowledge fast increasing. "I never saw an Indian in my life, and yet," said I, "I can tell you all about them." I read again and shewed him a coloured plate. "There," said he, "wife, is it not wonderful, that this gentleman, coming so many miles, should know these things from books only? See ye," said he, pointing to the Indian, "got him to a turn." In short, I never felt more interested for an hour or two to see how this man's mind thirsted after knowledge; and though he dreaded the appearance of so many books, he seemed, before he left us, as if he could spend his life amongst them.

Others also testified to the gracious life of the Birkbecks and Flowers—even William Faux, who, in 1819, rather surprisingly named Wanborough as the more progressive community.

The Flowers own a large and beautiful domain of prairie, containing unnumbered acres of fine land, beautified by British park scenery. The visitor, coming here out of the forest, fancies himself in England, especially if he looks at the country through the windows of Messrs. Flower's and Birkbeck's houses during the green and flowery season when the scenery presents a wide waste of grass, flowers, and shrubs of every hue. But the flowers have no fragrance, the birds no song. The sight of a flock of 500 Merino sheep and a large herd of cattle, all their own, is indeed a novel and unexpected pleasure in these wild regions; and, added to all these, the comfort of such houses and harmonious families, escaped from the embarrassments and anxieties of England to quiet rest and independence, makes it indeed a delightful spectacle.

Left Mr. Flower and Albion for Wanborough, a village rising on the estate of Mr. Birkbeck, and named after the village in Surrey where he last lived. Industry seems to have done more for this village than for Albion; every log house has a cleared inclosure of a few acres attached, and what is done is done by the occupants or owners, and not by Mr. Birkbeck; whereas, in Albion, all has been done by the purse of Mr. Flower. Both villages are the abode only of the humble mechanic. The farmers live on their quarter sections, and both are but scantily supplied with water at a distance.

Elizabeth Birkbeck wrote to her uncle back in England that late in September, 1819,

We have got into our new house, which is only partly finished; one of the upper rooms, which opens on to a balcony commanding a fine view over the prairie we have fitted up as our library. There Prue and I spend the chief of our time and receive our visitors. It is quite delightful to us to have our books round us again, and to have time to devote to them. The silk gowns which my dear Aunt sent to Prue and me are very much admired.

Adlard Welby brought a somewhat more jaundiced eye to bear about the same time, when he visited the settlement.

We did not fail to explore the retreat of Mr. Morris Birkbeck. A pleasant drive across the prairie brought us to the Flat, at one extremity of which Mr. Birkbeck has established himself. We found him busy superintending the building of his house, the site of which is within twenty yards of his erection of logs, a square building divided into two rooms, as I heard, for we did not see the interior of this *sanctum sanctorum* from whence have been issued relations of so many snug cottages with adjoining piggeries, cowsteads, gardens, and orchards; where the limbs of the poor emigrant were to find repose and his mind solace, not to mention the ranges of log rooms for the arch priest himself which were building two years ago. All—all have vanished "into thin air," except the humble primitive log building before mentioned. This serves the whole family, according to the cobbler's song,

For parlour, for kitchen and hall,

and furnishes a proof, though perhaps not sufficient for every one (the world is so incredulous), of Mr. Birkbeck's humility, for he certainly does not at present enjoy the *otium cum dignitate* whatever he may have in prospect.

Up to this log building with some meandering I drove; and seeing a little man who by description received appeared to be major-domo, I sent to tell him that an English traveller had called and begged to see his improvements; upon which he approached, and after salutation, turning towards and pointing to his primitive hut, observed that it was still his residence, to which so attached had he become that he should quit it with regret. He then drew my attention to his new house, which he said was building according to a promise made to his daughters; and he invited us to inspect it. Alighting therefore, he led the way over a sufficiently commodious dwelling, no part of which was yet finished but the library, placed at the gable end on the first floor and the approach to it up a high flight of stairs on the outside of the house. Here we found the Misses Birkbeck; they were engaged in some ornamental needlework, and received us like sensible, agreeable girls. Upon the table lay a flute, an instrument upon which one of them plays; and everything was well arrayed to give effect, as well as the sterling, good, and for a private library large assortment of books. A fine healthy boy, his son, came up and presented to us some bunches of wild grapes he had just gathered, the only refreshment I believe offered.

But there must have been rapid progress, for coming along in November of the same year, Faux was—for him—extremely cheerful when he wrote of the Birkbeck house that it

is very capacious and convenient, furnished with winter and summer apartments, piazzas and balconies, and a fine library, to which you ascend by an outward gallery. Every comfort is found in this abode of the Emperor of the Prairies, as he is here called. It is situated out of the village and on an elevation, having a fine view of his estate and the prairies generally in front. It is a pity that it is not built of brick or stone instead of wood; once on fire it will be inextinguishable, and the loss of comfort and property considerable and, moreover, irrecoverable. There is no limestone here for mortar but what is made, expensively, twelve miles off, of shells from the Wabash. Brick buildings are laid in muddy clay!

Whatever their approval of the living conditions of the two leading families, visitors were generally less enthusiastic about Albion and Wanborough. Faux's disgust was explicit.

I walked round Albion. It contains one house only, and about ten or twelve log cabins full of degenerating English mechanics too idle to work and above everything but eating, drinking, brawling, and fighting. The streets and paths are almost impassable with roots and stumps, and in front of every door is a stinking puddle formed by throwing out wash and dirty water.

I called on Mr. Cowling, late of Spalding, Lincolnshire, who with his brother is settled on a corner of a quarter section, living without any female and fast barbarizing in a most miserable log cabin, not mudded, having only one room, no furniture of any kind save a miserable, filthy, ragged bed for himself and his brother, who is lamed and prostrated on the floor by a ploughshare, and who, though unable to move, yet refuses a doctor. Both were more filthy, stinking, ragged, and repelling than any English stroller or beggar ever seen; garments rotting off, linen unwashed, face unshaven and unwashed, for, I should think, a month. Yet Mr. Cowling is a sensible, shrewd man, quite a philosopher, though filthiness is against the law of nature. "Here," says he, "a man learns philosophy and its uses!" He expects his sisters and brothers into this miserable abode. What a shock will such a spectacle be to their feelings!

And Welby gave a full account of the hardships a traveler faced in visiting Albion at this time.

The road was good, yet the length of way made it nearly dark when we drove up to the log tavern. Before the door and dispersed stood several groups of people who seemed so earnest in discourse that they scarcely heeded us; others, many of whom were noisy from the effects of a visit to the whiskey store, crowded round to look at us; and amidst the general confusion as we carried the luggage in (having first obtained a bedroom) I was not a little apprehensive of losing some of it. However, we got all safely stored, and taking the horses off led them into a straw yard full of others, for there was no stable room to be had; and what was worse no water, not sufficient even to sprinkle over some Indian corn which we got for them. The landlord did all that lay in his power, but our own fare proved little better than that of our horses, which spoke volumes on the state of the settlement; some very rancid butter, a little sour bread, and some slices of lean fried beef, which it was vain to expect the teeth could penetrate, washed down by bad coffee sweetened with wild honey, formed our repast. We asked for eggs—milk—sugar—salt; the answer to all was "We have none." The cows had strayed away for some days in search of water, of which the people could not obtain sufficient for their own ordinary drink, there being none for cattle, or to wash themselves, or clothes. After making such a meal as we could and having spread our own sheets, I laid down armed at all points; that is, with gloves and stockings on, and a long rough flannel dressing gown, and thus defended slept pretty well.

In the morning a request was sent to Mr. Birkbeck for some water, understanding that he had a plentifully supplied well. The answer sent back was that he made it a general rule to refuse every one. A similar application to Mr. Flower however met with a different fate, and the horses were not only well supplied but a pitcher of good water was sent for our breakfast. If the first was not punished for his general refusal the latter was rewarded for his grant by finding on his grounds and not far from his house, two days after, a plentiful spring of clear water, which immediately broke out on the first spit of earth's being removed. This real treasure I saw flowing; the discovery of it appeared miraculous in the midst of so general a drought.

Flower explains the unwashed condition of some of the settlers and the difficulty strangers had getting water, and adds other details of the early building at Albion.

The first efforts of the town proprietors to obtain water were signally unsuccessful. The first well dug was in the public square, and more than a hundred feet deep, and no water. The next a considerable depth, and but a limited supply. We knew not exactly where to dig to find water. The elevation of the town (being on the dividing ridge between the Great and Little Wabash) giving greater salubrity was accompanied by the inconvenience of deep digging for water. When ignorance is complete we are apt to take up with any superstition. I have often smiled at our resignation in following an old well digger, who claimed to be a water witch, with a forked hazel rod in hand, here and there, up and down, through the bushes, with solemn tread and mysterious air. The rod is to bend down of its own accord over the spot where water is to be found. After following the witch for a proper time, the rod bent down. We told him to go to work. The result was water at a depth of forty-five feet, not so deep and copious, but affording a moderate supply. This difficulty about water was all obviated afterward when the property was divided. Tanks and wells then became common as houses. But the want of water in the first instance was no light difficulty. Population streaming in before adequate preparations—add, to all the other inconveniences, the want of water, and it is almost fatal. When there were only two wells, I have known people to stand for two hours in the night to take their turn to dip their bucket full. Hence the efforts of the town proprietors to get an early supply.

One of the first things the town proprietors did after digging the wells was to contract for a large kiln of brick, for chimneys and hearths, to supply the various cabins now built and being built. Nothing gives more real and apparent comfort than a good chimney and a tidy hearth. They next built a markethouse, about seventy-five feet long, standing on a stone foundation, and covered by a shingle roof. One division was fitted up for the reception of books that were given by individuals in England as a nucleus for a public library, and was used for public meetings and public worship. When Albion became the county town the first courts were held therein. They cut roads east, west, north, and south, and built a bridge over Bonpas Creek that cost them five hundred dollars. Their last act of any notoriety was the building of the new courthouse and jail, which was done chiefly from their own subscription with a portion from the county. The proprietors, if they had done no more, would have done uniformly well, which is a little too much to be expected of human nature. They had some violent disputes and law proceedings which retarded business and was for a time injurious to the growth of the town. They dissolved partnership and divided the unsold property, and of course all disputes arising out of the association were ended.

My father took a lively interest in the growth of the town, and erected several buildings in which to carry on trades necessary to the existence of the town and the wants of the settlement. The year after his arrival he built a good two-story brick tavern. It was a remarkably dry fall, and the wells of the town were not more than sufficient to supply the inhabitants. But my father was not a man easily turned from his intentions. He ordered a barrel put on a sled, drawn by a pair of oxen or one horse, and all the water necessary to the building of that tavern was hauled nearly two miles in that tedious way. The next building for the benefit of the public was a mill. It was built as a treadmill, worked by four oxen, relieved by another four, and so kept constantly going. It soon became crowded with grists of the backwoodsmen and farmers. Besides this, wheat was bought and flour made for sale. Two other houses of hewn stone my father built, and he accomplished many other improvements in and about town.

Faux and Welby supply further impressions of how the town might strike a traveler arriving from an overland journey of a thousand miles and expecting to find English comfort on the widely heralded English Prairie.

FAUX

At four P.M. I reached the English Prairie, presenting a wide, rusty, black prospect, the fire having passed over it. I met Woods and Shepherd, the only two farmer-like men; saw no corn-fields, nothing done; rode into Albion at dusk, and called on speculator Pugsley and Mr. E. P. Fordham, who never means to return to England except rich or to be rich. If he fails here, he will turn hunter and live by his rifle on the frontiers. I supped and went to bed in a hog sty of a room containing four filthy beds and eight mean persons, the sheets stinking and dirty. Scarcity of water is, I suppose, the cause. The beds lie on boards, not cords, and are so hard that I could not sleep. Three in one bed, all filth, no comfort, and yet this is an English tavern—no whiskey, no milk, and vile tea, in this land of prairies.

At sunrise I rose from our filthy nest. Mr. Simpkins, a dirty idle wife, with sons and daughters, late of Baldock, Herts., are the managers of this prairie tavern. A better one of brick is building by Mr. Richard Flower, who owns the former, from which Simpkins is about removing to Evansville because he and family, though all poor, are above being at the beck and call of everybody and pleasing nobody; and besides (says Simpkins) the great folks are too aristocratical for me, and endeavour to oppress their countrymen.

WELBY

We now sallied out to take a view of the settlement, which is marked out not on prairie but on woodland only just partially cleared here and there where a house is built, so that there is yet but little appearance of a town. A very neat roofed-in building for a market first attracts the eye; at one end, parted off with boards and under the same roof is a very decent place of worship, which is at present of a size sufficient for the place.

While we were viewing this edifice a young Englishman
introduced himself with a welcome to us and hopes expressed
that I should settle among them; he was, I found, the medical
man of the place, and in himself certainly formed one inducement to stay, for he seemed to be a very pleasant com-
municative man. He possessed a very prettily finished picturesque cottage and seemed sanguine in his hopes of the
success of the settlement. We visited a wheelwright next,
one of the many who had been induced by Mr. Birkbeck to
emigrate soon after he himself left England. The man's story
is shortly this: he and his brother sailed for America, and
were induced by Mr. Birkbeck's "Notes" to leave the Eastern parts where good employment was offered to them and
to repair to the prairies. On arriving, he found none of the
cottages ready for the reception of emigrants which his
reading had led him to expect, nor any comforts whatever.
He was hired however by Mr. Birkbeck, and got a log hut
erected; but for six months the food left for his subsistence
was only some reasty bacon and Indian corn, with water a
considerable part of the time completely muddy; while Mr.
Birkbeck himself, at Princeton and elsewhere, did not, as he
might have done, send him any relief. On account of these
hardships the man left him, set up for himself, and now has,
he told me, plenty of work, but he seemed doubtful of the
pay.

FAUX

I was introduced to the young Birkbecks, riding through
Albion, and was struck by their polished and prepossessing
appearance. The young Birkbecks conducted us to the seat
of their celebrated father, whom we met near the house returning from shooting, dressed in the common shooting jacket,
&c., of an English farmer sporting over his own lands. Knowing my friend, he received us both very graciously, and with
a hearty welcome conducted us in to the ladies. He approached us at first as strangers, and, as is common with
him, with a repelling sternness and earnestness of manner
which seemed to say, "Who are you?" But this manner, if he

is pleased with appearances, soon dies away into smiling kindness and hospitality, which makes all at home. "If I am not," said he, "pleased with all who come, and I cannot, and will not, they go away abusing me and the settlement." Gentler and kinder manners, perhaps, to strangers indiscriminately coming from afar, would be no bad policy. Mr. Birkbeck is of a small, unformidable but erect stature, and swarthy Indian complexion. The contour of his face, with the exception of a fine nose, possesses little that is striking; and the face, viewed as a whole, indicates little of the exactness, ripeness, sweetness, and finished taste which are known to distinguish him.

He seems enviably happy in the bosom of his family, which consists of four sons and two daughters, mistresses of the lyre and lute and of many other accomplishments. Mr. Birkbeck, and every branch of this happy family with the exception of his son Richard, retire at ten every evening to their sleeping rooms, where a fire is kindled for them to read and study by half the night. "I am happy," said he, "in my family!" His favourite son Morris, a finished scholar, disliking a rustic life, is about returning to England. Mr. Birkbeck had not the advantages of his children, but still is master of the dead and several of the modern languages. He only a few days since returned from a tour through Illinois, by way of Kaskaskia, where he was chosen president of the agricultural society of Illinois, one grand object of which will be to rid the state of stagnant waters. He visited many settlements, but saw none so desirable as his own.

His hard words elsewhere notwithstanding, Faux even has pleasant things to say about the Flowers.

I was introduced also to Richard Flower, Esq., and engaged to dine with him and his family at their house in the prairie. This gentleman much resembles the celebrated Benjamin Flower, though of a finer person, but is fast fading away. The shock which he received by the death of a favourite son, a victim to the climate, has, together with some disappointments, greatly impaired the vigorous mind and body of this noble man and true fearless friend of liberty all over the world.

And of George and Mrs. Flower:

This gentleman is very polite, mild, gentle, and unassuming; trying scenes have made him rather silent and sombre. His lady seems the happiest and most elegant female I have ever seen, and perfectly suited to her present or any situation, being neither above the cottage nor below the palace. Well indeed might four gentlemen contend for the prize!

> *If some few failings to her portion fall,*
> *Look in her face and you'll forget them all.*

The gay, graceful, modest, hearty, anticipating kindness of this lady makes every guest feel himself at home and loth to depart.

Richard Flower, too, was writing about the superior state of society on the prairie.

Most of the persons who emigrate here are those who have diminished their former fortunes; persons who have received good education but are unable to sustain their stations in England. There is no arrogance in saying our circle of society is far superior to that in most of the villages in our native country. Except the parson, the squire, and the principal farmers, what is the society of many of the English hamlets but rude and uncultivated? Here it is different; for within the circle of a few miles there is more good company (I mean well-educated persons) than in the same circle in most parts of England.

We frequently find superior education and intelligence among the sons of the plough and the axe. A person lately offered me his services to split boards for me; we agreed for price. I observed a correctness in his pronunciation and manner of speaking apparently far above his situation. I attended him to the woods. He had with him two men younger than himself. The first singularity that appeared was, after taking off their clothes (having first ground their axes) a nail or two were driven into a tree on which were hung handsome gold watches. These men were well educated, understood geography, history, European politics, and the interesting events that now so much excite the attention of mankind. I went into my field the other day, and began a conversation with my ploughman; his address and manner of speech as well as his conversation surprised me. I found he was a colonel of militia and a member of the legislature; he was indeed a fit companion for men of sense. And where will you find persons of this class in England with equal intelligence?

Under the influence of such polished society, Faux grows so ebullient that he almost attributes true love to the benevolent effect of pioneering.

Not far from Mr. Woods live a Mr. Bentley and lady, late of London, who, here, with a little property, have turned farmers, doing all the labour in the field and loghouse themselves, and, it is said, seem very cheerful, happy, and healthy. In London he had the gout, and she the delicate blue devils; but here milking, fetching water, and all kinds of drudgery, indoors and out, have cured her, and ploughing him. He never, he says, loved her, or she him, half so much as in Illinois.

iii

THERE WAS A DARK SIDE to the picture as well. Temporary hardships were being overcome, there was friendly human intercourse in the towns; but out on the prairie or buried in the forest in an isolated cabin, a settler might feel different about the prospects of life. Fordham gives some indication of the terrible sense of aloneness that could descend on one.

You will never have a correct idea of what a wilderness is
till you come to visit me. It is no more like a great wood than
a battle is like a review. Whatever limits it may have on the
map, however quickly the eye may traverse the chart, or the
imagination may skim over the fancied desert—the traveller
and hunter find impediments which give to him notions of
extension.

To be at an unknown distance from the dwellings of man,
to have pathless forests of trees around you and intervening
rivers across which you must swim on your horse or on a raft,
whatever be the temperature of the water or the air—the
whispering breeze among the leaves, the spring of the deer,
or the flap of the eagle's wing are the only sounds you hear
during the day; and then to lie at night in a blanket, with
your feet to a fire, your rifle hugged in your arms, listening to
the howling wolves, and starting at the shriek of the terrible
panther: this it is to be in a wilderness alone.

And a letter writer who signed himself only "J. C." left a remarkable record of how terrifying the wilderness might be to a
London-bred amateur farmer trying to carve out a farmstead
among men wilder than the beasts they had replaced.

On my arrival in America, my spirits were exceedingly depressed by the bad news I heard on all sides respecting the
back country; however, I pushed forward, and have no reason
to repent. I arrived at Birkbeck's settlement on the 11th of
September, and purchased land in a few days; but the boys I
brought with me have occasioned me a great deal of trouble
and uneasiness. The one I engaged on my passage I was
obliged quickly to discharge—and the one I brought with me
from England, and whom I thought nothing would have induced to leave me, has turned out the most hardened, wicked
wretch imaginable. We are surrounded by numbers of backwoodsmen, whom Birkbeck truly calls "half savage hunters." These he has left my cabin, in my absence, to join;
wishing myself, his father, mother, brother, and all Englishmen the most hearty curses; declaring he was in a free country, where he could plunder and do as he pleased. For the

backwoodsmen have a strange notion that they are too strong for the law except in cases of money transactions. You hear of desperate characters in London; but these men beat them hollow in all species of crime. These are the men with whom Henry has associated himself, and particularly with a young but most desperate character who fancies himself freed from all moral obligations. He has espoused Henry's cause, and set the whole tribe of hunters in hostility against me. I have every reason to believe they have killed one of my horses, and that Henry is lurking about my plantation to destroy the other. The reasons he alleged for leaving me were that I had teased him with learning him to read and write, and reproved him for getting intoxicated—which they teach him are intolerable insults. It has been added that I have beaten him; but everyone acquainted with this country knows I dare not have touched a hair of his head, for children, from the age of six, are taught to resent such an injury with a stab, and are seldom seen here without a knife for this purpose.

That word liberty, but which I call licentiousness, is a curse to this country. Here, children of six and seven years old set their parents at defiance, and are supported in their rebellion by their neighbours. This state represents a melancholy picture of human depravity; parents encouraging their children in vice, and children threatening their parents like dogs. Law and order are odious to them.

In all new states there is a code of laws; but it takes some years to put them in force—and these characters, too strong for the gallows and the whipping post, indulge themselves in the most horrible crimes. I have mortally offended them by reprobating some of their evil propensities, and not permitting them to come to my house to get drunk. Last winter but one they shot twice at an Englishman, in his own house, for such a refusal; and one of the very men has since been made a magistrate—a murderer made a magistrate!

Last Christmas I expected the same fate; but I stood all day in the defensive, and I believe the number of my arms deterred them. They, however, denounce my destruction, and that of my cattle, which I expect going first—and for my-self I have been under the necessity of lying during the night with my arms by me, and my sword in my hand, for a long time together. I am five miles from Birkbeck, and therefore out of the reach of immediate assistance. My situation you will think a desperate one—and you must not be surprised to hear that they have shot me, or I some of them.

As our settlement increases, however, this nuisance will cease, for these fellows retire before the advance of popula-tion with the rest of the noxious animals. To my face they are very civil, when it serves their interest, for I am their lawyer and doctor and have given them every assistance in my power on all occasions without charge. But they are men with no ideas of gratitude—the Indians and wild beasts are far before them.

"J. C." was very likely Joel Churchill. It is gratifying to have this brief report of his subsequent success, as given by Flower.

Mr. Joel Churchill, an intelligent and educated gentleman from London, after trying farming in its roughest form in the woods some five miles south of Albion (first in a log house), soon built a store of brick and a stone dwelling house behind it. His business, by his good management and ap-plication, in a few years was much enlarged. To this he added the manufacture of castor oil. These businesses, on a larger scale, are now carried on by Mr. Churchill and his two sons, Mr. Charles and Mr. James Churchill, both married men.

George Flower also gives the only history of the other businesses early established in Albion, as well as brief notes on the various families that prospered there.

Of the trades first in order come the stores. Mr. Elias Pym Fordham, who had taken my little store, sold out to Mr. Olver, a merchant from Plymouth, England. In after years, Mr. Olver removed to the neighborhood of Pittsburgh, and opened the Edgeworth Institute, a seminary for young ladies; but he left behind him a capacious stone house of his own building.

Nearly forty years ago a young Scotchman in his teens rode up to my house and wished me to purchase his horse, saddle, and bridle, which I did for sixty dollars—a good price in those days. I built him a forge, which he rented at first and afterward purchased. With the proceeds of the horse he purchased iron and went to work. This was the beginning of Mr. Alexander Stewart, who, after some years of labor and industry, added to his blacksmith shop a store. Business and capital increasing, he soon went largely into the produce of the country, of which pork, corn, and wheat are the staples. He is also a principal proprietor of a large flouring mill at Grayville.

A store owned by an association of farmers was carried on successfully by Mr. Henry Harwick for several years. Mr. George Ferryman, from the island of Jamaica, came to us at the period of emancipation, thinking the island would be ruined; but he has since told me that the trade he left has largely increased. What is a little singular, Mr. Ferryman has twice removed from Albion with all his family. There must be some strong national sympathy at work to bring our migrating settlers back. Captain Carter, one of our earliest settlers, and more recently Mr. Henshaw, both went back to London, and both returned to Albion.

Englishmen returning to their native country after many years' residence abroad think the old country has changed since they left it, but fail to see the change in themselves worked by time, climate, and national associations of an entirely different character. One of our most respectable, an early though not of the earliest, settlers is Mr. Elias Weaver, one of Rapp's people, a German—left the Harmonites, quite a young man at the time of their removal, and came to Albion. Understanding the pottery business, my father built him a kiln, at which he worked some time; but he afterward changed to a business more to his liking, of which he also had some knowledge—a builder. He married, built himself a good house, and has assisted in the building of many others.

In 1821, Mr. Wm. Pickering, gentleman, from Appleton Roebuck, in the parish of Bolton Percy, Yorkshire, six miles

from the city of York, accompanied by his friend and cousin,
Mr. Thomas Swale, made their first settlement in the Village
Prairie. On the 9th of March, 1824, he became my brother-in-
law by marrying my eldest sister, Miss Martha Flower. Mr.
Pickering, like myself, returned to England. On his coming
a second time to this country he was accompanied by his
venerable father, Mr. Matthew Pickering. He also brought
valuable livestock—a fine bull of the purest Durham blood; a
thoroughbred Shetland pony; two rams and four ewes of the
Lincolnshire sheep, famous for producing in its highest perfection the long-combing wool of England; and four rams
and eight ewes of the thoroughbred Bakewell-Leicestershire
sheep. Mr. Pickering has ever taken a lively interest in everything of a public nature. He has served in the legislature, is
extensively known in our own state, and also known abroad.

Richard Flower proudly exclaims on the affluence achieved by
one of his servants who came with the family.

I wish you could visit my old servant T. S. on one of the
pleasantest situations in the world, with his nice garden, his
cows, pigs, and poultry about him; his wife and children contented and happy. Perhaps were you to come suddenly upon
him, eggs and bacon with a hastily got up chicken might be
your fare; but if you gave him a day's notice, you would see a
haunch of venison, or a fine cock turkey on the table. How
long would Tom have fagged in England, although he had
double his wages, before he could have possessed himself of
two hundred acres of good land and been placed in such
affluence? Here, indeed, it may be truly said that the hand of
the diligent maketh rich.

And George Flower identifies the man and gives further details
of the rapid rise in station of his family.

With my father's family came Mr. Thomas Shepherd, his
wife, two sons, and daughter. Thomas Shepherd had lived
with my parents from his youth, his father with my grand-

father (on my mother's side), and his great-grandfather with my great-grandfather. Such instances are not uncommon in England. In these cases the confidence between the employer and the employed is mutual, and the separation like the separation of blood relations. Mr. Shepherd had the care and management of my father's garden and of his riding horses, and some other arrangements about the house. Mrs. Shepherd had the exclusive care of the children of the family. Conscientiousness and integrity were the prominent traits in her character. The habit of reading, from her childhood, almost amounted to a passion with her. In a book she indulged at every opportunity. The habit of reading, aside from the information it imparts and the tone of quietude and reflection it induces, is eminently suited to those who have the care of children. Thus the children of our family had always the advantage of association with a conscientious, kind, and well-informed friend.

Some of the previous earnings of Mr. Shepherd were invested in a quarter section of land immediately after our arrival, within two miles of Albion. After staying with my father a short time, he went on his own property, which soon began to improve under his energetic industry. He did not live long to enjoy his dawning prosperity. The active labor which can be carried on continuously in cooler climates too often proves fatal under our hot sun and sudden changes. The son, also named Thomas, was soon old enough to work the farm for his mother. A few years afterward we see him a married man and father of a family. Mr. Thomas Shepherd is an excellent specimen of a practical farmer, strong, industrious, and intelligent. The monotony of labor is, in his case, mitigated by the perusal of useful books. The purely intellectual man, the exclusively hard-working or purely physical man are each of them but half a man. It is knowledge and industry combined that makes the well-balanced character.

Two sisters came with Thomas Shepherd, Mrs. Carter and Mrs. Ellis, both widows. Mrs. Carter, the elder, had been housekeeper in the family of Richard Flower for many years. Richard uses her

as an example of the rapid change in marital status that also occurred on the prairie.

Marriages here take place so frequently that we are certainly
in want of female servants; even our Mrs. C., who lived with
us upwards of twenty-five years and is turned of fifty, has
not escaped. She is married to a Mr. W., having first refused
Monsieur R., an Italian gardener, of very polite manners, and
who may be said to have seen a little of the world, as he
marched from Italy to Moscow with Bonaparte, back to
France, and proceeded from thence to this place. He was tall
and majestic in person, made very elegant bows to *Mad-
ame* C., and spoke English enough to assure her he had the
highest esteem for her and would marry her tomorrow if she
would consent. But all in vain; plain John Bull carried the
day. We have had ten or twelve marriages within three or
four months. This, I think, is settling the Illinois pretty fast.

And George Flower explains that Mrs. Ellis' second marital adventure was no less impressive than her sister's.

Mrs. Ellis was married in my house to Richard Field, one
of Wellington's old life guardsmen, who, turning his sword
into a pruning hook, engaged in the better occupation of cutting up corn and pumpkins instead of cutting down Frenchmen and their allies as he was wont to do in former days.

iv

THE HARD WORK OF SETTLEMENT continued, and more and more
settlers, attracted by the glowing reports they had read, drifted in
from other parts of the United States, and from England as well.
George Flower writes that

The members of our family often met at my house, but more
frequently at my father's to canvass some measure of interest
to the town or settlement. Myself, my father, my brothers-in-
law, Mr. Ronalds and Mr. Pickering, and sometimes an ad-

ditional friend or two, composed the party. Measures for the advancement of the town or country were then discussed— the erection of some public building, school, library, a new road, a petition to the legislature—and action in each case was often decided upon. If opinions were divided, we would take an appeal to the public sentiment, and a town meeting was called. These meetings and discussions were often discordant and sometimes stormy. However they kept things alive.

In 1819, the hunter class of backwoodsmen began to move off, to keep their true position between the receding Indian and the advancing white man. With all their faults, they were an interesting class. We were getting too populous and civilized for them.

Three brothers, Moses, John, and George Michaels, from one of the Eastern states—Connecticut, I think—were among our earliest settlers on the prairie three miles east of Albion. With them came two families of Browns, from the same section. Moses Michaels, for several years a magistrate, was our first representative in the legislature, that met first at Kaskaskia and afterward at Vandalia. A most striking example of a man being placed in the front rank without possessing a single qualification to lead or to command. Without one positive, his character was made up of all negative qualities. It may be observed in higher offices than those filled by our humble representative that men are often chosen for their moderate, rather than their superior, ability.

Other settlers, from the class of poor whites from slave states, came in and settled among us; and, now and then, a more substantial farmer from New York and Pennsylvania. It was curious to see the different appointments of these various American settlers. The eye could detect from whence they came as far as it could discern them.

When a large wagon came in sight, strong and complete, generally painted blue, drawn by four strong horses in high condition, its feed trough behind, tar buckets and water swinging beneath, laden with a full supply of bedding and household gear on which sat sturdy boys and buxom girls, all dressed in stout homespun clothes, a stalwart man in his deep-seated saddle driving, that wagon came from the Keystone State.

Another traveling establishment of a far different character was more frequently to be seen coming along—a little rickety wagon, sometimes a cart or light carryall, pulled by a horse as lean as a greyhound, scarcely able to drag the vehicle, which contains only a skillet, a small bag of meal, and a little piece of bacon; a gaunt, emaciated man and a large family, chiefly daughters, walking barefoot, and without a change of raiment. "Where from, good folks?" The answer is sure: from Alabama or Caroline. A more perfect picture of destitution can not be seen. Give them time, and with good soil, with freedom to work it, they will soon get on, if sober, which many of them are. Their only tools are an axe and a hoe, with, occasionally, a one-horse plow. They have no team to break up the prairie, and, necessarily, settle in the woods, girdle a few trees, and make a few rails, and get in a corn patch. After all, these are the best settlers we get from the South. Their little corn patch increases to a field; their first shanty to a small log house, which, in turn, gives place to a double cabin, in which a loom and spinning wheel are installed. A well with a sweep, a grapevine for a rope, a few fruit trees, and their improvement is complete. Moderate in their aspirations, they soon arrive at the summit of their wishes. The only difference between the roving hunters and these stationary settlers appears to be in the greater sobriety of the stationary class.

Quite a respectable man, a neighbor, told me that all he possessed was put into a bee gum, and carried by himself and wife when they came into the state on foot. We have some from the South with greater pretensions. But they neither plow, nor sow, nor build houses, nor make garments. The best of them get into the professions—a doctor or a lawyer— but their great ambition is to get to the legislature, and then to Congress.

Another class, from another quarter, and with other abilities, also come to us. Young men fresh from college, from the New England states. I have two examples now in my eye.

These two young men came to Albion, their wits their only fortune. I mean their legitimate wits; that is, the power of turning their acquirements to the best account, losing no opportunity. They too decline manual labor. One went to Carmi. He was a magistrate while there; afterward cashier of a branch of the State Bank at Mt. Carmel. The other at first took small children to teach, at two dollars a quarter, and taught them their A B C. Whenever he could get a little writing in the clerk's office, he employed himself there. He was soon seen on a horse, riding the circuit with the lawyers and becoming one himself. Tacking his political sails to suit the breeze, he got elected to the legislature, and afterward became governor of the state of Illinois. This is a class representing the active intellect of the country, possessing a great deal of tact and intelligence.

It is very curious to see how differently the Eastern American, the Southerner, and the Englishman proceed in their way of farming, where they all begin with little or nothing. The Southerner, as I have before stated, goes into the woods, girdles a few trees, and raises some corn and pumpkins. It is hard to say how he employs himself the rest of the year. Industry—that is, systematic and continuous labor—he seems utterly to avoid; but he gets along after his own fashion, and occasionally, by fits and starts, he will accomplish more than either of the others. But his periods of hard work are, for the most part, separated by long periods of inaction. The Eastern man, or Yankee, as we call him, shows great dexterity and good management in all he does. He has a certain sleight that seems to make his work go off rapidly and easily; and this quality is observable in the women as well as the men, in the housework as well as in the farmwork, and is very noticeable when contrasted with the mode of labor of most of the Europeans. If he meet with a difficulty he evades it, or lets it stand by until he is better able to contend with it. Industrious, economical, and with a thrifty experience, he seems to get along easily, and surpasses the Englishman at a great rate. The Englishman, unpractised in the ways of the country, does not take hold of things by the smooth handle. He plants himself squarely before his difficulties, he evades nothing but works hard and steadily to remove them—not always with dexterity; on the contrary, he often seems to take hold of things the wrong way. But the Englishman has a higher standard in his mind. He has seen well-cultivated farms and substantial and convenient farmhouses, mansions surrounded by verdant lawns kept as closely shorn as the pile on a Turkey carpet and the gravel walks kept as clean as the floor of the drawing room. These high standards he may not reach, but he approaches somewhat toward them. His improvements are more substantial, and he stays upon them. After some years, comparing the two, the Englishman has surpassed the American. In a few more, the American is gone; but the Englishman remains.

It is a noticeable fact that emigrants bound for the English Settlement in Illinois landed at every port from the St. Lawrence to the Gulf of Mexico. This arises from the fact that the laborers and small farmers of England are very imperfectly acquainted with the geography of America. Indeed, among all classes in England there is a very inadequate idea of the extent of the United States, and scarcely any of the nationality of each state. The child at school, looking at the map of England, sees all the counties and London as the metropolis of the kingdom. On the map of America, he sees the states and Washington as the metropolis of the republic. He feels that the states of America and the counties of England are relatively the same. I question if half a dozen maps are to be found in all England of the different states marked with county boundaries. It is a point not explained to him by his teachers. Thus the error grows up with him.

As various as their ports of debarkation were the routes they took, and the modes of conveyance they adopted. Some came in wagons and light carriages, overland; some on horseback; some in arks; some in skiffs; and some by steamboat, by New Orleans. One Welshman landed at Charleston, S. C. "How did you get here?" I asked. "Oh," he innocently replied, "I just bought me a horse, sir, and inquired the way." It seems our settlement was then known at the plantations in

Carolina and in the mountains of Tennessee. The great variety found among our people, coming as they did from almost every county in the kingdom, in complexion, stature, and dialect, was in the early days of our settlement very remarkable. Of the variety of places from which they came, I had some singular indirect testimony.

When a youth, I accompanied my drawing master on his annual sketching tour into the southern counties of Wales and adjoining counties of England. From some three hundred pencil sketches, we selected six for pictures in body color, an art I was then learning. Like many first productions of children, my parents put these, my first efforts, into frames and hung them up. By some means they came in our baggage, and were hung up in my cabins on the prairies. One day, the Welshman Williams, looking earnestly at one of them, asked me where that place was. I told him it was "Pont ne Vaughan," Glamorganshire, South Wales. "I thought it was, sir, or I should not have asked; and there stands the Widow Griffith's house. I have been there, sir, a hundred times." And there he stood, exclaiming sometimes in Welsh, sometimes in English, pleased at the representation that recalled to him the happy scenes of his youth.

On another occasion, my shepherd challenged another picture. "Is not that the River Severn, near Bristol, sir?" "Yes." "And there are the two islands called the 'flat' and the 'steep holmes,' on which I have gathered bushels of birds' eggs," said he. In this way were my early pictures nearly all recognized. That representations of places, taken nearly a half century before in secluded places in England, far apart from each other, should be sent into a wilderness of another hemisphere, there to be recognized by persons, some of whom were not born at the time the sketches were taken, seems a very strange thing.

In addition to George Flower's *History,* there are a few other scattered references to the activity taking place at this time. In 1820, Richard Flower writes about a project close to his heart— the public library.

Our library is now consolidated. I have conveyed all the books
presented to us in trust to the proprietors of the town for the
use of the Albion Library, writing the names of the donors
in them. Our little library is the admiration of travellers, and
Americans say we have accomplished more in one year than
many new settlements have effected in fifty—a well supplied
market, a neat place of worship, and a good library.

Birkbeck, too, had not entirely abandoned public projects.
When he fastened on Illinois as a place of settlement

it was inferred that the grand intercourse between this
western world and Europe would be through the Mississippi;
and that, consequently, the lower down the Ohio would
eventually be the nigher to Europe.

By 1818 his plan to approach Europe via New Orleans was maturing, and he wrote:

A naval establishment occupies our attention at present. We
Americans must have a navy. We are forming two pirogues
out of large poplars, with which we propose to navigate the
Wabash. By lashing them together and laying planks across
both, we shall have a roomy deck, besides good covered stow-
age in both, and take a bulky as well as a heavy cargo. And
we hope to have a shipping port at the mouth of Bonpas, a
considerable stream which falls into the Wabash at the point
where the latter makes a bold bend to the west and approaches within a few miles of our prairie.

The "navy" of course had to have commodities to export; in
spite of comments of visitors about the scarcity of farm produce,
the farms were beginning to yield harvests large enough to leave a
surplus for sale. When W. N. Blane came to the settlement in 1822
he could write that

The farms in the neighbourhood are increasing in magnitude
and number. The year I was there the settlers had exported
produce for the first time. The way they effected this was by

loading several flatboats with corn, flour, pork, beef, sausages, &c., and floating them down the Wabash into the Ohio, and from thence down the Mississippi to New Orleans, a distance of about 1,140 miles. The mere length of this navigation proves that the settlement is capable of great efforts.

So one of Birkbeck's dreams had come true.

Blane, like others who visited the settlement, tried to form an honest opinion about whether or not an Englishman would be wise to settle there. By the date of his visit, Birkbeck and Flower had at least had a reasonable time to put their ideas into action, and the results might be fairly judged. The difficulty of such an evaluation, however, may be seen in the subjects Blane singled out for mention. On the one hand, he wrote:

One of the principal inducements to settle at Albion in preference to any other place in the state is that there is a very clever English surgeon there, who, having had a regular education under Abernethy and walked the hospitals in London, must be a great acquisition to families in the neighbourhood. Persons who have not visited the Western states cannot have any idea of the general ignorance of the practitioners of medicine. A young man, after an apprenticeship of a year or two in the shop of some ignorant apothecary or at the most after a very superficial course of study at some school or college, is entitled to cure (or rather kill) all the unhappy backwoodsmen who may apply to him for advice. It would be well if they were all as harmless in their practice as Dr. Elnathan Todd, a person described in the *Pioneers*, an American novel, and whose character, drawn to the life, gives a good idea of one of these physicians. Indeed, to become a doctor in the backwoods it is only necessary to have a cabin containing 50 or 100 dollars' worth of drugs, with a board over the door affirming that this is Dr. M. or N.'s "store."

But on the other hand:

The lower class of English at Albion—that is, the common labourers and manufacturers—have, I am sorry to say, very

much degenerated, for they have copied all the vices of the
backwoodsmen but none of their virtues—drinking, fighting,
&c., and, when fighting, "gouging" and biting. In England,
if two men quarrel they settle their dispute by what is called
"a stand-up fight." The bystanders form a ring, and even if
one of the combatants wish it he is not permitted to strike his
fallen antagonist. This is a manly, honourable custom which
the people of England have good reason to be proud of. But
fighting in the backwoods is conducted upon a plan which is
only worthy of the most ferocious savages. The object of each
combatant is to take his adversary by surprise; and then, as
soon as he has thrown him down, either to "gouge" him—
that is, to poke his eye out—or else to get his nose or ear into
his mouth and bite it off. I saw an Englishman at Albion who
had a large piece bitten out of his under lip. Until I went into
the backwoods I could never credit the existence of such a
savage mode of fighting. I believe something of the same
kind was once customary in Lancashire; but it has, since the
days of pugilism, been totally exploded. This abominable
practice of gouging is the greatest defect in the character of
the backwoodsmen.

All of which, just or not, made its own contribution to the paper
warfare that had been rumbling around the settlement from its
earliest days. By the early 20's the settlement itself was sniping
back.

5

―――――――

"I would sooner live the life

of a gypsy in England."

ONCE DURING THE EARLY DAYS of their settlement, says
Flower, a man from the East landed from a boat at Shawneetown and put up at the village inn.

The first thing he asked of the landlord was if there was any
religion in the English Settlement. What the answer was I
don't precisely know; but it could not be very encouraging,
for the man muttered something and said then he would not
go there, turned round, and went on board the boat again, to
find some place that had a better character.

Why had this man asked such a question? Was it usual to
ask, when one got within a hundred miles of a place, if there
was any religion there? This was a puzzle. What could it
mean? It meant this: That a parcel of land speculators in
New York and Philadelphia, seeing that our settlement was
attracting emigrants whom they wanted to settle on their
land east of the mountains, set on foot every disparaging report as to health, success, provisions, morals, and religion,
plying each individual on the point at which he was most

sensitive. And this began almost as early as our first settlers
arrived. Of all this, we were for a time unconscious. It was
not until after their attacks appeared in print that we were at
all aware of the extent of these calumnies. And it took a long
time for a book or a pamphlet from the Eastern cities to
reach us in those days.

Not only did attacks shower down from New York and Pennsylvania but from England as well. The English onslaught began before there scarcely was a settlement. Directed at Birkbeck's *Notes
on a Journey* it was, if anything, more vicious than the American,
and was aimed both at Birkbeck and his adopted country.

The *Quarterly Review,* for instance, taking a stance of self-
satisfied sarcasm and recalling Birkbeck's Quaker attachment, addressed him habitually as Friend Morris. Of an episode in *Notes
on a Journey* its reviewer wrote:

On the way to Vincennes our Friend loses himself, and is
obliged, in the phraseology of the country, *"to camp out."*
This agreeable adventure, which would sicken an English
gipsy of "camping out," leads quite naturally to a lofty
panegyric on the superior advantages of travelling "in that
vast western wilderness" compared with those to be found in
this country. "Let," says Mr. Birkbeck, "a stranger make his
way through England—let him keep at a distance from every
public road" (made for his accommodation), "avoid all the
inns" (established expressly for his convenience and comfort)
and perversely scramble over hedge and ditch "in quest of
such entertainment only as the hovel of the labourer can
supply, and he would have no more cause to complain of the
rudeness of the inhabitants" than of the werewolves of the
wilds of Indiana! If we could conceive a traveller to be guilty
of such gratuitous folly we should then say that as his application to the day labourer for "entertainment" could only be
looked upon as a deliberate insult on his poverty, he would
deserve whatever rudeness he might chance to experience.
In somewhat of a similar spirit Mr. Birkbeck adds—"when
we have been so unfortunate as to pitch our tent near a
swamp, and have mismanaged our fire, we have been teased

by moschetoes; but so might we, perhaps, in the fens of Cambridgeshire." The traveller must have a strong predilection for the *teasing* of moschetoes who would sleep in the fens of Cambridgeshire when by turning a few yards to the right or left he might obtain shelter under a roof. Certainly these are pleasant proofs of the inferiority of England to America.

The same reviewer, softly slipping the gears of his logic, could use Birkbeck's remarks on the backwoodsmen to damn all Americans.

These men, it would seem, though persevering as savages in the pursuit of their game, are as indolent too. This indolence, Mr. Birkbeck says, "they cultivate as a privilege," and he repeats, over and over again, that "indolence is the easily besetting sin of the Americans." The supreme felicity of a true-born American is described to be inaction of body and inanity of mind. If the picture be overcharged, it is not we, but our Friend Morris, who has painted it.

And he was not above insinuating that a Morris Birkbeck in the backwoods was a step toward the violent overthrow of the existing federal government.

Old America, to the eastward of the Alleghany Mountains is very soon likely to become, as our Cambridge Friend expresses it, "the thinnest part of the wedge." Under such circumstances, and considering the character of the people who are flocking to the other side of the Alleghany chain, the opinion is by no means chimerical that "New America" will be induced shortly to shake off her allegiance to the parent states and set up a congress of her own. A few such settlers as Morris Birkbeck (who seems to think that every little society of men ought to govern itself) will marvellously expedite the separation.

It is not surprising that the colonists began to suspect they were the victims of a vast plot. Whether right or not, Flower believed that H. B. Fearon's early volume of travels "was edited and published by the poet laureate, and so worded by him as to give an unfavorable turn to everything American in the eyes of the English emigrant. To sum up, the British Government lent the weight of its influence against us."

Even if this tiny backwoods community was beneath the notice of the majestic British Government—which seems likely—it was a great threat to Eastern landowners, as Flower says, principally in New York and Pennsylvania and also those who were exploiting the development of Canada. In itself the English Settlement meant nothing; its population at this time could not have been greater than a thousand people counting the backwoodsmen, and all of these could easily be lost to other regions. But the reason it had to be put down was that its leaders were highly articulate men whose books and pamphlets were read by thousands. And while Birkbeck and the Flowers naturally favored their own settlement, they also promoted the West as a region. Birkbeck's *Notes on a Journey* was published both in Philadelphia and London, and in two years following the London publication such was the demand for it that it had to be reprinted eleven times. His *Letters from Illinois*, also published in Boston and Philadelphia, passed through seven editions in London; and in addition both books were printed at Dublin and Jena, and the first also at Cork.

Fearon's *Sketches of America* was the earliest book in print to attack the settlement. As Flower says, "He never saw it." Yet, despite its strictures, even this book turned the favorable attention of some Englishmen toward the settlement. Flower tells us that

With Mr. Samuel Thompson, the father-in-law of Mr. Fearon, of London, I became acquainted when last in London in 1817. Mr. Thompson was the head of a religious sect then called the Free-Thinking Christians. The opinions of himself and followers are to be found in his many published works. Radical in politics, heretical in religion (according to the orthodox standard), Mr. Thompson and some members of his family and church then thought to leave England. America generally, and our settlement in particular, at that time engaged their attention. So nearly were the minds of himself and friends made up for a removal that they sent money by me to buy land. The land was bought. Fortunately for them, I think, they changed their minds and never came. In after years Mr. Thompson's two sons, F. B. Thompson, the younger, and Sam'l Thompson, the elder brother, both came out as permanent settlers and inherited their father's land and property in Albion.

Those interested in the settlement tended to be radical and heretical in more ways than one, and the charges and counter-charges that flew back and forth—from the settlers, from visitors, and from armchair geographers—soon amounted to a paper war. Nearly every book and pamphlet dealing with the settlement, whatever its descriptive content and whatever the authenticity of its observations, contributed in one way or another to the skirmish.

On the side of the settlement and under the generalship of Birkbeck appeared his own *Letters from Illinois* (1818), Richard Flower's *Letters from Lexington and the Illinois* (1819), Birkbeck's *Extracts from a Supplementary Letter from the Illinois* (1819), John Melish's *Information and Advice to Emigrants* (1819), John Woods' *Two Years' Residence in the Settlement on the English Prairie* (1822), Birkbeck's *An Address to the Farmers of Great Britain* (1822), Richard Flower's *Letters from the Illinois* (1822), and—important strategical aid from a rather unexpected quarter—James Hall's *Letters from the West* (1828), by perhaps the best writer the Illinois frontier produced, Judge Hall who edited the *Illinois Monthly Magazine* and as a circuit-riding lawyer had visited Albion in its early days. George Flower remained relatively aloof from the verbal strife, his only direct contribution being a sixty-four page pamphlet called *Errors of Emigrants,* and that published in 1841, when the shooting was over. His *History,* written twenty more years later, is, however, the last word in the whole argument, and is a sustained defense after all passions had cooled. These titles do not include the many open letters printed in newspapers, some of them later collected into the books and pamphlets listed above. Nor are the many reviews included—principally of Birkbeck's books and those of travelers— especially in the British periodical press—though they too played an important part in the squabble.

The lines of attack pursued by the critics of the settlement ranged from the absurd to the profound. No second- or third-hand report was too improbable to be picked up and repeated in print by someone. Climate, for instance, was a subject on which everyone had an opinion, and related to it was the question of the healthfulness of the location. Depending on when he visited the settlement—summer or winter—the critic found the climate either too hot or too cold. And he didn't have to visit it at all to know that it was unhealthy—Birkbeck had admitted that people had died there; the critics seemed to expect immortality.

An interesting if unfair anecdote comes from Adam Hodgson, and is a good example of the cords of innuendo some critics managed to get out of slivers of truth.

I lately met a gentleman who has been travelling extensively through the Western country. He did not visit Mr. Birkbeck's settlement but saw two English families returning from it sickly and debilitated; their inability to preserve their health there being, as they alleged, their principal reason for leaving the colony. He also met an English gentleman of property who had been to examine the place with a view of taking his family thither: he said the sight of it, and a conviction that it was unhealthy, decided him at once to relinquish the idea.

All represent Illinois in general as a most unhealthy state, where the people for the most part are pallid and emaciated, and exhibit the languor and apathy which follow frequent or long-continued intermittents. I became sadly too familiar with this melancholy spectacle on my southwestern route; scarcely one family in six in extensive districts in the Carolinas, Georgia, Alabama, Louisiana, and Mississippi being exempt from fever and ague; and many of them exhibiting tall young men of eighteen to thirty moving feebly about the house completely unfitted for exertion after fifteen or eighteen months' residence, or rendered indolent or inefficient for the rest of their lives. In Georgia and Carolina we were told in a jocular way that it was not uncommon for a person who was invited to dinner on a particular day, Wednesday for instance, to begin reckoning "Monday—Tuesday—Wednesday—No; I cannot come to you on Wednesday, for that is my fever day."

In addition to the writers already mentioned—Fearon, Faux, Welby, and Hodgson, all of whom were more or less antipathetic

Morris Birkbeck, proprietor of Wanborough and co-founder, with George Flower, of the prairie settlement. This, the only known likeness of Birkbeck, appropriately pictures him at his portable writing desk, from which issued a stream of books and pamphlets in defense of the settlement and the West in general. Though exaggerated, it was the opinion of one visitor that "no man since Columbus has done so much towards peopling America as Mr. Birkbeck." From Flower's *History of the English Settlement.*

George and Mrs. Flower, as they were represented in the mid-1850's by a primitive portrait painter who signed his canvases D. Roster. The tight-lipped expression on both may well be the result of the painter's idiosyncrasy, but there was cause enough for it in the financial failure of the settlement; the Flowers had left Illinois in 1849 with a few pieces of furniture, some family plate, and $2.50 in cash. The paintings are owned by the Chicago Historical Society.

A cartoon equivalent of such vicious attacks on the West as William Cobbett's. This woodcut was printed many times in the 1830's as a warning to settlers, but it had originated at least a decade earlier. In the first versions the well-dressed gentleman says that he is going to Ohio. The barefoot fellow with the weeping wife and smirking sons had failed there too. Land speculators with holdings farther east quite naturally wished to discourage settlement in the Mississippi Valley.

The National Road, begun in 1811, here showing a tavern near its eastern end in Maryland. Open for traffic as far as Wheeling when Birkbeck published his enticing *Letters from Illinois* in 1818, it became a main artery for immigration to the settlement and other Western communities. Before George Flower gave up his Illinois holdings, the road had already reached Vandalia; East and West were linked by a two-way means of transportation far less hazardous than the journey by flatboat down the Ohio River which Flower and other early settlers had been required to make. English travelers agreed, however, on the hazards of American inns which seldom offered clean, decent accommodations or good food.

"The Pioneer's Home" as imagined by F. F. Palmer and lithographed by Currier and Ives in 1867. A roof such as that on the cabin would never turn water. But this touch is no more phony than the bucolic cheer and groaning abundance pictured; that they never existed matters less than the fact that people continued to want to believe the pioneers lived this way. Birkbeck, the man who raised pigs on paper, was accused by his Eastern critics of representing such a dream of Western life as actuality.

Mouth of the Fox River as it empties into the Wabash, where
Birkbeck was drowned in 1825. Even with full discount for the
overheated imagination of European travelers, this aquatint
shows the grotesque vegetation of the gloomy river bottoms
through which visitors had to find their way to reach the sunlit
prairies. After Charles Bodmer, reproduced in *Travels in the
Interior of North America*, by Maximilian, Prince of Weid-
Neuweid, who visited this region in 1833.

This engraving, also after the Swiss Charles Bodmer and printed in Maximilian's *Travels*, shows the virgin forest which surrounded the prairies. In the distance is the village of Harmonie in Indiana from which the English settlers drew many of their supplies. Birkbeck was drowned returning from this village, then only recently purchased by Robert Owen from the German Rappites and renamed New Harmony. For many years after the settlement, pigs and cattle were allowed to forage, half wild, in the forests.

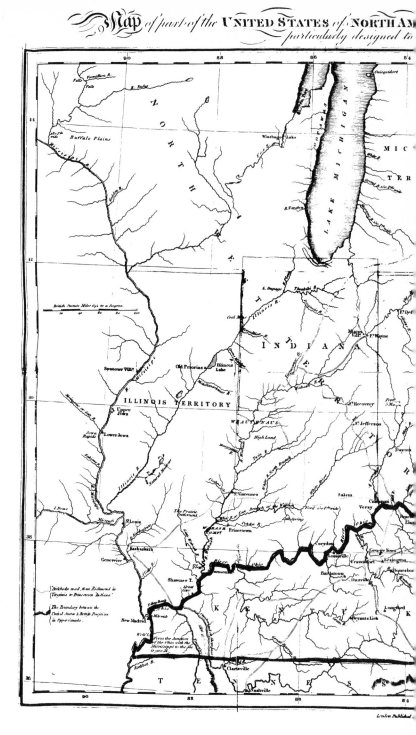

Route of Birkbeck and Flower in 1817 from the Atlantic coast to the Illinois Territory, where they made their settlement. Flower had come this way the previous year when he searched out the prairies, and afterwards, in 1818, he descended the Ohio from

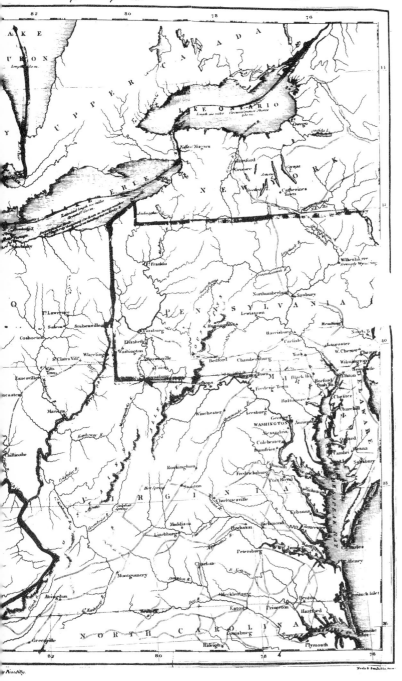

Pittsburgh to Shawneetown with his family and household possessions. Reproduced from the London (1818) edition of Birkbeck's *Letters from Illinois*. Apparently, detailed maps of the Northwest Territory were not readily available in 1818 in London.

"Interieur d'un flat boat"—actually a keelboat—sketched by
Charles Alexandre Lesueur aboard the "Boatload of Knowledge"
which drifted down the Ohio in 1826 bearing the group of scien-
tists and intellectuals who were to make New Harmony famous
as a leading cultural center of the West. For twelve years Lesueur
explored the surrounding country from this base, leaving in his
sketches as complete a record as any artist produced of the Old
Northwest. Though about 1,200 of his drawings and water colors
of American scenes are preserved at the Muséum d'Histoire Naturelle in Le Havre, none relate directly to the settlement on the
English Prairie—a fact that may attest to its waning significance
after Birkbeck's death.

bon repos a shan ½

bon repos - dit bon pas = Creek South Wabash

Lesueur's sketch, made in May 1826, of the hamlet he calls "Bon
Repos"—on Bonpas Creek, near the English Settlement. The tow-
ering trees left standing suggest something of the character of the
virgin forests which the settlers preferred rather than the open
prairie as sites for their homes.

A panoramic view of Princeton, Indiana, made by Lesueur in June 1827. Ten years earlier, Birkbeck had wintered in Princeton while Flower returned to England to recruit settlers and acquire additional funds. Even more primitive then, this settlement was preferable to the loneliness of the bleak prairie winter. The enforced separation of this winter may have led, as Flower believed, to the estrangement between the two families which resulted in the establishment of adjacent villages—Birkbeck's Wanborough, and Flower's Albion.

For twelve years Lesueur explored the surrounding country from his base at New Harmony on the Wabash, leaving in his sketches as complete a record as any artist produced of the Old Northwest during this period. About 1,200 of his drawings and water colors of American scenes are preserved at the Muséum d'Histoire Naturelle in Le Havre (these reproductions are from an American Philosophical Society microfilm), but none relate directly to the settlement on the English Prairie—a fact that may attest to its waning significance after Birkbeck's death.

"Shooting for the Beef," painted in 1850 by George Caleb Bingham in Missouri, represents a backwoods pastime known as well in Illinois. While the backwoodsmen here contend for the placid prize standing nearby, they or others like them might have looked with wonder two decades earlier at the recreation of the English settlers on Boltinghouse Prairie. These marksmen could be the very squatters displaced by the flood of Englishmen who played cricket for amusement and hunted deer with greyhounds.

This Kennedy and Lucas lithograph gives the impression of an English visitor, A. Rider, of a Western camp meeting. With similar British reserve, George Flower observed that such religious expression was "more pandemonian than paradisical," though he thought "the whole affair was well suited to the times and to the people." Birkbeck, Quaker turned freethinker, and Flower, equally tolerant of all religions, drew attack for the "godlessness" of their community.

Park House, viewed from the north side. This water color by
George Flower shows the eleven-room mansion he constructed
for his parents at a time when most of the settlers were still living
in rude log cabins. It too was constructed of logs, with this side
stuccoed to resemble stone. Built in 1819, the house was the pride
of the settlement and the marvel of the backwoodsmen. It took
its name from the thirty acres of open woodland on which it
fronted, and its interior boasted such refinements as papered
walls and a piano said to be the first brought across the Allegheny
Mountains. After the Flower family lost possession of the house
it passed through several ownerships, and was destroyed by fire
sometime after the Civil War. Birkbeck's imposing house built of
timber and brick nogging, of which no picture remains, was
pulled down even before Flower's death.

to the settlement—other critics of some importance were John S. Wright, who wrote *Letters from the West; or, a Caution to Emigrants* (1819) in defense of New York State as a place for settlement; George Courtauld, who wrote an *Address to Those Who May Be Disposed to Remove to the United States of America . . . Including Remarks on Mr. Birkbeck's Opinions* (1821); James Strachan, *A Visit to the Province of Upper Canada* (1821); John Lorain, *Hints to Emigrants; or, a Comparative Estimate of the Advantages of Pennsylvania and of the Western Territory* (1819); C. B. Johnson, *Letters from the British Settlement in Pennsylvania* (1819); Isaac Holmes, *An Account of the United States of America* (1823); Charles F. Grece, *Facts and Observations Respecting Canada and the United States* (1819); and William Cobbett, *A Year's Residence in the United States* (1818). These titles do not include the even more ephemeral newspaper articles and book reviews.

Much of what the critics had to say was repetitious, and is tedious reading today. From the disadvantage of not having seen the settlement they were attempting to annihilate, many had to content themselves with washing the same dirty linen over and over. But a few selected examples will show the directions the attack took.

Charles F. Grece, who grandly signed himself a member of the Montreal and Quebec Agricultural Societies, devoted not a little of his pamphlet to a fulsome dedication to "His Grace, Charles, Duke of Richmond, Lenox, and D'Aubigny, Knight of the Most Honourable Order of the Garter, Captain General, and Governor in Chief of the Canadas, &c. &c. &c." But for His Grace's benignant inspiration, Grece could never have set pen to paper, for, he said,

The unostentatious display of your Grace's Virtues—the justice and humanity of your Administration—and the fostering care and zeal for the welfare of these Provinces, which you have ever manifested since you were first appointed to the high office you now hold, as Captain General and Governor in Chief of the Canadas—are the strongest characteristics of true greatness; and inspire me with confidence to request your acceptance of this little work.

Should this book be honoured by your Grace's perusal, the Author, trusting in the Truth of his Statements, and in the

Experience on which those statements are founded, will feel but little anxiety for his fame as a writer. Indeed, the chief honour to which he aspires, as the Author of this work, is, that he may secure your Grace's approbation.

Probably Grece got his wish for the duke's approbation and no longer was anxious about his fame. His text, no less toadying than his dedication, struck the right tone of submission to higher wisdom. Well he knew the secret reasons scoundrels departed from the emerald shores of Britain.

It cannot with propriety be denied that one of the main inducements to emigration has its origin in political prejudice and animosity. Restless and dissatisfied at home, and impatient of those restraints which the wisdom of Government has imposed upon the turbulent spirits of the idle and the disaffected, many persons assume the character of republicans; and, under professions of great zeal for the rights of man, forsake their native country and retire to the United States.

Besides these theorists in politics, the sanguine speculators in commerce, and the visionary experimentalists in agriculture, all turn their attention to the transatlantic shores of republican America.

There are other motives even more equivocal than these to expatriation. There are not a few of the emigrants who leave Great Britain from having exposed themselves to the justice of its laws.

All these fly to the United States, as to an asylum; but, alas! how miserably have multitudes of emigrants already found themselves disappointed! What bitter regrets have succeeded their brightest hopes and golden dreams! Still, however, the emigration mania has not been cured. Such plausible and fascinating writers as Mr. Birkbeck tend to keep alive the hazardous and often fruitless desire of emigration. Experience alone effectually undeceives; but how frequently does it happen that knowledge of this kind comes too late! Seeing, therefore, that nothing but experience can offer an effectual check to self-expatriation, and, moreover, considering it a duty which I owe to the country of my birth, as well as to those distant portions of its dominions which I have adopted and where I have resided, with my family, many years, I have attempted to divert the tide of emigration from the remote tracts, and wilds of the back settlements, and other regions of the United States to the more hospitable, contiguous, and accessible districts of the lower and upper Canadas.

And with that the cat was out of the bag. Why go to America when it was so much easier to come to Canada?

The emigrant from Great Britain who has resolved to make choice of the Illinois must, of course, cross the Atlantic Ocean. The emigrant to the Canadas must do the same. This voyage is usually performed in about five or six weeks. Both these emigrants may sail nearly all the way to Quebec or Montreal. The one who is bound for the Illinois must then traverse a country, sometimes indeed by inland navigation but generally in wagons or on foot, of about two-thirds the distance from the Canadas as the Canadas are from Great Britain. By the time, therefore, that the Illinois emigrant has arrived at the place of his destination, the Canadian emigrant might be comfortably seated by his own fireside, resting from the fatigues of his voyage.

There were other compelling reasons as well, among them patriotic ones.

The delusions of such visionaries as Mr. Morris Birkbeck cannot be too severely reprobated. Next to the crime of downright falsehood is that of telling, in certain cases, only half the truth. Mr. Birkbeck, though compelled at times to admit a disagreeable fact, has stifled many important truths in the most shameful and culpable manner. Nor has Mr. Fearon, though without doubt the most honest and candid writer on this subject that has hitherto appeared, always adhered to the duty of telling the whole truth. He has, however, this to be said in his favour—if he has omitted all notice of the Canadas it has been owing, in all probability, to the nature of his

instructions from the thirty-nine English families who sent
him out on a kind of voyage of discovery to the United States
and their dependencies only. Mr. Fearon's friends wished to
forsake the government and laws as well as the country of
Great Britain.

If the emigrant to the Wabash country could find advantages to reward him for his labour which he could not
find in the Canadas, he would perhaps be justified in making
choice of those distant and trackless districts. I say perhaps,
for I much question whether any subject of Great Britain can,
upon a general principle of reasoning, justify his conduct in
deliberately adding to the strength and resources of a rival
nation whilst there are extensive, rich, and fertile territories
belonging to his own country, inviting the hand of cultivation, and claiming the exertions of all those who may be induced to quit the immediate soil that gave them birth to seek
their fortunes in distant regions. Your citizens of the world, I
fear, for the most part are but indifferent members of particular communities. And it may be said of the natives and subjects of England generally, if they are not for their country
they are against it. It is impossible to remain neuter when
patriotism, or the love of one's country, is the question.

And besides, the climate of Illinois was dreadful. Here Grece
launches an artful argument that others also used, striking directly at the root of Birkbeck's well-known sentiments about
slavery.

Mr. Birkbeck appears to have laboured as much to withhold
as to convey information; and that not only with respect to
the difficulties he had to encounter in travelling to the place
he fixed upon but also with respect to the place itself. He has
not told us that the climate of the Wabash country is such as
to prevent the most laborious parts of agricultural employments from being performed by Europeans on account of its
heat. He has not told us that the system of slavery must be
adopted there if cultivation be carried on to any great extent.
There is something very disingenuous in all this. Mr. Birkbeck must have known very well that the labour of plough-

ing, harrowing, hoeing, sowing, reaping, housing, &c.,
could not be well performed by those who have been accustomed to the air and climate of Great Britain. How great
has been the astonishment of many to find that this same
English Prairie is indebted to the sweat, the toil, the groans,
the heartbreaking pangs of slavery! Indeed, there is good
reason to believe that the Western territory will forever be
subject to that species of labour, the heat of the climate
being too great for white men's constitutions. In the months
of July and August the heat is absolutely intolerable.

John Lorain, writing the same year as Grece, but in defense of
Pennsylvania over Illinois, also thought it improbable that a white
man could live in the English Settlement. He, however, had a
"scientific" explanation for the debilitating climate.

It so happens in unhealthy countries such as the Illinois that
the gaseous effluvia arising from the fermentation and de-
composition of the remains of dead animals and vegetables
predominate so exceedingly over the oxygen and other constituents which form a healthy atmosphere that bilious complaints very generally prevail. Whole families are frequently
severely afflicted by them at one or nearly one and the same
time; and the bile is so often copiously distributed through the
system that the skin is tanned a sickly looking yellow by it;
and so effectually by frequent repetition of the fall complaints
that notwithstanding the persons thus affected may remove
early in life to a healthy situation, their skin has been so
thoroughly and permanently stained that it commonly continues yellow, and an attentive observer may generally determine that they emigrated from an unhealthy country or
neighbourhood.

Petulant over what he fancies are Birkbeck's sneers at American
culture, Lorain slashes out that

It is a fact too notorious to be controverted that too many
even of those Englishmen who remove to this country with
apparent hostility to the political situation of their own, as

did Mr. Birkbeck, seem to think they derive so much information, merely from being born and brought up in it, that they are not only capable of teaching us everything necessary for us to know but also licensed to calumniate, and very unjustly abuse us, whenever they consider doing this will increase their own consequence.

But what bothers him most, and the nub of his explanation for why immigrants pass over Pennsylvania without stopping, is the original argument that they are too lazy to spread manure. If there is one subject that encourages Lorain's muse to soar, it is dung. And, giving the devil his due, he has to admit that Birkbeck himself had some sensitivity to the marvels of manure; he only lacked complete dedication.

The frontier farmer may consider the hauling and spreading of dung a very laborious business, and ought to be avoided; especially, as it but too commonly happens, that his father and very likely his grandfather too have taught him by precept and example to build a cabin, clear land, plough and crop perpetually until the grounds are so much exhausted as no longer to produce crops worth half the value of the labour bestowed upon them. After this very extensive and inconsiderate injury has been done to the soil, these cultivators remove further back in the fruitless search of a soil that will never wear out. As they find, however, that the very deep and rich bottom lands in the Atlantic states have been in general already settled, and a very great many of them long since worn out, they bend their course to the Western country, determined to risk the effects of agues, fevers, cholera morbus, and the whole train of fall complaints to which such level, flat countries are subject, as well as to withstand the tormenting annoyance from swarms of mosquitoes, prodigiously increased in size and vigour by the very great excess of the same evils which produce the diseases so destructive to man.

Now it is evident that the frontier farmer encounters all those evils and more rather than employ a reasonable proportion of his time in gathering, saving, hauling and spreading manure. It clearly appears, however, that Mr. Birkbeck is better informed than to save the labour of employing manure, for he tells us he means to apply dung for his wheat after the second crop of corn. But as he does not consider it prudent to take more than two crops of corn and one of wheat before recourse is had to manure, what could have induced him to sacrifice his own health and that of his posterity, when if he had settled on any of the hill and dale lands in the interior of the Middle States and given the same attention to manure, he would have gathered more produce from the same breadth of soil?

Another common line of attack was that used by Adlard Welby.

A party proposed to each other coolly to go and shoot neighbour * * * * * who had behaved ill to them at sundry times. It was agreed upon; they went to his field, found the old man at plough and with unerring aim laid him dead! Mr. Flower himself related to me this atrocious affair, and I did not hear that any punishment was ever talked of. Such is the state of things in this Western paradise! A beautiful garden indeed it is from the hands of nature, and with but a little industry a most desirable country to dwell in—with a people who do not shoot each other. But for a man of orderly habits and civilized manners to leave his every comfort, plunge into this wilderness, and sit himself down among a set of half savages far more expert than he can be in everything essential to such a life!—'tis a strange anomaly, and I think "cannot come to good."

This was the kind of story that had been circulating since the earliest days of settlement, when Henry B. Fearon wrote:

Small provocations insure the most relentless and violent resentments. Duels are frequent. The dirk is an inseparable companion of all classes; and the laws are robbed of their terror by not being firmly and equally administered. A general character of independence, both as to the means of living and habits of society, appears universal. Here, no man is either thought or called "master"; neither, on the other hand, is there found any coarse vulgarity. A cold, selfish indifference is the common characteristic of the labourer and the judge.

To which James Hall made the apt reply:

I presume that the reviewer who asserts that "a dirk *is* the constant companion of every gentleman in Illinois," could justify himself under the authority of some traveller into Nova Scotia or Brazil, and by a reference to the times when gentlemen were scarce in those regions and Indians and wild animals abundant. But let that pass—we are a quarrelsome people in Illinois because the people at the lead mines in Missouri were so ten years ago, and because a pugnacious Methodist knocked down an unpolite fellow who told him he lied!

Birkbeck, too, taking a somewhat larger and more abstract view, argued that neither England nor the East could understand conditions in the West.

We are on the eastern limits of a country differing essentially from all that has hitherto been cultivated in the United States. The people to the east of us are incapable of imagining a dry and rich wholesome country, where they may enter at once on fine lands prepared for cultivation without the enormous expense of time and labour in clearing which has been bestowed on every acre between this and the Atlantic. The inhabitants of the old states are profoundly and resolutely ignorant of the advantages of our prairie country. Books are written in the East to prove the wretchedness of the prairies, by persons who have never approached them within five hundred miles; and English writers of the same description, some with names and some without, can obtain more credence than is granted to me, from that description of readers. On the whole, I do not think it worthwhile to undertake the conviction of these people. The settlers here who prosper—that is to say, those who possess good morals and common discretion—will, in course, tell their experience to their friends and connections in England and invite them to follow their example; these again will invite others. This is now going on in all directions. Some write for their former neighbours or the residue of their families; others push back to the old country to conduct them out. Numbers who come to try their hands at a new settlement are wholly unfit for any place in this world, new or old, unless it be to supply the requisite quota of evil which in this imperfect state adheres to all places. These are the people sometimes most likely to be heard, whilst those who go on well and wisely are little noticed. Their adventures are at an end; they "keep a pig" and live happily. A volcano is a fine subject when in action, but the interest ceases with the eruption.

Most of the critics, however, cared little about real understanding. Very few came to see for themselves; the title-page maxims of Welby, "Nothing extenuate—nor aught set down in malice," and of Faux, "intended to shew men and things as they are," were as rare as they were inaccurate. The critics cared less to understand than to persuade—persuade those interested in Illinois that they should settle elsewhere.

The most pugnacious of the lot was William Cobbett. It is true that Cobbett had dispatched Thomas Hulme to the settlement as his personal emissary, and included Hulme's journal in his book. When Hulme failed to damn the settlement as roundly as his employer wished, however, Cobbett was not above "editing" his journal into the direction it should have taken. Hulme promptly pointed out the changes—trifling though they were—and a friend of the settlement, John Melish, put his denial into print in a pamphlet called *Information and Advice to Emigrants*. So the battle raged, back and forth.

Richard Flower writes, "When I passed New York, I heard a popular writer say, 'I'll be damned if I don't write down Birkbeck and the settlement.'" The writer was, of course, Cobbett. His malignity seemingly motiveless, he was said to be in the payment of New York land speculators. Perhaps he was. Cobbett himself always maintained that he owned not an acre of American land, never intended to own any, and had only the interest of his English countrymen at heart. Perhaps this was true also. His changeable political sympathies, as everyone recognized at the time, made all things possible for him, and his quixotic projects were legion. In the book intended to undercut Birkbeck, he devotes as much space to a panegyric on the rutabaga, or Swedish turnip, whose cultivation happened to be an enthusiasm of his at the moment.

Faux reports this exchange with Birkbeck:

Cobbett now became the theme. I said he had sent the bones of Tom Paine to be enshrined at Botley. "He cannot be such a fool?" "His writings have been useful, and extensively read," said I. "Yes, that is true, but he sticks not to truth; he is a caricaturist, and a dishonest man." He then showed me his manuscript reply to Mr. Cobbett's attack. In giving my opinion of it, I pointed out what I conceived to be a grand omission, that of not noticing "no market for a surplus produce," and said, "he will fasten upon that." "Yes, he probably will, but that is a general question applicable to the whole Western country." "He will," said I, "have a rejoinder for you." "Well, I must write again."

Caricaturist he may have been, and possibly dishonest as well, Cobbett nevertheless produced some of the most readable invective to come out of the paper war. Addressing Birkbeck directly, he entered the fray brimful of wrath and turnips.

It is very true that you decline advising anyone to go to the Illinois, and it is also true that your description of the hardships you encountered is very candid; but still, there runs throughout the whole of your *Notes* such an account as to the prospect, that is to say the ultimate effect, that the book is, without your either wishing or perceiving it, calculated to deceive and decoy. You do indeed describe difficulties and hardships. But, then, you overcome them all with so much ease and gaiety that you make them disregarded by your English readers, who, sitting by their firesides and feeling nothing but the gripe of the borough-mongers and the tax gatherer, merely cast a glance at your hardships and fully participate in all your enthusiasm. You do indeed fairly

describe the rugged roads, the dirty hovels, the fire in the
woods to sleep by, the pathless ways through the wilder-
nesses, the dangerous crossings of the rivers; but there are
the beautiful meadows and rich lands at last; there is the fine
freehold domain at the end! There are the giants and the
enchanters to encounter, the slashings and the rib roastings to
undergo; but then there is, at last, the lovely languishing damsel to repay the adventurer.

It is the enchanting damsel that makes the knight encounter the hairbreadth scapes, the sleeping on the ground,
the cooking with cross sticks to hang the pot on. It is the
prairie, that pretty French word which means green grass
bespangled with daisies and cowslips! Oh, God! What delusion! And that a man of sense; a man of superior understanding and talent; a man of honesty, honour, humanity, and
lofty sentiment should be the cause of this delusion!

I, my dear sir, have seen prairies many years ago in America as fine as yours, as fertile as yours, though not so extensive. I saw those prairies settled on by American Loyalists,
who were carried with all their goods and tools to the spot,
and who were furnished with four years' provisions, all at the
expense of England; who had the lands given them; tools
given them; and who were thus seated down on the borders of
creeks, which gave them easy communication with the inhabited plains near the sea. The settlers that I particularly
knew were Connecticut men. Men with families of sons.
Men able to do as much in a day at the works necessary in
their situation as so many Englishmen would be able to do in
a week. They began with a shed; then rose to a log house; and
next to a frame house—all of their own building. I have seen
them manure their land with salmon caught in their creeks
and with pigeons caught on the land itself. It will be a long
while before you will see such beautiful corn fields as I saw
there. Yet nothing but the danger and disgrace which attended their return to Connecticut prevented their returning,
though there they must have begun the world anew. I saw
them in their log huts, and saw them in their frame houses.
They had overcome all their difficulties as settlers; they were

under a government which required neither tax nor service
from them; they were as happy as people could be as to ease
and plenty; but still they sighed for Connecticut; and especially the women, young as well as old—though we, gay
fellows with worsted or silver lace upon our bright red coats,
did our best to make them happy by telling them entertaining
stories about old England while we drank their coffee and
grog by gallons, and ate their fowls, pigs, and sausages and
sweetmeats by wheelbarrow loads; for, though we were by
no means shy, their hospitality far exceeded our appetites. I
am an old hand at the work of settling in wilds. I have, more
than once or twice, had to begin my nest and go in, like a bird,
making it habitable by degrees; and, if I, or if such people as
my old friends above mentioned, with everything found for
them and brought to the spot, had difficulties to undergo, and
sighed for home even after all the difficulties were over, what
must be the lot of an English farmer's family in the Illinois?

Can our people live without bread for months? Can they
live without beer? Can they be otherwise than miserable, cut
off as they must be from all intercourse with, and hope of
hearing of, their relations and friends? The truth is that this
is not transplanting, it is tearing up and flinging away.

What society can these people have? 'Tis true they have nobody to envy, for nobody can have anything to enjoy. But
there may be, and there must be, mutual complainings and
upbraidings; and every unhappiness will be traced directly to
him who has been, however unintentionally, the cause of the
unhappy person's removal. The very foundation of your plan
necessarily contained the seeds of discontent and ill will. A
colony all from the same country was the very worst project
that could have been fallen upon. You took upon yourself the
charge of Moses without being invested with any part of his
authority; and absolute as this was, he found the charge so
heavy that he called upon the Lord to share it with him, or to
relieve him from it altogether.

Even harder to take were Birkbeck's own statistics flung back in
his teeth.

A house, you say, "exceedingly convenient and comfortable, together with farm buildings, may be built for 1,500 dollars." Your own intended house you estimate at 4,500, and your outbuildings at 1,500. So that if this house of the farmer (an English farmer, mind) and his buildings are to be "exceedingly convenient and comfortable" for 1,500 dollars, your house and buildings must be on a scale which, if not perfectly princely, must savour a good deal of aristocratical distinction. But this *if* relieves us; for even your house, built of pine timber and boards, and covered with cedar shingles, and finished only as a good plain farmhouse ought to be, will, if it be thirty-six feet front, thirty-four feet deep, two rooms in front, kitchen, and washhouse behind, four rooms above, and a cellar beneath; yes, this house alone, the bare empty house, with doors and windows suitable, will cost you more than six thousand dollars. I state this upon good authority. I have taken the estimate of a building carpenter. "What carpenter?" you will say. Why, a Long Island carpenter; and the house to be built within a mile of Brooklyn, or two miles of New York. And this is giving you all the advantage, for here the pine is cheaper than with you; the shingles cheaper; the lime and stone and brick as cheap or cheaper; the glass, iron, lead, brass and tin, all at half or a quarter of the prairie price. And, as to labour, if it be not cheaper here than with you, men would do well not to go so far in search of high wages!

Let no simple Englishman imagine that here, at and near New York, in this dear place, we have to pay for the boards and timber brought from a distance; and that you, the happy people of the land of daisies and cowslips, can cut down your own good and noble oak trees upon the spot, on your own estates, and turn them into houses without any carting. Let no simple Englishman believe such idle stories as this. To dissipate all such notions, I have only to tell him that the American farmers on this island, when they have buildings to make or repair, go and purchase the pine timber and boards at the very same time that they cut down their own oak trees and cleave up and burn them as firewood! This is the univer-

sal practice in all the parts of America that I have ever seen.
What is the cause? Pine wood is cheaper, though bought,
than the oak is without buying. This fact, which nobody can
deny, is a complete proof that you gain no advantage from
being in woods as far as building is concerned. And the
truth is that the boards and plank which have been used in
the prairie have actually been brought from the Wabash,
charged with ten miles rough land carriage. How far they
may have come down the Wabash I cannot tell.

Thus, then, the question is settled that building must be
cheaper here than in the Illinois. If, therefore, a house 36 by
34 feet cost here 6,000 dollars, what can a man get there for
1,500 dollars? A miserable hole, and no more. But here are
to be farm buildings and all, in the 1,500 dollars' worth! A
barn 40 feet by 30 with floor and with stables in the sides cannot be built for 1,500 dollars, leaving out wagon house, corn
crib, cattle hovels, yard fences, pig sties, smokehouse, and a
great deal more! And yet you say that all these and a farmhouse into the bargain, all "exceedingly comfortable and convenient," may be had for 1,500 dollars!

Now you know, my dear sir, that this is said in the face of
all America. Farmers are my readers. They all understand
these matters. They are not only good but impartial judges;
and I call upon you to contradict, or even question, my statements if you can.

However, here they are in this miserable place, with the
ship bedding, and without even a bedstead, and with 130
dollars gone in land and house. Two horses and harness and
plough are to cost 100 dollars! These, like the hinges of the
door, are all to be of wood I suppose; for flesh and blood and
bones in the form of two horses for 100 dollars is impossible,
to say nothing about the plough and harness, which would
cost 20 dollars of the money. Perhaps, however, you may
mean some of those horses, ploughs, and sets of harness
which, at the time when you wrote this letter, you had all
ready waiting for the spring to put in your hundred acres of
corn that was never put in at all! However, let this pass too.
Then there are 220 dollars left, and these are to provide

cows, hogs, seed corn, fencing, and other expenses. Next come two cows (poor ones), 24 dollars; hogs, 15 dollars; seed corn, 5 dollars; fencing, suppose 20 acres only, in four plots, the stuff brought from the woods nearest adjoining. Here are 360 rods of fencing, and if it be done so as to keep out a pig and to keep in a pig or a horse or cow for less than half a dollar a rod, I will suffer myself to be made into smoked meat in the extremely comfortable house. Thus, then, here are 213 out of the 220 dollars; and this happy settler has seven whole dollars left for all "other expenses," amongst which are the cost of cooking utensils, plates, knives and forks, tables, and stools; for, as to tablecloths and chairs, those are luxuries unbecoming "simple republicans." But, there must be a pot to boil in. Or is that too much? May these republicans have a washing tub? Perhaps, indeed, it will become unnecessary in a short time, for the lice will have eaten up the linen and, besides, perhaps real independence means stark nakedness. But, at any rate, the hogs must have a trough, or are they to eat at the same board with the family? Talking of eating puts me in mind of a great article, for what are the family to eat during the year and more before their land can produce? For even if they arrive in May, they can have no crop that year. Why, they must graze with the cows in the prairies or snuggle with the hogs in the woods. An oven? Childish effeminacy! Oh! unleavened bread for your life. Bread, did I say? Where is the "independent family" to get bread? Oh! no! Grass and acorns and roots; and, God be praised, you have plenty of water in your wells, though perhaps the family, with all their "independence," must be compelled to depend on your leave to get it, and fetch it half a mile into the bargain.

To talk seriously upon such a subject is impossible without dealing in terms of reprobation, which it would give me great pain to employ when speaking of any act of yours. Indeed such a family will be free; but the Indians are free, and so are the gypsies in England. And I most solemnly declare that I would sooner live the life of a gypsy in England than be a settler with less than five thousand pounds in the Illinois.

And if I had the five thousand pounds and was resolved to exchange England for America, what in the name of common sense should induce me to go into a wild country when I could buy a good farm of 200 acres, with fine orchard and good house and outbuildings, and stock it completely, and make it rich as a garden, within twenty miles of a great seaport affording me a ready market and a high price for every article of my produce?

Thus it is to reckon one's chickens before they are hatched; and thus the Transalleghenian dream vanishes. You have been deceived. A warm heart, a lively imagination, and I know not what caprice about republicanism have led you into sanguine expectations and wrong conclusions. Come, now! Confess it like yourself; that is, like a man of sense and spirit, like an honest and fair-dealing John Bull. To err belongs to all men, great as well as little; but to be ashamed to confess error belongs only to the latter.

Great as is my confidence in your candour, I can, however, hardly hope wholly to escape your anger for having so decidedly condemned your publications; but I do hope that you will not be so unjust as to impute my conduct to any base self-interested motive. I have no private interest; I can have no such interest in endeavouring to check the mad torrent towards the West. I *own* nothing in these States, and never shall.

ii

BIRKBECK, OF COURSE, had been striking back all the while. Yet, exaggerated as the claims of his critics often were, he had to some extent to back down from his former grandiose assertions. A significant letter of his to John Melish, a Philadelphia bookseller, written December 12, 1818, answers the major charges brought against the settlement, and even admits one previous error—not by any means, though, the kind of retraction Cobbett demanded.

Dear Sir:

The interest for this colony expressed by yourself and many other respectable individuals personally unknown to me makes ample amends to my own feelings for the petty hostilities practised against us; but on public grounds I gladly avail myself of the opportunity your letter affords me of contradicting a few of the false reports which have been circulated to our disadvantage. Yours is not the first intimation we have received of a design as wicked as it is foolish to slander us down. At Evansville, on the Ohio, a point of the river nearest to us, two worthy delegates on this extraordinary mission are said to have commenced their operations about the beginning of August. They betrayed themselves by overacting, like the "three men in plain garb" with Major B. You will do me a favour by informing that gentleman that our settlement is not "blown up," but on the contrary is very prosperous. We now number about three hundred where, eighteen months ago, there were two families. We have good health and good spirits; good water, good land, and good provisions. We have probably suffered less by sickness than any settlement under similar circumstances, certainly less than any settlement under my observation, and this we may fairly attribute to the superior salubrity of the situation. My own family has enjoyed extraordinary health, and I have not been confined an hour by sickness of any kind since I entered the country.

The copy of my letters you were so good as to transmit has arrived. I had learnt from Mr. Carey some particulars of the delays and difficulties attending their publication in this country. Receiving the approbation of liberal men, I pay little regard to the censure of others. In fact, their sinister proceedings give currency to truth, which is "mighty, and will" eventually "prevail."

Sentiments have been imputed to me of hostility to my native country. How unjustly every faculty of my soul bears witness! I hate her enemies, it is true, as I hate the enemies of mankind, the enemies of every country; and those are the persons who are aggrieved by our simple and successful effort to emancipate ourselves, perceiving that the evil they foster is beginning to work its own remedy.

And because I deprecate the formalities practised among mankind in lieu of religion I am charged with being a foe to

religion. It is the bond which connects the soul of man with
the Supreme Intelligence "in whom we live and move and
have our being." It is the love of God, increasing our good will
to each other. It is a principle of action aiding the moral sense;
a divine sentiment impelling us to those pursuits which reason
approves, and restraining us from evil. If I have written in
disparagement of this principle, I plead guilty.

There is an error of some importance in my *Letters*, and I
wish that a correction of it could accompany the publication.
In my estimate of the expenses of cultivating these prairies I
have not made sufficient allowance of time, for the innumerable delays which attend a new establishment in a new country. I would now add a year of preparation, which will of
course make a material deduction from the profits at the commencement of the undertaking.

Your giving publicity to the above in the way you find
most expedient will oblige,

Dear sir, your obedient servant,

M. Birkbeck

Melish himself writes:

"Who shall agree when doctors differ?" When two such
men as Mr. Cobbett and Mr. Birkbeck differ so completely
in opinion as to facts and arguments regarding a business in
which both profess to be adepts, what are their countrymen
at a distance, or even those newly arrived in the country, to
think of it?

Now upon the merits of the case, the first view that presents
itself is that Mr. Birkbeck has greatly the advantage of Mr.
Cobbett, in having seen and examined both sides of the
question. Mr. Birkbeck came first under my notice in consequence of the publication of his tour in France. I was much
gratified by the liberality of his sentiments and the correctness of his views; and I was no less gratified by the correctness of his remarks in his *Notes on a Journey to Illinois*. His
Letters came under my observation in manuscript long before
they were published. I was of opinion that they were written
in a masterly style and contained valuable information. I was

glad to see the calculations of a practical farmer as to what could be done with capital in a country of which I thought very highly; and was of opinion that the publication of them would afford important information to emigrants, particularly from Britain. My reason for this opinion was that these sentiments accorded, generally speaking, with the views which had occurred to me in consequence of a personal examination of the Western country. The letters lay over unpublished at the time that Mr. Hulme returned from his visit to Mr. Birkbeck's settlement. He was of opinion that it was important to publish the letters. The general facts accorded with his personal observations. The letters were shortly after published, and had a rapid sale, both here and in Britain; and they are certainly an important addition to our stock of knowledge regarding the Western country.

That they are entirely correct I will not assert. But that the general facts are true I can have no more doubt than I have of the Western country being an exceedingly fine field for emigrant farmers, whether from England or any other country.

The late Dr. Paley has a most ingenious remark concerning the utter impossibility of an animal with four senses judging of a fifth which it has not. It can form no conception of it, and no reasoning can make it clear to its imagination. It would therefore be arrogance in the extreme for such an animal to reason on a sense that it did not possess itself. But it is almost equally arrogant for a writer, no matter what his abilities are, to reason as to a country he has never seen. Mr. Birkbeck remarks correctly that the people of Philadelphia have no conception of the Western country. I have fifty times made the same remark, and I aver that no person can form an adequate conception of the Western country unless he view it personally. Mr. Cobbett, with all his great powers of mind, can no more judge of the subject than a blind man can judge of colours; and his attempt to give a view to others of what he has no correct view himself leads him into more errors in this little volume than I have ever seen in any equal number of pages.

The truth is, Mr. Cobbett is erroneous in his conclusions
regarding the Western country altogether. There is no such
country for emigrants in the world. In point of soil, and
climate, and natural advantages it stands almost unrivalled.
It is very true that there are fine situations in the Atlantic
states also; and it no doubt suits Mr. Cobbett's views better
to be near a city than farther back in the country; but he has
no right to find fault with others who prefer a settlement
back in the country, even if it should be in Illinois.

By 1822, Birkbeck had prepared a formal defense of his views,
which he dispatched as a pamphlet aimed at the ultimate jury in
the debate, a pamphlet titled *An Address to the Farmers of Great
Britain,* some portions of which follow.

My old countrymen!

The accounts I receive from various parts of Great Britain
of your distressed condition are too consistent with each
other and with my own painful anticipations to admit in my
mind a doubt of their authenticity. Wretched pauperism,
which before my departure had possession of the cottage, has
entered the farmhouse and is prowling round the mansion
of the landlord! Such is the sad report which reaches me in
my retreat.

Five years ago I quitted our common country, believing
that the sufferings which are now so general were impending
and that they were only to be avoided by flight. It then lay
upon me as a duty to communicate, as an example for others
if successful, if not as a warning, the motives, the progress,
and the result, whatever it might be, of my enterprise. This
duty I have performed faithfully. Nothing less should have
induced me again to come forward in defense of my own
veracity than a recurrence of the same duty which prompted
me at first to lay my proceedings before the public.

Happily for myself and my family, we have escaped in
time. We have made good our landing. And shall I not,
when I can render no further help, lift up my voice and
cheer my old messmates with words of encouragement?

Peace and independence in the evening of a laborious life

—these I have obtained. My children are settled around me, with the like prospects as the reward of their industry. I may add with perfect confidence that these blessings await as many of you as choose to embrace them, subject of course to the contingencies to which all human affairs are liable. They are to be attained now at a cheaper rate, inasmuch as you would have to encounter fewer difficulties than we had.

Here are, now, mechanics willing to be employed, stores prepared to furnish all you require, mills to grind your corn and saw your planks, houses and allotments ready for your labourers until you can provide for them. Here are men also of like feelings and habits with yourselves. This is no longer a trackless wilderness, but a settled country abounding in the necessaries and even comforts of life.

Much pain has been taken to impress on the public mind, from motives sufficiently obvious, that my undertaking has failed and that I am a disappointed and ruined man. To me this is of little importance; but it is of much to you. It is astonishing that people endowed with common sense should allow themselves to be biased by vague report, and rely upon evidence of the most trivial nature in an affair of so great moment as their establishment for life. There are persons who have, in their own country, betrayed no deficiency in the management of their affairs; but on their arrival in this they seem to lose their discretion. They will give entire credence to the statements of strangers who are interested in misleading them, and turn their backs on the testimony of friends of approved fidelity.

From the shores of Virginia to this place, I had to explore a vast country, always looking out for an opportunity of settling. I have also traversed this state in various directions; and it is with a feeling of self-gratulation which your candour will rather sympathise with than condemn that I can now assure you that, had I again to choose, this would be my residence in preference to any other situation that I have seen or heard of.

Thus, my old friends and fellow labourers, I have once more thrown myself before you, and probably for the last

time. Such of you that know my character in England, in
your estimate of my first impressions might very fairly allow
something for political bias and a good deal to errors of judgment. You might suppose me mistaken, but you would not
doubt my sincerity. Five years of probation have now matured those first impressions into matter of fact and experience in which I cannot be deceived. As such I present it to you
coupled with my best wishes.

Birkbeck's sincerity was beyond doubt. But—as his critics
charged—he had a marvelous knack for slipping around the painful edges of hard truths. Coming along in the same year that
Birkbeck published his *Address,* W. N. Blane gave a judicious
summary of the change in circumstances that Birkbeck preferred
to ignore.

With regard to Mr. Birkbeck's *Letters,* everyone who
has lately been at the settlement must allow that the description he has given of the advantages of the situation is somewhat exaggerated. But I also believe that everyone who
knows Mr. Birkbeck must be perfectly convinced that his
exaggerations were unintentional; and this I am sure would
be granted even by those who have found to their cost that it
is much more difficult to increase one's capital in Illinois than
in England.

When Mr. Birkbeck first arrived in this state, land, and
particularly produce, bore a much higher price than at present. Hence this gentleman, being rather an enthusiast and
viewing only the bright side of things, described the country
in a manner which, even at the time, was not literally correct.
But the transition from war to peace, from an annual expendi-
ture of 33,000,000 dollars to 13,000,000, combined with the
opening of so much new territory, and with other fortuitous
circumstances, has now reduced the Western farmers to great
distress. Indeed the agriculturists of all the Western states
have suffered nearly as much as the same class of people in
Great Britain. Mr. Birkbeck has participated in the general
calamity, as it is well known that he does not possess as many
dollars at this moment as he did pounds sterling when he left

England. But for this, which was his misfortune and not his fault, he has been greatly and unjustly calumniated in several publications.

iii

HERE THE PAPER WAR may be said to end. Judge James Hall pronounced the funeral obsequies over the fallen heroes of both sides in a typical Western tall tale.

A weary wayfarer illustrated his remarks upon the badness of the roads by relating the following curious fact. He was floundering through the mire, as many an honest gentleman flounders through life, getting along with difficulty but still getting along; sometimes wading to the saddle girth in water, sometimes clambering over logs; and occasionally plunged in a quagmire. While carefully picking his way by a spot more miry than the rest he espied a man's hat, a very creditable beaver, lying with the crown upwards in the mud, and as he approached was not a little startled to see it move. This happened in a dismal swamp where the cypress waved its melancholy branches over the dark soil, and our traveller's flesh began to creep at beholding a hat move without the agency of a head. "When the brains are out the head will die," thought he. "And when the head is out, the hat, by the same rule, should receive its quietus." Not being very superstitious, and determined to penetrate the mystery, the solitary rider checked his nag and, extending his long whip, fairly upset the hat—when, lo! beneath it appeared a man's head, a living, laughing head, by which our inquisitive traveller heard himself saluted with "Hullo, stranger! who told you to knock my hat off?" The person thus addressed was so utterly astonished as not to be able for a moment to understand that the apparition was no other than a fellow creature up to the neck in the mire; but he no sooner came to this conclusion than he promptly apologized for the indecorum of which he had been guilty, and tendered his services to the gentleman in the mud puddle. "I will alight," said he, "and endeavour to draw you forth." "Oh, never mind," said the other, "I'm in rather a bad fix it is true, but I have an excellent horse under me who has carried me through many a worse place than this—we shall get along."

If this story proves the badness of the roads, I think it also demonstrates the goodness of the horses and the perseverance of their riders. That it is true is not for me to assert, as I get it at secondhand—but I will venture to asseverate that it is as true as one half of all that has been written in relation to this country; and if it be in itself but half true I am privileged as a traveller to relate it.

Between Princeton and Mr. Birkbeck's in Illinois, Mr. Hulme says, "we had to cross a swamp of half a mile wide. We were obliged to lead our horses, and walk up to our knees in mud and water." If this be true, I suspect that Mr. Hulme is the first sane man who was ever known to be so fond of grovelling in the mire as to dismount from his horse at a time when the services of that animal were most requisite. If he had walked upon the hard ground and kept his feet dry by riding through the swamp, his sanity would be less questionable; but his conduct, as he exhibits it, smacks too much of the character of that of the man in the fable who carried his ass because people censured him for making the poor ass carry him. "Before we got half way across," he continues, "we began to think of going back; but there is a sound bottom under it all, and we waded through as well as we could."

The gentleman under the hat found a sound bottom too, but had to go much deeper for it than Mr. Hulme; and if the latter had heard this story previous to his adventuring into Illinois he would have known the advantage of having a good horse under him, and could never have been induced to quit his saddle under such circumstances.

As a companion to this anecdote, I might relate that of Captain R., who is said to have emerged from a prairie through whose high grass he had been wading with five hundred rattlesnakes hanging by their teeth to each leg! These things may be so—I have been in the Western country six years, and have not seen six rattlesnakes; and I have travelled thousands of miles on horseback without ever finding the mire so deep that my horse could not keep his head above the surface; but other gentlemen may have met with more adventures.

There is another snake story, the relater of which was almost as valiant among these reptiles as Samson among the Philistines. "I killed a hundred of them," said he, "in a few minutes, each as large as my leg." "I do not dispute it," replied his friend, "but would be better satisfied if you would fall a snake or two." "There were *ninety*, I am sure." "Say fifty." "No, I can't; I am convinced there were *seventy-five*, and I'll not bate another snake to please any man!"

We might perhaps say these are petty lies, not greater than are told by all travellers; but if such be the case, I cannot but think that all travellers might fall a snake or two with advantage.

6

―――――――

"I had a most curious adventure."

EARLY IN 1819, Elizabeth Birkbeck wrote to her uncle back in England:

When we left England we expected to lead a very retired life in the backwoods of America, but this on the contrary proves to be a very busy retreat—scarcely a day passes without some amusing event taking place; some arrival or some departure in which we are all interested. We never entertained half so much company at old Wanborough as we have received in these humble little cabins.

Besides the British visitors who came to inspect the settlement and to decide whether it was a fit place for an Englishman to live, other travelers who passed through the area on whatever mission felt the need to make some comment about a place so notorious. The Germans Ferdinand Ernst and Karl Postl passed this way, in 1819 and 1826 respectively, but had little to say that had not been noted already by the English. Neither thought highly of the fertility of the soil, and Ernst was chagrined to find no crops planted or orchards under cultivation. Ernst had at least read Birkbeck's books, and had decided that *Notes on a Journey* was "in conformity with the truth" but *Letters from Illinois* was "not sufficiently well founded." The American Henry Schoolcraft, hurrying down the Wabash in 1821, never got far enough from the river to see the settlement but agreed nevertheless that it presented "a vivid picture of English industry and English comfort." In 1830 came the Scotsman James Stuart, who "took a more comprehensive view than most travelers," said Flower. Possibly so, but the thing that impressed him most when he visited George Flower was that his was "the only house in America where I saw egg cups."

There were other visitors who left no written record of their visit. Two of them, opposite in station and even in method of travel, are mentioned by Flower.

Among the many tourists that, from time to time, visited our settlement, one of a class common in Europe but rarely if ever seen in America appeared among us in 1824. As a pedestrian tourist, performing all his journeys on foot, he could see more of persons and places than if conveyed by stage or carried on horseback.

On a summer afternoon, a gentleman of middle age and middle stature, with a small knapsack on his back and a light walking stick in hand, came to Park House, and introduced himself as Mr. D. Constable from England. I had a slight knowledge of the name, and gained a complete knowledge of the family from his brother, who visited me some years afterward. We all spent a pleasant evening together. The next day he passed on, as unostentatiously as he came, to see other people and other places. He spent several days in the settlement, staying a little time with those of congenial minds and similar tastes; and, no doubt, during those few days he obtained more information and correct impressions than more pretentious and less observant travelers. The most remarkable thing about Mr. Constable was his unremarkableness. His dress and address were as plain and simple as they could be, not to be singular—nothing absolutely wanting; but nothing superfluous could be detected about his dress or personal appointments. A superficial observer would pass Mr. Constable by, as an ordinary man, almost unnoticed. In conversation he did not press inquiry, or argue strongly, and

never followed argument into controversy. He did not much
care for what you thought, but liked to hear what you knew,
and would freely give you any information that he thought
would be of service to you. But with all this simplicity, he
possessed a talent of discovering what his companions knew
and thought.

In his little knapsack, besides his two shirts, one handkerchief, one pair of socks, razor, and soap, he carried a
numerous pack of cards. Each card had on one side a portrait, and on the other a short biography of the person represented. Both men and women, eminent in any way, were here
pictured; and, according to the opinion he wished to elicit,
he made his selection of the cards—say a dozen or more—
and, taking some favorable opportunity of showing, perhaps
to some member of the party, a portrait in which he or she
would feel an interest, it would naturally pass from hand to
hand, and the others would be asked for, and would receive
some comment; some remark in approbation or censure of the
life or opinions of the person represented would escape the
spectators. If he wished more distinctly to learn the religious
or political opinions of any one of the party, he would show
portraits of some eminent divines, and of Voltaire, Rousseau,
Pitt, Fox, Mirabeau, Paine, Jefferson, Adams, Hamilton, and
so on, with others famous in science or notorious for crime.
Thus, in five minutes from some run of argument or casual remark, he would be in possession of the opinions, predilections,
and prejudices of all his associates; and this was no small
acquisition to one who wished to pass on his way smoothly,
without conflict with his fellows. He would enter the humblest
cabin and chat with its inmates. Traveling in this unostentatious way, he saw more of the whole people. It was not his
fault if his entertainers did not gain something, however short
his stay. If he saw a sick child, he would name some remedy
or palliative within its parents' reach. If the woman was
cooking, he was likely to tell her of some simple preparation
for a palatable dish, or point out some plant that she had
never thought of cooking before. For he was a vegetarian, or
ate little or no animal food. If a man was at work with a

clumsy tool, he would show him how it might be improved, and often sit down and whittle it into right shape.

Constable was of the utilitarian school, and thought more of individual than political reform. He thought that extravagance in one part of the community made want in the other; if all the misspent labor in the fooleries of fashion and useless ornamentation was directed to the creation of something useful or necessary, this change would of itself go far to remove the suffering from want. He lived up to his opinions. As a bachelor, he occupied but two rooms, one for a parlor, the other for a bedroom. In England it is not the habit to use by day the same room that you sleep in by night. In his parlor were a few chairs, a table, and a shelf of books. On the sill of the window, near to which he usually sat, was a small pulley, over which ran a cord with a hook at one end. About noon, at the sound of a well-known voice of a boy from a neighboring tavern, he lowered his hook into the street, and pulled up a small basket containing a loaf of bread, a pint of beer, a slice of butter or cheese, a lettuce, or some vegetable or fruit in season. His simple repast over, as the boy returned he lowered his basket and empty pewter pot, both to be filled and drawn up for his next day's dinner. His breakfast and evening meal—a cup of tea and piece of dry toast—he prepared himself at his own fire. Whatever was left of his income at the end of the year he gave away, either to relieve individual wants, or to strengthen some benevolent institution. He belonged to no political party, nor to any religious sect; yet was alive to every proposed reform, political or social.

A few years afterward, Sir Thomas Beevoir and Lady Beevoir, of Beevoir Castle, England, made us a visit. Their mode of traveling was by a light phæton drawn by a well-matched pair of black ponies. These Sir Thomas drove from Washington City to Albion, and afterward across the state of Illinois to St. Louis, and from thence descended to New Orleans. He was unattended by any servant. He walked to Park House immediately after his arrival at Albion and introduced himself. At his departure, on his arriving at a

very tall white gate that stood between the lawn and the park,
to the surprise of everybody he lightly laid his hands on the
top bar, and with the greatest ease sprang over the gate without opening it. On relating the circumstance to a neighbor, a
Norfolk man who formerly lived in the vicinage of the Beevoir
family—"Ah!" said he, "it is just like them. The Beevoir family are all muscular and long limbed." He then related that at
the parish church he attended, the living had been given to
one of the Beevoir family, who officiated every Sunday. "He
was a remarkable man," said he; "his arms were so long that
when he stood upright he could with ease button up his own
knee breeches, which are just at the join of the knee and a little
below. He delighted in all country sports, but his particular
fancy was the ring. A strong man himself, a well-trained
pugilist, his great length of arm gave him such an advantage
that but few adversaries dare encounter him; but withal, a
well-educated man and a good preacher."

English milords, English eccentrics—anybody might show up at
the settlement during the days when it was a tourist attraction
second only to Niagara Falls. Getting there was often an adventure in itself. W. N. Blane, arriving in the winter of 1822 from
Vincennes, the jumping-off place for most visitors, wrote of typical
difficulties.

From Vincennes, I turned to the left in order to cross White
River below the junction of its two forks and proceed through
Princeton and Harmonie to Birkbeck's English Settlement
at Albion. The road, or rather path, to the ferry on White
River runs chiefly through low flat barrens, with here and
there a patch of prairie. Upon arriving at the bank, I found
the ice running so thick and in such very large cakes that the
boat could not cross. Some men with a drove of hogs had
already waited there two days, and the ferryman said that I
had very little chance of being able to cross for a day or two,
and perhaps not for a week. I therefore determined to cross
the country in a westerly direction so as to meet the Wabash
just above its junction with White River.

Upon inquiring of the ferrymen if there were any house in

the neighbourhood at which I could stop, they informed me that there was only one, which belonged to a Scotch gentleman who had lately settled in this part of the country. "But although," said one of them, "I am certain he does not keep open house, yet perhaps as you are a stranger he will allow you to stay there tonight." As it was getting late I determined to lose no time, and accordingly, after a ride through the woods of about two miles, I found myself at the settlement.

The house, which was of a much better description than any I had lately seen, was situated on a gentle rise, overlooking the river and surrounded with a large space of cleared land. I dismounted, and upon opening the door was delighted to see six or seven men in Highland bonnets sitting round a blazing fire. I mentioned to the gentleman that I was a stranger and should feel much obliged to him for a night's lodging for myself and my horse; upon which he immediately, with the genuine hospitality I have so often experienced in his native land, said that I was welcome to stay there and to partake of whatever his house afforded.

He had left Perthshire at the head of twenty of his countrymen, and had fixed himself on this spot; and although he had only been here eight months had already put everything into very good order.

My fare was sumptuous, compared to what it had been for some time past; and moreover I had a good bed to sleep in, with a pair of fine clean sheets. I went away in the morning after receiving an invitation from my worthy host to repeat my visit if I should ever pass again in that direction.

The path from hence to the Wabash lies through a thickly wooded country abounding in game. I expected to have had much difficulty in crossing the river; for though there was a ferryboat, it had been drawn ashore and was frozen to the ground. Fortunately, however, I found a man going over in a flatboat with some cattle. The Wabash just above had closed up and frozen over, so that here, where the stream was very rapid, there was little or no floating ice. After crossing, I rode along the right bank to Palmyra. This most dirty, miserable little village was once the county town of Edwards County,

Illinois, an honour which it lost in consequence of the superior healthiness of Albion.

After stopping a night at Palmyra, I proceeded along a road which was in a very bad state, and which was very difficult to find. About two miles before arriving at the Bonpas River is one of the largest and worst swamps I ever passed through. I can form no idea of its length; but it is full two miles broad where the road crosses it. At the Bonpas, five miles from Albion, I found a wooden bridge, which is a great convenience to travellers, as they would otherwise often have to swim the stream, both the banks of which are steep and slippery.

On arriving at the far-famed settlement of Albion, I found that it by no means merited all the abuse I had heard of it in England. The town is indeed small, but has at any rate a very pleasing appearance as contrasted with most of those in the backwoods.

I was hospitably received by Mr. Birkbeck and Mr. Flower. They both have large houses. That belonging to Mr. Flower is a peculiarly good one, and is very well furnished. One room in particular was carpeted, and contained a nice assortment of books and a pianoforte—all luxuries of great rarity in these remote districts. The inn is a well-built brick house, and might have been made very comfortable; yet, although kept by an Englishman, it has none of the characteristics of an English inn but, on the contrary, partakes largely of those of the backwoods, so much so indeed, as to be a subject of remark even to the Americans. I staid here several days without having clean sheets.

While at Albion I read all the books and reviews that had been written both for and against this settlement. One traveller describes it as an earthly paradise, another as a miserable unhealthy swamp. The truth is about midway between these extremes.

James Hoby, traveling in the other direction some years later, nearly came to grief, probably in the same swamp in Bonpas bottoms.

In leaving Illinois I met with an adventure, the consequences of which were providentially unimportant. I had been expressly cautioned against driving over a long corduroy or gridiron sort of bridge, in crossing a vast mud hole where the water was now deep, and the logs and trunks of trees were rotten. My directions were to keep in the water to the left. We naturally supposed we were to proceed by the side of the bridge, whereas it was meant that we should diverge far into the forest, keeping the track of other wheels, which we did not observe. When we reached the deepest part of the mud, the poor exhausted horse stuck fast, and every effort only rendered the case more hopeless and desperate. He began to plunge, and threatened to lie down. It happened that a horseman with a flock of sheep was in the road; I implored his assistance still further to dilapidate the bridge by rolling toward us two or three logs. By these I contrived to leave the wagon, and being left by the friendly traveller to my own resources, I completed my raft by using more timber, so as to venture on lightening the Dearborn of my luggage. This was no sooner effected than my young driver, screaming at the top of his voice, "Ah! Joe, Joe (the name of the horse), you rascal you, what are you about, Joe!" vanished out of my sight. They were soon far away in the wood, and in due time made their appearance at the end of the bridge, in a plight as forlorn and ludicrous as can well be imagined. All was speedily adjusted, and we reached the Wabash at La Valette's Ferry.

Though neither Blane nor Hoby found a man in the mud under a floating hat, others did report adventures in the vicinity of Albion that Judge Hall might say should fall a snake or two. Leaving Vincennes, Adlard Welby got sidetracked by a place he calls Marvel Hall, an establishment so mysteriously foreboding yet so splendid that one wonders whether the tale owes more to experience or to gothic romances. He writes that

both ourselves and horses sufficiently rested, we made the necessary inquiries and preparations to proceed to the English Prairie in the Illinois State; from thence intending to visit the German settlement called Harmonie on the Wabash, and returning to winter at Vincennes. Receiving however, meanwhile, a pressing invitation to accompany a gentleman to his country house about twenty miles distant, it being represented as little deviating from our intended route, I accepted of it; the more inclined perhaps because of his pleasing manners and his being a native of the northern part of my own country. Having however a little apprehension as to the fitness of the roads for wheels, I inquired of him whether they would permit a carriage to travel; and all my doubts were removed by his answer that they were as good as the town street where we happened to be standing.

It was a beautiful day in the latter part of September that we started on this expedition in my Dearborn, our friend on horseback leading the way. We drove along a good turf road across the fine plain of Vincennes, fully expecting to get on as smoothly and pleasantly as a gig party on a Sunday excursion. We were not long suffered to enjoy these pleasing anticipations however, for our guide suddenly turned into the wood, and the wheels came bump upon our old acquaintance a stump road.

While we are getting on slowly upon it, I will just give a slight description how such tracts are formed. Imagine a woodland in a state of nature; through this, guiding themselves by compass, people get on as they can, chopping a piece of bark from the trees in the line, which they call "blazing," as a direction to those who follow with tools to cut down the trees between those blazed, which they do at about a foot to a foot and a half from the ground, leaving the stumps and brushwood standing. In a short time this latter gets worn away, but the stumps remain a long while; and between these, horsemen, wagons, and other carriages proceed, steering between, or bumping upon them, which is at times unavoidable, and progressing at most not more than three miles an hour.

But to return to our adventure; for our companion calls, and presses me to urge forward the horses—advice needless to give, for alas! we could not adopt it. The small track became more blind; our guide appeared to be confused. And not a little to my dismay and vexation, instead of a road as good as

a Vincennes town street, we were at length entangled in
woodland, brushing through breaking boughs, going in and
out through bogs, and lifting the wheels over dead fallen
trees as we could. In this situation, as difficult to retreat as
advance, I knew not what to do and began to suspect some
foul play; but recollecting the respectable character our companion bore at Vincennes, I dismissed the thought, and being
both myself and servant armed I resolved to try to proceed.
So calling in a peremptory tone to our friend in advance to
keep in sight, for I fancied he seemed to be uneasy at his
situation, and he at times disappeared, I asked him, not if this
was his excellent road—I was too vexed for that—but how
much farther such difficulties would be found. He answered,
not far, that we were near the river, and that we would cross
it at a nearer ferry than he had at first intended. Adding he
would ride on and get the boat ready, he vanished, after pointing the way we were to follow.

I now thought he was gone and had left us in the lurch;
however we got on by degrees, and at length had the pleasure
to see the riverside and our friend waiting for us with the
crazy ferryboat, into which with some difficulty we got the
carriage. Our difficulties were now to cease, he said, and a
good road the rest of the way was to reward our exertions.
For better assurance of these good tidings I endeavoured to
obtain some information from the boatmen as we crossed the
Wabash; but they proved to be Canadian French, and we did
not sufficiently understand their *patois* to gain any satisfactory
account from them.

We landed safely; and after rising the river bank actually
did find a tolerable good woodland road for some miles, until
it approached without much hinderance a small settlement
dignified with the name of Palmyra, a place which to all appearance need not hope for the prosperity, much as it may
fear the lot, of its prototype. Here we found a log tavern, however; and we halted to consider what to do, for the day was
closing and I remembered there would be no twilight. In this
dilemma I again suffered myself to be guided by our companion, who represented that at this log inn we should not

find any accommodations either for ourselves or horses beyond shelter, that his house was now but three short miles
farther upon a good road, and that he had provided everything for our comfort as well as that of our cattle. Yielding to
these pressing arguments, the rather too as he seemed a little
chagrined at my hesitation, I once more trotted on, which the
horses could well do for about half a mile beyond the settlement. But how shall I describe what followed! Our guide
turned again into the wood, calling out that it was his private
road; and private indeed we found it, for we soon lost all
track and light together.

There was now no retreating, so summoning up more resolution from despair I urged and encouraged my good little
horses, and they dragged the carriage at the constant risk of
our necks through brushwood, over fallen trees, down and up
precipitous banks and deep gullies, which I could scarcely
discern and which if I could have seen should not have attempted; until I became so enraged at the man's deception
that had he given the least provocation I believe I should have
shot him. However he luckily avoided this by keeping a little
in advance and mildly calling out now and then to direct the
way, saying we were very near; and indeed, long after day
had departed, we halted at a gate. Here he advised us to get
out and walk, as the way up to the house for wheels was circui-
tous. Out therefore we got, when I perceived approaching,
carrying a light, a human figure in form, dress, and manner
as wild and complete a ruffian as ever Shakespeare portrayed.

To this being, whose appearance and the friendly shake of
the hand given him by my conductor did not tend to relieve
my mind from suspicions of I knew not what, I was fain to
give up my horses. He returned a surly answer in French to
Mr. ***** who had said something I did not understand,
and receiving the reins from me jumped into the carriage and
drove away; but not alone, for I directed my man to go with
him, a service he probably did not much relish but which in
my then state of mind I thought necessary.

I now explored my way towards a light, and soon came up
to a portico which had the appearance of being built in good

style. Here too I had the satisfaction to meet the carriage, which I had no sooner come up to than a voice which seemed of stentorian power hailed me from the portico with a torrent of words, amongst which what struck me most was, "You have got here but you will never get away again!" My host, who had approached to press me to enter his house, seemed to put this off with a smile not quite easy; and I declined quitting my horses, being determined to see them into the promised stable. But upon expressing this intention the ill-omened voice again thundered, "Oh, there is no place for your horses but this. They will be safe enough; they cannot get out."

"But they are warm," said I; "have had a long pull ever since noon without bait, and will catch cold out of a stable."

"Can't help it" was the answer; but just after he added, "to be sure there is a log place, but it has no roof!"

My host now again returned to invite me in; and under his assurance that the horses should have every care taken of them, and knowing that my own man would do his best for them, I reluctantly gave up the point; mounted a flight of steps, crossed the piazza, and entered a room not calculated to make amazement cease.

It was spacious, lofty, well-proportioned, and finished in every part in the very best style of workmanship. A good wood fire blazed upon a beautiful polished grate, the appurtenances to which were equally handsome. A marble chimney piece, the tables, chairs, the supper table, and lights supported in handsome branches, all which is commonly seen in good houses was here, surrounded by primeval wilderness—an accomplishment so wonderful that it seemed not to be within any powers short of those of necromancy, and when my mind glanced back upon the way we had been led I might fairly suspect the person who had done it to have some credit at the court of his Satanic Majesty. Such thoughts however were well dispelled by a neat supper, served in a manner corresponding with the appearance of the place; and by the aid of some excellent wine our spirits began to flow as the impressions of the day's adventures were, for awhile, lost in social converse. Our host I found to be a man of the world, knowing

perfectly well how, and practising that which he knew, to be
agreeable; full of anecdote, which he gave well. And after
keeping it up to a late hour we retired to rest in a handsome
adjoining chamber.

Rising with the early sun, refreshed from the harass of the
preceding day, I walked out anxious to explore the lodgings
of my four-footed companions, not much expecting to find
that "every care" had been taken of them. Indeed after a considerable search I at length discovered the place of their confinement, in an inclosure of logs without the slightest roof. Of
course they looked piteously, for the nights had become rather
keen and frosty. Perhaps it may be thought by some readers
that too much has been said of the dumb servants; but let those
who think so either take a journey during which their lives
shall constantly depend upon the steadiness of their horses, or
at least let these objectors reflect that during such daily
acquaintance a sort of mute friendly understanding takes
place between the driver and his cattle—they will then no
longer wonder at his anxiety for their welfare.

And here let us bring this strange adventure to a close. We
passed two days very pleasantly, during which we met with
the most attentive hospitality, and I am unwilling to search for
other motive, though perhaps it might principally be to induce
me to engage in aid of a scheme to build mills upon a favourable situation on the Wabash River. This I mention in order to
take the opportunity of cautioning emigrants against engaging in the schemes, generally delusive, of the old settler or
the American.

Sometimes, because of their ignorance of the countryside, British
tourists rushed headlong into perilous encounters. W. N. Blane
tells this pungent anecdote:

I had a most curious adventure, and one that caused me for
some time afterwards a great deal of vexation. While crossing
a small prairie I observed coming towards me in the middle
of the path a beautiful little animal about two feet long, of a
dark colour with longitudinal white stripes down its back, a

bushy tail, and very short legs. Intending to catch it, I immediately galloped forward to prevent its escape. To my astonishment, however, it did not attempt to run away, but stopped in the middle of the road, as if it had been tame. I came close up to it so that my horse's forefeet almost touched it, when it drew up its back and looked up at me but still did not offer to escape. I at first intended to dismount and catch it; but considering that I could do nothing with it and that perhaps it might bite me, I determined to leave it alone and content myself with admiring it.

It would have been well for me if I had done so; but after having finished looking at it, a spirit of mischief (I can attribute it to nothing else) prompted me to lean forward on my horse and strike it over the back with a small whip I had in my hand. Scarcely had the whip touched the animal's back, when, turning its posterior towards me and lifting up its hindleg, it discharged a Stygian liquor the odour of which I shall recollect till my dying day. In an instant the whole prairie seemed to be filled with a stench that is beyond all description. It was so powerful, pungent, and sickening that at first it nearly made me faint, and I galloped away from the brute with all possible expedition.

I had previously supposed that I had, in the course of my life, smelt very bad odours; but they were all perfumes compared to this. No one who has not experienced it can form any idea of such a horrid stench. Most fortunately, from the position in which I was, my horse had received the whole of this infernal water on his breast, and none of it had touched my clothes. If it had, I should have been obliged to destroy them; for I was afterwards informed that no process or length of time will remove the smell from woolen cloth.

This adventure happened early in the morning, and made me so sick that I could not eat any breakfast. Indeed I was ashamed to go into any house, well knowing how offensive both I and my horse must be. I rode my horse into the rivers, had him washed with soap and water, &c., &c.; but nothing would do. For a week afterwards I could never get upon him without perceiving, in a most disagreeable degree, the stench

of my little enemy. The man of the house at which I stopped
in the evening immediately observed the offensive odour with
which I was infected. When I told him my adventure, and
how I intended to have got off my horse to catch the animal,
he laughed most heartily, and informed me that it was called
the skunk or stinkard, and was common in that part of the
country. He had no sooner mentioned the name than I recollected that Dobrizhoffer, who has left so interesting an account of the Abipones, met with even worse treatment from
one of these animals than I did.

It is a most wonderful defense that nature has given to this
little animal by which it is enabled to repel at once the largest
and most formidable enemies! Let all who may chance to
meet one beware of insulting it.

In the autumn, travelers were sometimes privileged to see one
of the grandest spectacles offered by the prairies—a prairie fire.
Even the settlers, whose lives and property were menaced by the
fires, could not help remarking on their grandeur. In the middle
of a letter he is writing, Elias Pym Fordham breaks off his description of the quality of the land to say:

Since I began to write this letter I have been interrupted by a
tremendous fire in the prairie which, driven by a strong south
wind, threatened our habitations. By the exertions of about
40 Americans we saved everything but a haystack.

It was the most glorious and most awful sight I ever beheld. A thousand acres of prairie were in flames at once—the
sun was obscured, and the day was dark before the night
came. The moon rose, and looked dim and red through the
smoke, and the stars were hidden entirely. Yet it was still
light upon the earth, which appeared covered with fire. The
flames reached the forests, and rushed like torrents through.
Some of the trees fell immediately, others stood like pillars of
fire, casting forth sparkles of light. Their branches are
strewed in smoking ruins around them.

While I was with G——'s people, burning a trough round
his house, I saw the fire approach my own. It almost had surrounded it. I ran with my utmost speed, and found I could

not get round the fire. A small opening appeared in one part, and I dashed through, though not without singeing my hunting shirt and scorching my moccasins with the glowing ashes. A small creek near my house stopped the fire. There are five large fires visible tonight, some many miles off.

Blane, too, wrote movingly about a fire he witnessed.

It is customary with the Indians and hunters to set fire to the long grass for the purpose of compelling the game to take shelter in the woods, where they can more easily get at it. They do this in the autumn or winter when the grass, which is often four or five feet in height, becomes dry. Now the last autumn had been very wet, and on that account the prairies had not all been fired, so that when I passed through, the grass in many of them was still unburnt. I had often heard of the grand spectacle they present when on fire, and was fortunate enough to witness it.

I observed a very thick smoke issuing from a small belt of wood on the edge of the prairie, about two miles ahead of me and just where the road entered the forest. The wind was blowing towards me very violently, and in a minute or two the flames dashed out of the wood into the long grass of the prairie. That on the right hand of the road had been burnt before, and accordingly I rode a little off in that direction. The flames advanced very rapidly, continued to spread, and before they had arrived opposite to the place where I stood formed a blaze of fire nearly a mile in length.

How shall I describe the sublime spectacle that then presented itself? I have seen the old Atlantic in his fury, a thunderstorm in the Alps, and the cataracts of Niagara; but nothing could be compared to what I saw at this moment.

The line of flame rushed through the long grass with tremendous violence and a noise like thunder, while over the fire there hovered a dense cloud of smoke. The wind, which even previously had been high, was increased by the blaze which it fanned; and with such vehemence did it drive along the flames that large masses of them appeared actually to leap

forward and dart into the grass several yards in advance of
the line. It passed me like a whirlwind, and with a fury I shall
never forget.

I was always forcibly struck by the melancholy appearance
of a burnt prairie. As far as the eye could reach, nothing was
to be seen but one uniform black surface, looking like a vast
plain of charcoal. Here and there by the roadside were the
bones of some horses or cattle which had died in passing
through, or the horns of some deer which had been killed.
These, bleached by the alternate action of fire and rain,
formed by their extraordinary whiteness a most remarkable
contrast to the black burnt ground on which they lay.

I afterwards saw several prairies on fire but was not within
two or three miles of them. They produce a beautiful effect
during the night, the clouds immediately over them reflecting
the light and appearing almost on fire themselves. When, during a dark night, there are two or three of these meadows on
fire at a time the effect is of course very much heightened; and
the whole heavens are then tinged with a deep and sullen red.

I have heard the hunters in the state of Missouri describe
the grand spectacle offered to their view when the Indians,
every autumn or winter, set fire to the large prairies that extend almost to Mexico. Here the flames, having nothing to
stop their fury, blaze on for many days and nights together,
and are only checked at last either by a heavy fall of rain or by
the blowing of the wind in an exactly contrary direction.

ii

VISITORS WERE NOT the only ones to find adventure on the prairies. The settlers also enjoyed leaving their work for a day or two
at a time and exploring the wild, unsettled regions to the north.
Elizabeth Birkbeck, like women everywhere, knew that the spoils
of the chase were not uppermost in the minds of men setting off
to hunt. In a letter of 1819 she writes:

Some of the gentlemen of our settlement are projecting a
hunting expedition in quest of bears and deer—but I believe
chiefly in quest of adventures. They will equip themselves

regularly for camping out and go back into the unsurveyed lands where, as yet, there are no inhabitants and the bears and the wolves and the panthers are as yet undisturbed in their haunts.

Later, when the first labors of pioneering were over, an intrepid woman like Mrs. Flower might accompany her husband on a backwoods pleasure trip. George Flower tells of the hardships and satisfactions of such excursions that he and Mrs. Flower took.

Each of us well mounted and equipped with well-filled saddlebags, we started northward on a fine July morning. For the first twenty miles the country was settled thinly—six or eight miles between cabins. North of the trace leading from Vincennes to St. Louis the country was yet more thinly settled—from ten to twenty miles between house and house. We had difficulty in finding the little cabin we were in search of for our first night's lodging, and but for a small column of blue smoke betraying its locality in a small clump of brushwood we should have passed it by. When found, it was of the smallest class of cabins. After a supper of corn bread, milk, and venison, we rested for the night on one of the two beds, the whole family taking to the other. Before mounting the next morning, we were struck with the occupation of our host. He was greasing his wagon with good fresh butter. He might as well do so, he said, for when he took it to Lawrenceville, ten miles distant, he could only get five cents a pound for it, and that in trade.

After riding across a prairie for about twelve miles, our horses being much tormented by the prairie flies, we rested for some hours at a house in a point of timber, the last timber we should meet in a day's journey. About five in the afternoon we mounted again. The direction we traveled, with scarcely the indication of a track, was due north, keeping the timber about two miles to the right. A few miles ahead, and a little to our left, stood a grove of timber covering one section of land in the open prairie. It was appropriately called Island Grove.

Clouds, black and portentous, had been long threatening.

The rain came down in torrents. The north wind blew in our faces with such violence that for a time the horses could not face the storm. We had to allow them to turn round. Pursuing our way northward, night overtook us. The feeble rays of a young moon added but dreariness to the scene. The wind, growing more and more cold, pierced through our wet garments. It was about nine at night when we came to the track of the National Road, just being laid out and worked. This greatly relieved our anxious watchings, for we feared that we had passed over it and were wandering northward in the interminable prairie. Following its course westward, we were suddenly arrested by a broad sheet of water which we dared not enter and could not go round.

The moon set. We were in darkness. Wet through, exposed to a keen north wind, without the slightest shelter, we stood by the side of our horses and waited the termination of this dreary night. I at length yielded to sleep on the wet and sodden ground. My wife, with greater resolution, kept watch on foot, holding the horses' bridles in her hand, sometimes putting her fingers under the saddles to catch a little warmth and sometimes waking me from what she feared might be a fatal slumber. One sound only was heard during these hours of dreary darkness, the dismal howl of a solitary wolf. At break of day, so stiff and cold were we that we could with difficulty mount our horses. Both ourselves and horses shook and trembled as with an ague.

We had to proceed about six miles, through mud and water, before reaching a small roadside cabin kept by John Ganaway. A good breakfast and two hours' sleep set all to rights, and we proceeded on our way none the worse for our late exposure. Such incidents were of common occurrence to travelers on the prairies in those days.

These encounters with the elements were not always so happily got through, especially in the winter season. Mr. Hugh Ronalds and his young son were traveling on the prairies, about thirty miles northwest of Albion, with a covered carriage and a pair of horses in the winter season. On coming to a creek frozen over, in attempting to cross on the ice, the horses broke in; but the ice was too strong and the creek too deep to allow the horses to get through. It was necessary to detach the horses from the carriage and to break the ice to allow the horses to struggle out on the opposite bank, in doing which Mr. Ronalds became wet to his middle. Before he could arrange the harness on the horses, his clothes became quite stiff, his legs seemed to be encased in boards. A house near the creek, the view of which was an additional inducement to risk the crossing, was found to be entirely deserted. No fire or the means of making any. Under these circumstances it became a struggle for life. Mr. Ronalds, becoming weak from cold and suffering, desired his son (a lad of nine years) to make for a house about three miles across the prairie and send back aid if he should arrive there. He, with aid of men and women, returned and met his father. Mr. Ronalds proceeded at a slow pace with the horses. He soon became insensible. When met by the party from the house, he was standing between the horses, holding on by the harness, but nearly insensible and very numb. Covering him with blankets, and carrying him when he could no longer walk, they arrived at the cabin and put him to bed, stiff and unconscious. It was long before friction and warmth induced circulation or sign of life. The process of freezing, or dying, was attended by no remembered pain; but in returning to life he suffered much agony.

If a family party desired to make a journey of some distance —say two or three hundred miles—a wagon was found to be the most safe and comfortable conveyance. Wishing to visit a friend who had settled a few miles north of Peoria on the Illinois River, more than two hundred miles distant from Park House, an old friend and neighbor, Capt. James Carter, wishing to see the country north, accompanied us, brought with him a wagon and a pair of oxen, to which I added another yoke. This was furnished with provisions and cooking utensils and some bedding. My own covered wagon, drawn by two stout and active horses with a driver sitting on the near saddle horse, conveyed my family, two sons and one daughter, with Mrs. Flower and an infant at her breast. Two saddle horses,

one furnished with a sidesaddle, for any of us to ride by way
of change, completed our cavalcade. Proceeding thus leisurely
along, we passed over some of the most beautiful prairies in
the centre of the state. Pulling up at evening near some pleasant grove, we lighted our campfire and cooked our evening
meal. As the evening advanced, we spread our blankets on
the ground, and with feet to the fire took our night's rest.
Breakfast over next morning, we proceeded onward through
the day. A fresh venison ham, milk from some farmhouse,
or a prairie fowl occasionally shot by one of the party gave us
the most wholesome and invigorating food. Including our
short visit, we were six weeks going and returning, living day
and night during our journey in the open air. The fine autumn
weather continued with us until the last day of our return. On
the afternoon of that day we were ushered into my own park
gate by a gust of sleet and rain. We all returned with renewed health and spirits. The freedom from care, the gentle
exercise in the open air, the ever-changing scene, the varied
beauties of the landscape gave renewed health, appetite, and
happiness. On entering my park and pleasant dwelling, I
confess to a feeling of approaching care. We were again in
harness, performing the drudgery of civilized life. These
journeys give a fair specimen of the primitive mode of traveling in the early years of our settlement in Illinois.

But at any time a man might escape the drudgery of civilization to go hunting with his backwoodsmen friends, those grown-up
Huck Finns whose irresponsible freedom was a standing reproach to civilized lives dulled by quiet desperation. Fordham,
like all cultivated men who knew the frontier firsthand, had no
romantic illusions about the hunters' way of life, especially as it
affected women exposed to it. Yet he liked these "entertaining and
interesting companions" and was fond of slipping away with them
for a few days of masculine recreation. Thus he presents the
hunter:

Clothed in dressed not tanned buckskins; a homemade, homespun hunting shirt outside, belted to his waist with a broad
belt, to which is appended a knife with a blade a foot long; a

tomahawk or powder horn, in the belt of which is sometimes a smaller knife to cut the patch of the bullet; a bullet pouch; moccasins on his feet; a blanket on his saddle; and a loaf of Indian corn. Thus equipped and accoutered he enters the trackless woods, without a compass or a guide, but what appears a kind of instinct. He is fearless of everything, attacks everything that comes in his way, and thinks himself the happiest and noblest being in the world. These men have kindly feelings. I should expect to receive more sympathy from them in real distress such as they could understand, than from more enlightened and more civilized men. They never swear. Their women never sit at table with them—at least, I have never seen them. I cannot speak in high terms of the manners or of the virtue of their squaws and daughters. Their houses contain but one room and that used as a sleeping room as well by strangers as by the men of the family, they lose all feminine delicacy and hold their virtue cheap.

And later, speaking of a backwoodsman identified only by his initial (who may well have been Captain Birk), he writes:

He is a fine fellow. There are traits of kindness in his character which soften down the sterner features of a ranger. Three Indian with their wives were killed at the south end of the English Prairie 15 months ago. B—— had moved them off his hunting ground, but would not kill them, in pity of their wives. Three others 25 miles farther off came after them, killed all six, and buried them in our prairie. B—— said his hand should never be stained with woman's blood.

I have been at these hunters' cabins and found them almost without food of any kind. A deer or a turkey has been brought in at nightfall; each has cut off the part he liked best, stuck it on a sharpened stick which he has inserted between the logs of the chimney, and so roasted it. The best skins and blankets have been chosen for me. The broken fiddle and a cup of metheglin made of wild honey have been produced; and dances, songs, and mirth have lasted till past midnight. I have been obliged to get up and dance with them, such has been the intolerable noise. Living all together in one room, they have no notion that silence is necessary to a sleepy man; and, having no society and no regular engagements, night and day are alike to them.

Flower also liked to visit the hunters, and he got some good stories from them while the broken fiddles played.

At the house of one of these men, a noted character of that day—John Lewis of the trace—said that he had seen in his hunts the tracks of an enormous elk. For months of search he had failed to get sight of the gigantic animal that had made these tracks of such unusual size. The fortunate day came at last. Himself concealed by a point of wood, the huge animal appeared in full view, grazing in the open prairie. Mustering all his woodcraft for concealment and approach, he succeeded in bringing down the animal at the first shot. He produced the horns; when set on their prongs, a tall man could walk under them without touching. This patriarch of the prairies met his death in 1818 or 1819.

Upon another occasion at the same house, a party of Indians, accompanied by their agent, arrived. They were from some tribe far distant in the interior, on their way to Washington. They were regarded with some curiosity, and much admired as a fine specimen of their race—tall, thin, muscular men, of delicate features, with small hands and feet. There happened to be present a party of backwoods hunters, men of strong-set frames, used to fights of every description, and noted good wrestlers. Their number being equal to that of the Indians, someone expressed the wish to see a friendly combat or trial of strength in a wrestling match, to see who could throw the other. With the consent of the agent, who explained to the Indians the nature of the proposal, the arrangement was soon made. Weapons being carefully removed from both parties, they met man to man. To the astonishment of the spectators, the Indians threw all their antagonists again and again, and with such dexterity and apparent ease that the white men could never get an opportunity to close with them.

Birkbeck, too, collected tales about the Indians, most of whom had already retreated far enough west to be something of a curiosity in the settlement.

Our frontier position affords us many opportunities of obtaining information on Indian manners and customs from persons intimately acquainted with them, men who have fought with them and traded with them. A neighbour of ours has just returned from a trading expedition up the Red River, about seven hundred miles southwest of this place, among the Iotans, Cados, and Choctaws. He relates an event which occurred about Christmas last, at a place he visited, highly illustrative of the virtues and the vices of this untameable variety of the human family.

Their simple necessaries of food and clothing are supplied as heretofore by the chase; but the skins of the various animals they kill have acquired, since their intercourse with the whites, a new value, and *they* have acquired a taste for one fatal luxury, ardent spirits. For these they barter their skins and furs. They indulge in them to dreadful excess; and thousands on thousands perish through intoxication and the frantic broils which it continually occasions.

In one of these frays a Cado bit off the under lip of a Choctaw, both young men. The latter was so drunk that he did not know who had been his antagonist; he lost his lip, got sober, and returned to the chase as usual. Sometime after as he was attending his beaver traps with a comrade of his own tribe, his companion divulged the secret and told the name of the Cado who had disfigured him.

The Choctaw could not sustain the disgrace when vengeance was practicable. He immediately sold his whole property, his beaver traps, his rifle, and his horse. For these he obtained forty bottles of whiskey. Thirty-nine bottles he consumed with his friends, Iotans, Cados, and Choctaws, indifferently, in a grand debauch which lasted a week, but reserved one bottle secreted for a special purpose. After this, when again sufficiently sober, he joined a party among whom was his devoted foe—fell upon him with his knife, and dispatched him. He then coolly took from his pouch some red paint and smeared himself with it preparatory to his death, which was a matter of course, as blood must be avenged by blood, saying he should be ready to die by ten o'clock the next day, but he wished to be shot by one of his own nation. The Cados were merciful; they told him he should not be shot by one of them but by one of his own tribe, a friend of his own selection. He chose his friend, and he desired them to accompany him to a certain spot in the woods. They did so, and he directed them to dig a grave for him there.

The next day he was missing; they sought for him at the appointed hour, and found him sitting at his grave, his bottle of whiskey by him. He drank a part of it, and told them he was ready. He kept his seat, and holding up his arm pointed to the place on his side where the ball should enter. The friend took aim—the gun missed fire. He gave a slight start, but said nothing. Again he raised his arm—again the gun snapped. He jumped up with some exclamation, took another draught of whiskey, and seated himself in the same place. The flint being chipped and all ready, once more he presented his side. And the fatal ball sent this brave man to an untimely grave.

Sometime after they were talking over the melancholy affair and the *friend* declared he was glad to shoot him, for he was not his friend in reality. The spirit of savage justice was roused again; one of his companions immediately fired at him but missed—thanks to the whiskey both for the danger and the escape. However, they confined the false friend one whole week whilst they sat in council on the case. At length he was acquitted of murder and liberated, as he had only taken a devoted life, though with the heart of a traitor to his friend.

Not all adventures took place in the backwoods and unsettled regions. Flower relates one that occurred near Albion.

A friend of mine, with a companion, were riding together in a large open prairie one hot summer's day. On one side of them the wood was four miles distant, on the other three. As they rode up a steep and grassy mound, a wolf was coming up on the other side. Both wolf and horsemen met on the top with equal surprise, no doubt; for both parties came to a sudden halt, gazing at each other. In a moment, the wolf was making off for the nearest woods, with the horsemen after him at full speed. They soon overtook him, and attempted to ride him down. But the horses, perhaps from an instinctive fear of his fangs, would never step upon him. In this way they continued the chase for a long time. At length, the wolf, exhausted and faint, lay down. My friend dismounted to dispatch him by a blow on the head from his heavily loaded whip. The horse, free from restraint and made frantic by the flies, galloped away, my friend's companion riding after, endeavoring to catch him and bring him back. My friend was now alone with the wolf. As he raised his arm to give the fatal blow, the wolf sprang to his feet, with his bristles erect, showing all his terrible fangs. Wolf would allow of no retreat, but springing at the throat of the man, was knocked down by a blow from the heavily loaded whip. Three times were these attacks given and received by wolf and man. At the last blow given, the load in the handle of the whip fell out. My friend was now without weapon. With great presence of mind, he threw himself upon the wolf, seizing him by the nape of the neck with one hand, and throwing upon him the whole weight of his body. Both came to the ground, man on top, still grasping him fast by the skin of his neck. Such was the strength of the wolf that he rose up with the weight of the man upon him, walking and staggering along, until the disengaged hand of the man pulled up one of his legs and threw him again. This struggle between wolf and man, with alternate advantage, continued some time, until the companion returned with both horses. For a time they were at a loss, being destitute of all weapons. At last a small penknife was found with which the wolf was bled to death by severing his neck vein—my friend holding on like grim death to the last moment, his face, in the struggle, often coming in disagreeable proximity to the jaws of the wolf.

Equally dangerous but less pleasant to recall were the encounters the settlers had with drunken backwoods rowdies. It was bad enough when the rowdies emptied their rifles into the prize livestock of the settlement, worse when they shouldered their way into the homes of frightened settlers. Faux remarks that

the Illinois rowdies, as they are called, are rather troublesome. They come rudely with their hats on into the parlour, and, when drunk, threaten Mr. Flower's life; but they are great cowards; firmness and a fearless resolution are necessary in dealing with them. One of a large offended party came drunk to Mr. Flower's house and said he would enter and shoot him. Mr. Flower got his rifle and pointed it at the fellow, on which he rushed up and put his mouth madly to the muzzle, and said, "Fire!" Mr. Flower then laid it down, seeing the effect was not good, and some less drunken members of the party dragged the fellow away. Law has no influence over these rowdies. Violence must be opposed to violence.

The Flower family has bought out a good many of these wretches. One, however, more violent and lawless than any yet known, still remains, of the name of Jack Ellis, the son of an old and industrious settler from Indiana, who says that he expects this son will sometime murder his mother and that if God does not take him, he, his father, must kill him himself.

This rascal, with several others, in addition to their hunting go round stealing free Negroes, on pretence of being employed to find runaways. The poor blacks are thus cruelly taken and sold at New Orleans. I saw Jack with his rifle after a Negro in the employ of Mr. George Flower, who had armed the poor fellow in defense of himself against Jack, whom the settlement wish to be shot.

Flower gives another escapade in which the renegade Jack Ellis figures.

A man named Clark, in a grog shop, stabbed a man named Hobson. A fellow named Perry, as accessory after the fact, was found guilty and condemned. During Perry's imprisonment, whilst under sentence of death, there lived near to Albion a young fellow of vagrant habits who spent most of his time about grog shops and getting into fights. His youth and strength made him the bully of the place. The condemned Perry was the owner of a good rifle. All the backwoodsmen knew the qualities of their neighbors' rifles. From the frequent shooting matches with each other, the range, power, and accuracy of all the rifles roundabout were known. Perry's rifle had a good reputation, and was coveted by the young vagabond Jack Ellis. Jack, conferring with the prisoner, agreed to get up a petition, take it to Vandalia, and endeavor to procure a pardon from the governor. If he succeeded, Perry was to give him his rifle.

Jack set about the business with considerable tact. He took a sheet of paper with a proper heading, and secretly and silently sped away to Vandalia, a dreary ride of seventy-five miles, the weather bad and waters out. When at Vandalia he was in no hurry to present himself to the governor, but, as usual with men of his stamp, first went to the grog shop. He soon told his story to the loafers hanging about the place, and, in exchange for his drams, they gave plenty of signatures to his petition. The governor signed, little thinking that the majority of the signatures were procured at some doggery within fifty steps of his own lodgings. Jack, returning with the pardon, had fairly earned his rifle.

In his interview with Perry, after his return, a curious scene took place. Perry, brought from a neighboring jail, was chained to a beam in a house, where Jack announced the success of his mission and demanded his rifle. This Perry flatly refused. He expostulated on the unreasonableness of the demand. What was he to do without his rifle? Might as well take his life as his rifle! How was he to live? It was unreasonable, inhuman, and much more to that effect. "Very well," says Jack, "no rifle, no pardon; here goes the pardon into the fire." It went, but not into the flames, but onto the ashes close by. Perry, in his terror, gave up the rifle, adding to it all his other earthly possessions, an axe and a cow and his old woman too, a faithful paramour who had stood by him in his

life of crime and trouble. Jack was not exacting, merely taking cow, axe, and rifle, generously leaving the old woman.

But there was another party to be appeased—the public.
Disappointed of the exhibition for which they had especially
come, they became furious. Men and women had come in
from forty miles around, on horseback, on foot, and in numerous sledges (many wagons were not then in the country), a
great crowd. On learning that Perry was out of their reach,
they raged and cursed at everybody and everything generally,
and Governor Coles in particular. If the governor had been
there he would have been in danger that day. Consoling themselves with whisky and a score of fights, they gradually dispersed. The murder of Hobson terminated in the transfer of a
cow, an axe, and a rifle from an old ruffian to a young black-
guard, and in giving to Perry a new piece of furniture. Perry
claimed the coffin and the rope that was to hang him, which
the county had procured for his especial use. They were given
up to him; the former became a fixture in his cabin as a corner
cupboard, the latter a happy memento in his rural hours. Jack
did not live long to use his rifle. An insolent assault on a very
quiet Englishman procured for him a blow which gave him
his quietus. He did not die for months, but he never recovered
from that blow.

And so the community was rid of Jack Ellis, at least, without the
expense of hanging him.

iii

WHAT WERE THE CONSEQUENCES of these travelers' tales—most of
them, perhaps, in need of falling a snake or two? Besides holding
interest in their own right, these were the experiences that helped
form the opinions of both travelers and settlers about the country,
about the people in it, and about the desirability of Illinois as a
place to live. Surely most of the visitors were ready to generalize
on rather scanty evidence. Judge Hall reminded them that

It is always to be recollected that "the Western country" is an almost unlimited region, embracing every grade of society and civilization from the mere frontier, where the hunter erects his solitary cabin in the bosom of extensive forests, where no axe is heard but his own, where he wages war with the savage, or mingles with him in the chase, to the polished circles of Lexington, the crowded marts of Cincinnati and Louisville, or the populous and refined neighbourhoods which are now numerous in almost every Western state.

It was often the backwoods rowdies and hunters they had in mind when they sketched the outlines of the American national character, the nearly impassable swamps and dangerous animals still at large when they advised Englishmen—as most of the travelers did—not to exchange civilization for the wilds. For finally, all the contemporary writing about the settlement aimed to illuminate the question of whether an Englishman would be wise to emigrate or not. The people the immigrant would have to live among and the kind of land he would have to live on were necessarily the crucial factors. The land could be described, and the proof of its fertility lay in what Birkbeck and Flower were able to raise on it. The great imponderable was the race of men who inhabited it.

Hence it is not surprising that nearly all these writers had more or less to say about the Americans, whom they took to be almost a unique social species. Even bluff old John Woods, having described the flora and fauna, heaves himself bodily up to the expected task, well aware that he is taxing his analytical powers in the effort.

I will now give a slight and very brief sketch of the American character; but in speaking of our American neighbours, it must be recollected that the greater part of them are backwoodsmen. My family have several American neighbours at Birk's Prairie from whom they have received the most friendly treatment, and those with whom I have had dealings have been uniformly civil and obliging. As we live at the entrance of Wanborough, we have frequently the first offer of game and other provisions brought for sale, and whether we buy or not we never receive the slightest incivility from them. In selling, they always take care to ask enough, as they can fall their price with a good grace; in short, they are Jews in this respect, nor are they very punctual in their payments.

Most of them are well acquainted with law, and fond of it on the most trifling occasions; I have known a lawsuit brought for a piggin or pail of the value of 25 cents. Another failing in their character is drunkenness; and they are extremely quarrelsome when intoxicated. Many of them are sometimes truly industrious, and at other times excessively idle. Numbers of them can turn their hands to many things, having been accustomed to do for themselves in small societies. They are a most determined set of republicans, well versed in politics, and thoroughly independent. A man who has only half a shirt, and without shoes and stockings, is as independent as the first man in the States, and interests himself in the choice of men to serve his country as much as the highest man in it, and often from as pure motives—the general good, without any private views of his own.

One of the most penetrating observations on this subject was made by Birkbeck when he himself was still a traveler trying to find order in the welter of sensations that assailed him on his trip from Virginia to Illinois.

It is a phenomenon in national character which I cannot explain, but the fact will not be disputed, that French politeness remains until every trace of French origin is obliterated. A Canadian Frenchman who, after having spent twenty years of his prime among the Indians, settles in the backwoods of the United States, still retains a strong impression of French good breeding. Is it by this attractive qualification that the French have obtained such sway among the Indians? I think it may be attributed with as much probability to their conciliating manner as to superior integrity, though the latter has been the cause generally assigned.

This tenaciousness of national character under all changes of climate and circumstances, of which the French afford many remarkable instances, is the more curious as it is not

universal among nations, though the Germans, I am told, afford examples equally strong. This country gives favourable
opportunities for observation on this interesting subject.

What is it that distinguishes an Englishman from other
men; or is there any mark of national character which neither
time, climate, nor circumstances can obliterate? An Anglo-
American is not English; but a German is a German, and a
Frenchman French to the fourth, perhaps to the tenth generation.

The Americans have no central focus of fashion, or local
standard of politeness; therefore, remoteness can never be
held as an apology for sordid dress and coarse demeanour.
They are strangers to rural simplicity; the embarrassed air of
an awkward rustic, so frequent in England, is rarely seen in
the United States. This, no doubt, is the effect of political
equality, the consciousness of which accompanies all their
intercourse, and may be supposed to operate most powerfully
on the manners of the lowest class; for high and low, there
are and will be even here and in every society—from causes
moral and physical, which no political regulations can or
ought to control.

In viewing the Americans and sketching in a rude manner,
as I pass along, their striking characteristics, I have seen a
deformity so general that I cannot help esteeming it national,
though I know it admits of very many individual exceptions.
I have written it, and then erased it, wishing to pass it by; but
it won't do. It is the truth, and to the truth I must adhere.
Cleanliness in houses, and too often in person, is neglected to
a degree which is very revolting to an Englishman. America
was bred in a cabin; this is not a reproach, for the origin is
most honourable, but as she has exchanged her hovel of unhewn logs for a framed building, and that again for a mansion
of brick, some of her cabin habits have been unconsciously
retained.

And of the visitors, the most judicious answer to the great question of emigration for the British was that given by the thoughtful
W. N. Blane, who had read all the printed arguments for and

against the settlement, had made his personal inspection tour, and
arrived at a balanced, independent judgment in which even
Birkbeck and Flower might have found only a little to quarrel
with.

I by no means advise my countrymen to emigrate to Albion, or
indeed to any other place whatsoever. On the contrary, I am
convinced that anyone who has even a prospect of making a
decent livelihood in England would be a fool and a madman
to remove to the Illinois.

To a family man who finds his property and his comforts
daily diminishing without any prospect of their changing for
the better, the English Settlement may be an object worth
attending to; though, for my own part, should I ever be
obliged to emigrate (which I trust in heaven will never be the
case), I should give a decided preference to the state of New
York, or to Canada, or Pennsylvania, for reasons to be mentioned hereafter.

A bachelor has no business in the backwoods; for in a wild
country, where it is almost impossible to hire assistance of any
kind, either male or female, a man is thrown entirely upon
himself. Let any one imagine the uncomfortableness of in-
habiting a log cabin, where one is obliged to cut wood, clean
the room, cook one's victuals, &c., &c., without any assistance
whatsoever, and he will then feel the situation of many unhappy young men who have come to this settlement, even
from London, and quite by themselves. To a family man the
case is different. When isolated from the world, as every one
must expect to be who goes to the backwoods, he has an immense resource in domestic enjoyments, and particularly in
the care and education of his children. How different from the
solitary inhabitant of a log cabin in this most solitary country!

But even the married emigrants cannot be perfectly happy.
How often have I observed the love of their native land rising
in the hearts of those of my exiled countrymen whom I have
met with in different parts of this vast continent! When I have
spoken to them of England, and particularly if I had been in
the countries or villages where they once dwelt, their eyes

have glistened, and their voice has been almost choked with grief. Many a one has declared to me that it was with the most heart-rending anguish that he determined to abandon his home and his relations. But what could he do? Poverty stared him in the face. Many a one has told me, over and over again, that were the tithes and poor-rates taken away, or were they even only diminished so that he could make a shift to live, he would return to his native land with the most unfeigned joy.

Supposing a man intends to emigrate, he should contrast the good with the bad, and will then, from his own sentiments, be able to determine what course to take. A man in England enjoys numberless little comforts which he does not appreciate. Moreover, with moderate temperance, he has the certainty of enjoying good health. But when he goes to the backwoods of America, he has everything to do for himself; he has a difficulty even of obtaining shoes, clothes, &c.; and he then begins to call luxuries what he once considered only as necessaries. He lives in a log cabin, cut off as it were from the world, and in all probability suffers from the prevailing diseases of the country. As to the specious accounts and calculations that he is to increase his capital and make his fortune, so far is this from the truth that if he once invest his money in land, he is compelled to remain, out of inability to dispose of it. Money and land are not, as in England, convertible; and it often happens, that land in the backwoods cannot be disposed of at any price.

Nevertheless, I must allow that emigration offers some great advantages. In the United States a man, instead of renting a farm, can, for a small sum of money, become a respectable landholder. He will no longer be pestered every quarter-day for rent, and tithes, and poor-rates. There is indeed a land tax, but it is so trifling that it may be left out of any calculation, not being annually more than one farthing per acre. The emigrant becomes here independent. He is even considered as a member of the great political body; for, as is the case in the state of Illinois, after residing six months he is entitled to vote, and at the end of five years, by becoming a citizen, is eligible to any office or place in the whole United States, President only excepted. Though the gain of the colonist be but small, his mind is at ease. His fortune cannot well diminish, and with moderate industry may slowly increase. At all events he can look forward without anxiety to the establishment of his family.

As, however, everyone views things in a different light, I most earnestly recommend all persons intending to emigrate to visit the country before they move their families to it. Indeed it is a duty which the emigrant owes them, to see the place he intends to remove them to. The whole expense of a journey from England, even to Illinois and back again, might, by taking a steerage passage across the Atlantic, be easily included in £100, a sum which a man with even a small capital could not grudge in so momentous a concern as that of emigrating. I have, moreover, no hesitation in saying that the £100 would be well laid out, even should he afterwards determine to emigrate. By going through the country he would have an opportunity of seeing several states and could judge which would best suit his ideas of comfort and profit. He would inform himself accurately about the life of the American farmers, and about the value of land as connected with the healthiness of its situation, and of its proximity to a market or a navigable river. He should also inform himself concerning the methods of cultivation; for it must be considered that although an English farmer may know very well how to raise wheat and oats, he is perfectly ignorant of the culture of cotton, tobacco, and particularly of Indian corn, which is the grand staple of the Southern and Western states, and of which 500 bushels are raised for every bushel of any other grain. Indeed most of the small backwoods farmers do not cultivate anything else.

If four or five families from the same part of England wish to emigrate, they would do well to send first of all one of their own number, a poor man but upon whom they could rely. His journey would cost much less than £100—perhaps only £50 —for, on arriving at the other side the water, he might travel on foot and yet go as far in three days as a horseman would in two.

By adopting such a plan the emigrant may become independent of books, which at most are but fallacious guides—everyone, in his views of a strange country, being influenced more or less by his former mode of life.

A poor man would, I think, if willing to work, live more comfortably in the state of New York, or in Pennsylvania, than in the Illinois; but then he could not so easily become an independent landholder.

There is one class of people, however, whom I must on no account dissuade from emigration; I mean the poor Irish. Never, in all my travels, have I seen any set of people who are so wretched as these. The poorest Swiss or German peasant is rich and well off compared to them. Persecuted, and put almost out of the pale of the law on account of their faith; obliged, when almost starving, to stint themselves in food in order to support a religion they abhor; living on roots, often not having enough even of these, and probably not tasting bread or meat once a year—surely such men cannot but find any change advantageous. I verily believe that the poorer class in Kerry are no better off and no more civilized than when Ireland was first conquered by Earl Strongbow. If they could emigrate en masse they would become superior beings; and I would strongly advise every one of them who possesses the means of getting to the seaside, to work or beg his passage over, and go where he may, so that at all events he may quit his native island—that den of human wretchedness.

7

"Our rational amusements."

A NEW COMMUNITY, established in a region as well known by rumor as by truth, surrounded by alien people with strange customs—these circumstances gave the English much to write about of an adventuresome but less heroic stamp than bare-handed fights with wolves or battles against prairie fires. Assuming their readers, in England especially, would be interested in the milder exploits of daily life in the new settlement, both settlers and visitors crammed their pages with details of social history, some of which still hold interest. From roads to roasting ears, fences to frolics, cows to courts, their record of how life was lived is replete with vignettes of pioneering.

The first thing to strike the attention of the English accustomed to metes and bounds was the method of land survey used in the old Northwest Territory. Birkbeck, who admired its logical neatness, took time to inspect its manner of operation, as he journeyed from Virginia to Illinois, and described the way land was purchased in Ohio.

The tract of country which is to be disposed of is surveyed and laid out in sections of a mile square, containing six hundred and forty acres, and these are subdivided into quarters, and, in particular situations, half quarters.

The country is also laid out in counties of about twenty miles square, and townships of six miles square in some instances and in others eight. The townships are numbered in ranges from north to south, and the ranges are numbered from east to west, and lastly the sections in each township are marked numerically. All these lines are well defined by the axe in the woods by marks on the trees. This done at a period of which public notice is given, the lands in question are put up to auction, excepting the sixteenth section in every township which is reserved for the support of schools and the maintenance of the poor. There are also sundry reserves of entire townships as funds for the support of seminaries on a more extensive scale, and sometimes for other purposes of general interest. The lots which remain unsold are from that time open to the public at the price of two dollars per acre, one-fourth to be paid down and the remaining three-fourths to be paid by installments in five years, at which time if the payments are not completed the lands revert to the state, and the prior advances are forfeited.

When a purchaser has made his election of one or any number of vacant quarters, he repairs to the land office, pays eighty dollars or as many times that sum as he purchases quarters, and receives a certificate which is the basis of the complete title, which will be given him when he pays all. This he may do immediately, and receive eight per cent interest for prompt payment. The sections thus sold are marked immediately on the general plan, which is always open at the land office to public inspection, with the letters A. P., "advance paid." There is a receiver and a register at each land office, who are checks on each other, and are remunerated by a percentage on the receipts.

John Woods fills out the picture with an account of the specific practice in Illinois.

In surveying the land on the north side of the Ohio River, a point was taken on the river and a line run from that point due north till it reached the north side of the United States, as far as the Indian title to the land was extinct. This line was called the first principal meridian, and was begun somewhere in the state of Ohio. The second principal meridian, I believe, was in the state of Indiana; and the third principal meridian in the state of Illinois, at the mouth of the Ohio. This third meridian was first run north till it reached the Indian boundary line, about seven miles to the north of the English Prairie. And the land was laid out into ranges of six miles wide on the east and west side of the meridian line, these ranges running from the Ohio River to the Indian boundary line; and the ranges are called first, second, third, and range east or west as the case may be.

Next the ranges were run into townships six miles wide, beginning at the Indian boundary, called the base line, the townships running the width of the ranges, and the first line of townships from the base line called town one. The second line town two, and so on to the Ohio River.

The townships are then laid out in sections of one mile square; thus a township contains six square miles, and thirty-six sections are in each township. They are named section one, two, three, and so on. If the sections are in the woods they are marked near the corners on the trees, and if in the prairies by stakes. They are offered for sale in quarter sections of a hundred and sixty acres; and are called northeast, northwest, southeast, and southwest quarters.

When a part of the country is surveyed and offered for sale, notice is given in the public papers for some months previous, with the time and place of sale. At the sale the lots are put up, beginning with the lowest number, at two dollars per acre; and if there be no bidder, another lot is put up, and so continued till the sale is ended. If a bidding be made the lot is sold; if more than one bidder, then the highest is the purchaser. He must then pay down one-fourth part of the purchase money, one-fourth more at the end of two years, one-fourth more at the end of three years, and the remaining fourth at the end of four years; and if it be not then paid the land reverts to the government and the money paid down forfeited. At the time of sale the purchaser receives a certificate of the quarter purchased, and of the money paid thereon, with the times of payment of the other installments. These installments bear interest from the day of purchasing at six per cent, but if they be paid on or before they respectively become due, no interest is demanded thereon. But should the payment be delayed only one day after it becomes due, interest is demanded from the day of sale. If a person at the time of sale should pay the whole of the installments, after the first he receives eight per cent discount on the sum so paid, according to the length of time of each installment; or if at any time before the installments are due, discount is allowed according to time.

As many people who have speculated in land have let their interest run, much will be due at the end of four years; but should the installments and interest be paid on the day the last installment becomes due, the interest will be saved on the fourth installment; but four years' interest are due on the second and third installments. That is $38.40, but one day later will make it $57.60.

If not paid at the end of four years, I have reason to think some time is allowed before the land reverts to the government. But the interest still runs on till the day of payment; and if the arrears be not paid, the land and all its improvements, if any, return to the government.

The above was the plan on which the public lands were disposed of; but by an act of Congress a new plan has been adapted, by which all credit on public land is done away, and the price reduced to $1.25 per acre, or $200 for a quarter section; that is, for land that has been offered by public auction.

I have every reason to conclude that much remains due on the land entered in most of the Western states, and some will, most probably, be forfeited to the government, as much of it was entered on speculation and still remains in a state of nature.

Faux observed that

The land here seems very tempting to a British farmer, quite ready for the plough without any hewing or cleaving, or a

blade of grass to obstruct the plough. The fire has laid the
surface black and bare as a stubble ground burnt in the fens
of England.

And that

Many acres are enclosed by a ditch and rail fence formed by
stakes, bands, and split rails, which will oftener need repairing than the worm fence without being so complete a protection. Less timber, however, is needed in this mode.

Once on the land, the English, more than the Americans, were
concerned about putting up substantial fences. In this effort Birkbeck made a notable contribution, for, as Faux implies, fencing
first became a serious problem when American agriculture
reached the treeless prairies. The Virginia worm fence made of
split rails had become the customary farm fence in the wooded
areas of the East, except for those with stone to dispose of, where
stone walls were raised. But on the prairie, and especially when
agriculture pushed beyond the Mississippi River, some substitute
for rails had to be found. The prairies of the English Settlement
were near enough to timber that the problem was not yet crucial
here. Yet it is noteworthy that in Illinois, where the fence problem
was eventually solved by the invention of barbed wire, Birkbeck
was among those who began the first experiments in new methods
—a thing he could do because his farming experience in England
had not closed his mind to all but the ubiquitous rail fence.
    The early visitor Thomas Hulme, who "very much admired"
Birkbeck's fences, described them thus:

He makes a ditch four feet wide at top, sloping to one foot
wide at bottom, and four feet deep. With the earth that comes
out of the ditch he makes a bank on one side, which is turfed
towards the ditch. Then a long pole is put up from the bottom
of the ditch to two feet above the bank; this is crossed by a
short pole from the other side, and then a rail is laid along
between the forks. The banks were growing beautifully, and
looked altogether very neat as well as formidable; though a
live hedge (which he intends to have) instead of dead poles
and rails upon top would make the fence far more effectual

as well as handsomer. I am always surprised that this mode of fencing is not adopted in cultivated districts, especially where the land is wet or lies low; for there it answers a double purpose, being as effectual a drain as it is a fence.

And Birkbeck himself discussed his fences in a paper he presented at a meeting of the Agricultural Society of Illinois, adding that "such a fence is absolute against cattle, and as much so against hogs as anything short of a stone wall." The cost he estimated at 83 cents per rod. He knew, too, that such fences, serving the dual purpose of enclosure and drainage, would counter one of the frequent criticisms of prairie land, the claim that it was too damp for good farming or even healthful living. Faux remarked that such "ditching and fencing removes the cause of fogs which hang over the low prairies," though he thought that "this fence will not be imitated by any American." And Birkbeck again was providentially equipped by past experience to bring this innovation to prairie agriculture. His son wrote back to England in 1819: "My father has enclosed about 350 acres of most excellent land and has been ditching it most thoroughly, although it was scarcely wanted, except in a few places. Ditching, if you recollect, was my father's favourite operation, and he would never rest until he had completely secured any spot which *appeared* even likely to be ever wet."

Apparently not many Americans did follow Birkbeck's example, for the reason Faux gives:

It is useless to fence much more land than is cleared, because until the country is cleared round about the autumnal fires would destroy the fences. The cattle, therefore, must range in the woods until some small inclosures for pasture can be made.

And in the absence of adequate enclosures, livestock permitted to roam the woods and prairies had to be identified by some permanent mark. Woods tells how this was done.

Beasts, sheep, and pigs are all marked in their ears by cutting and notching them in all possible directions and forms, to the great disfigurement of many of them; yet these marks

are absolutely necessary in this wild country, where every person's stock run at large. They are not sometimes seen by their
owners for several months, so that without some lasting mark
it would be utterly impossible to know them again. Most people enter their marks with the clerk of the county in which
they reside, and no person is then allowed to use the same
marks if living in the same county and within five miles of the
person who has previously entered the same marks. The
county clerk's fee for entering a mark is twelve cents and a
half. And no person is allowed to dispute his marks with
another of the same marks unless his are also entered at some
county office.

ii

MANY ACTIVITIES COMMON to all pioneer communities in America
naturally struck the newcomers with surprise and were worth setting down for the amusement of readers back in England. John
Woods' book is especially rich in such reports. For instance, he
writes about animals new to him, or those especially numerous.

Ground hogs are scarce; I have seen but one. It was larger
than a large cat; it had a large head that a little resembled the
head of a pig; in colour like an English badger; the legs very
short, with long strong claws. It was fat, and said to be good
eating; the person who had it did not eat it, but stripped it for
the sake of its skin, which he was going to tan to make shoes
for his wife. He put it into some very strong lye to take off the
hair, and afterwards he intended to put it into a vat with some
oak bark. I have seen several of the Americans tanning hides
and skins in a trough made from a large tree, the inside hol-
lowed out and the skins put in and covered with some small
pieces of oak bark and water. These troughs are covered to
keep off the sun and rain. I do not know how long they are in
tanning their skins, but I have not, anywhere in America, seen
any good leather of their own manufacturing.
    Ground squirrels are handsome little animals, mostly run-

ning on the earth, fallen trees, and rails, and are as mischie-
vous as rats. Tree squirrels are of two or more sorts, and are
eaten here. A party of eight Americans, in May this year, had
a squirrel hunt for a trifling wager. They were equally
divided, and started at daylight with their rifles; and that
party which produced most squirrels by the middle of the
next day was to win the wager. They each took a different
ground to hunt on, each had a man to attend him to see all
was fair. Three of them hunted on and near my land. I knew
them all; and I saw one of them several times during the
hunt. He was of the winning side; he killed 41. The whole
number killed by his party was 152, by the other 141; total
293. Although more than 100 squirrels were killed on my
farm and near it, it did not appear greatly to lessen them.

And he writes about the way Americans handle their national
grain, Indian corn.

The green ears are eaten boiled or roasted, the latter mostly
by the Americans, who call all green ears roasting ears. The
price of corn last fall was mostly 50 cents a bushel delivered,
and now 50 cents in the place. But near us there is very little
to be procured at any price. On the Wabash, where the country has been longer settled, it is lower and plentiful. It is
gathered in October and November, when they only take off
the ears; but as the ears are covered with a large husk, they
carry them as they are to the corn crib, and then all the neighbours collect together to help to husk it and put it into the corn
crib. This is a high day with the Americans, and is called a
husking frolic. Plenty of whiskey is generally to be found at
one of these frolics. I never was present but at one; I suppose
there were near forty people present. I did not stop, but I
understood it concluded with a dance. We did not make any
frolic in husking our corn, but did it ourselves; but the Americans seldom do anything without having one.

This brings him to generalize further on how Americans get together to get their work done.

They have husking, reaping, rolling frolics, &c., &c. Among
the females they have picking, sewing, and quilting frolics.
Reaping frolics are parties to reap the whole growth of wheat,
&c., in one day. Rolling frolics are clearing woodland, when
many trees are cut down and into lengths, to roll them up
together so as to burn them, and to pile up the brushwood
and roots on the trees. I think this one is useful, as one man
or his family can do but little in moving a large quantity of
heavy timber. Picking cotton, sewing, and quilting frolics
are meetings to pick cotton from the seeds, make clothes, or
quilt quilts; in the latter, the American women pride themselves. Whiskey is here too in request, and they generally
conclude with a dance. Raisings are a number of men getting
together to raise a piece of building; that is, to lift the logs
on each other. This is practised by the English as well as the
Americans; nor is whiskey here omitted.

Commenting on the roads leads him naturally to a national trait
of character long attributed to Americans—their restlessness—
and finally to the sights a man might see in his backwoods travels.

The roads are all natural roads, yet always free from ruts and
perfectly smooth when dry. I have heard the land round us
is much like some in Lincolnshire; but of this I cannot judge,
as I never was there. I never found any land in Surrey that
hoed or dug so light as this does when it has once been well
broken up. The colour of it is rather brown, but much blacker
when wet; and in appearance it bears the most resemblance
to peat mould of any soil I ever saw in England.

Many of the people here have been extensive travellers; and
to have resided in three or four states, and several places in
each state is not uncommon. A man who boarded a short time
at my house said he was born in old Virginia; that he removed, with his father, over the mountains into new Virginia, but left his father before he was twenty; that he married and took up his abode in the wild parts of South Carolina and built a cabin, the first in that part of Carolina.

People settling round him, he sold his land and removed into Kentucky; and on the land he disposed of in Carolina, a town soon sprang up of 300 houses and seven large stores. In Kentucky he stayed some years; but settlers arriving and seating themselves near him, he again moved off into the wild part of Indiana, near Rockport, where he now resides; but he expressed a wish to come into the Illinois, as he said the country round him was not healthy for cattle.

A person who lives in Birk's Prairie who has been there four years, and who has planted a small orchard, had a few apples last year, the first he ever grew, although he had planted six orchards before the present one. His wife says she has had twelve children, but never had two born in one house, and does not remember how many houses they have inhabited since they were married. Yet they think they are now fixed for life; but several of their sons are gone to the Red River, 700 miles to the southwest.

Since I have been here, I have travelled more than I ever did in the same space of time in England. In a journey I took to Palmyra to record my own and my son's cattle marks, I saw a muster of Edwards County militia near Bonpas bridge. They amounted to several hundred men, under the command of Colonel Jourdan. There were five or six companies, but much the largest one was from our township, under Captain Cadwallader Jones. The militia at this muster did not cut a very warlike appearance, being all drest in their customary clothes, except some of the officers, who had uniforms. They all find their own arms, mostly rifles; a few had fowling pieces, and a very few only sticks. There are four musters, besides this general yearly one, of the whole county.

Thus skipping along from topic to topic as association brings them uppermost in his mind, John Woods gives a comprehensive picture of the minutiae of pioneer life. Too honest to comment on what he had not seen for himself, he had to omit certain activities we expect to find. Some gaps are filled by other writers. Birkbeck tells something of another pioneer industry.

The season for sugar making is now commencing; some has already been made in this neighbourhood. There are several species of the maple from which sugar may be extracted. The hickory, and I believe some other trees, contain sugar of excellent quality; but the Acer saccharum, or sugar maple, affords the great supply of this article. In a favourable season (calm weather, frosty nights, and sunny days), I understand one hundred pounds of sugar may be collected from fifty trees; and one man, with great assiduity, may perform the work in about eight days where the trees stand conveniently near to each other. Auger holes are bored through the bark into the wood about three feet from the ground, from which a tube, formed perhaps of cane, conveys the limpid and slightly sweet liquor into small troughs. Hard by a range of iron kettles are steaming away; in these the "sugar water" is evaporated to a syrup of proper consistency. When in this state, it is placed in a tub with holes in the bottom, and the process of graining (an imperfect crystallization) is performed very handsomely, and a delicious molasses runs off through the holes. It is, however, generally grained very imperfectly in the kettles by stirring it till it is cool. The great consumption of this article in Kentucky, Ohio, and Indiana has been chiefly derived from the sugar maple; but cane is now cultivated with success in Louisiana, and cane sugar in large quantities is brought up the river and can be afforded cheaper, I believe, than that from the maple. The price this season of the latter is twenty-five cents per pound.

And Blane remarks on another backwoods source of sugar.

It is a favourite amusement at a particular season of the year to go bee-hunting, and great quantities of honey are then collected. This the settlers, for the most part, use instead of sugar. I have been surprised at the number of gallons of honey that a single bee's nest will sometimes yield. The bees make their nest in the hollow of a tree, and continue to increase their comb until the hollow space is quite or nearly filled. The honey is obtained by chopping down the tree, and killing or driving off the bees with branches.

In most respects it was a good life the settlers described. Birkbeck could write:

We are now feasting on wild turkeys. We have not sat down to dinner for the last month, I believe, without a fine roast turkey. They weigh about twelve pounds, and are sold five for a dollar. Some weigh twenty-five pounds—I have heard of thirty. They are fat and tender; better, I fancy, than Norfolk turkeys; but I must not be too positive on this nice point.

One annoyance, however, was the currency problem. As Woods explains it:

One unpleasant circumstance is the paper currency of this part of the United States, and it requires some experience to know what notes to take. The paper money is of two kinds, called land-office and current money; land-office money is bank paper that will pass at the land office, but this money frequently changes. Current money is bank paper that will pass in trade, but is not payable at the land office, and is often from ten to twenty per cent below the value of land-office money. It is common to make a price according to the sort of money to be paid, and there are some articles in most stores that are only sold for land-office money.

The United States Bank notes and silver are mostly sought for, as the credit of that bank is better than that of any other, and they will sometimes bear a premium of two per cent above the price of silver, as notes are more convenient to send to the Eastern states to pay for merchandise, &c. But there are many people who prefer silver, and I find I can purchase many articles a great deal more reasonable with silver than with the best paper money.

I have never yet lost but one dollar note, nor have I discounted a single one. Discounting of notes is called shearing, and is sometimes much practised.

But even this state of affairs was not as bad as it once had been in Indiana, according to the example of Gresham's law palmed off on W. N. Blane by a leg-pulling Hoosier.

While I was passing through a point of wood running into one of the prairies, two raccoons, who had come out to enjoy the fine weather, ran up a small tree so near me that had I been inclined I could easily have killed them both. These animals are very numerous, and their fine and soft skins are worth about 20 cents each. I was much amused by a story told me about these skins. "Money was at one time so scarce in Indiana that raccoon skins passed current, being handed from one person to another. But some Yankees (New Englanders) forged these notes by sewing a raccoon's tail to a cat's skin, and thus destroyed the currency."

iii

THE COMMUNITY LIFE which developed in the English Settlement in its early days was a blend of English and American practices, sometimes a blend in which the ingredients were held in uneasy combination. The wiser settlers sensibly looked to their American neighbors for methods which experience had shown were best adapted to the environment. Flower mentions Joseph Applegath as an example of one who profited from the lessons of humble teachers.

Mr. Applegath was a bookseller in London, a man of good education and general information. He was a striking instance with what comparative ease a well-informed and cultivated man can change his occupation and even his habits of life. From knowing nothing of farming or country life of any kind, for several years he followed it energetically and successfully, acquiring the habit of labor which in general seems to go so hard with those unaccustomed to toil. One secret of this was, he had nothing to unlearn and no prejudices on that subject to eradicate. He looked over the fence of his neighbor to see how he did a piece of work, and copied after him. In a few years he retired from habitual labor, but not from active employment; he frequently gave familiar lectures to young people in Albion on useful or scientific subjects, made easy to their comprehension by his simple language and arrangement.

Others were not so adaptable. Richard Flower, too old to change his ways gracefully, never became reconciled to a life without servants or to the Americans' bumptious contempt for domestic service. This quarrel with the Americans was partly a semantic squabble. Faux tells that

Mr. Flower, senior, one day found it necessary to have his family carriage ferried over the river in a flat which had only one man to manage it and get the carriage on and off. Much delay being the consequence, and the man unable to do alone, Mr. Flower complained, and said, "If you do not go and tell your master to send more help, I will fine you for detaining me." The fellow very rudely said, "I have no master, nor shall I go for more help. I am not a servant." "How is that," said Mr. Flower, "the proprietor hires you; you serve him, and he pays you. I am not above assisting you, and being your servant; and you shall pay me too." When landed on the other side, Mr. Flower had two dollars demanded. "Very well," said he, "I have done half the work, and therefore I charge one dollar for my service!" The fellow leered and looked humbled.

The elder Flower, it seems, devoted not a little of his time to humbling haughty servants and to speculating on the cause of this —to him—queer quirk of American character. He wrote:

A good sempstress, earning a dollar per day, will soon quit servitude and put on the airs of American independence, with an addition of some little insolence; but a cure is not infrequently wrought, and that by various easy methods.

A gentleman hired a female servant of this sort who would insist, as a condition, on sitting down at the dinner table with the family. Her Christian name was Biddy. The condition was consented to, and a project for cure at the same time engaged in. A party was invited to dinner, and Biddy took her place at the table, being above waiting or being in any degree more than a help. When anything was wanting, a gentleman arose from table and offered it to Miss Biddy. Miss Biddy was asked to drink a glass of wine, first by one gentleman and then by another. Miss Biddy was desired not to trouble herself about anything, and was ceremoniously treated, till she felt the awkwardness of her situation and said the next day to her mistress, "Madam, I had rather give up dining at your table"—which she did, continuing in their service for some time. I have had to do with people of the same cast, though not quite so foolish as Miss Biddy. I have hired persons to certain employments, and they have been discontented and spoiled by their notions of equality. "Very good," said I; "we, then, are equal. I like the idea much; it pleases me greatly. You, of course, mean to take no money of me for what you please to do for me; and if that is the case, I shall be as perfectly satisfied with your notion of things as you appear to be. But if you take my money, you must perform the service I have pointed out to you." This perfect notion of equality does not suit, although it is too reasonable to be much objected to.

It is generally supposed that this high notion is of republican origin; but it is the contrary, and originates in the insolence of those who keep and domineer over slaves. Anything that a black is made to perform is pronounced unfit for whites; and, although many who have held slaves as their property are far inferior in understanding to the slaves they hold, and are sometimes reduced to poverty, they deem it degrading to perform any work that a slave can perform. And those persons who, like myself, are far from thinking all men equal in character are little disposed to engage with such persons in any service.

iv

THE ENGLISH SETTLERS managed to preserve many of the old amusements in their new home. Several accounts mention cricket matches, and Woods remarks that "the Americans seem much pleased at the sight of the game"—baseball had not yet been invented. William Owen, coming to visit with his traveling companion Donald Macdonald, mentions an afternoon of sport that must have been an incongruous sight on the prairie.

23 December 1824. A very beautiful day; a little frost. After getting Miss Ronalds mounted and riding with her to Mr. Pickering's to get another sidesaddle I was obliged to walk back a mile, as my horse, which I had fastened to a paling, got his head out of the bridle and ran home before me. I and a party of ten or a dozen persons started on horseback with about an equal number of dogs of all kinds, greyhounds, halfbreeds, bulldogs, pointers, etc., to course for deer on the prairies. After starting two deer, we called on Mr. Orange, whose farm is at the southwest extremity of the prairie—before Mr. Flower's house—here named the Boltinghouse Prairie, but commonly called the English Prairie. We found here Mrs. Orange and Mrs. Jolly, cousin of Mr. Beckett, a very pretty, lively woman. After leaving Mr. Orange's and riding through a great deal of brush and underwood, in doing which we saw a rabbit or hare and squirrel and killed an opossum, we returned to Boltinghouse Prairie and had some capital runs after eight or nine deer—which we started at two different times—for several miles. We got home about half past four without catching any deer, as the grass on the prairie was so long that the greyhounds never got sight of the deer, although we from our horses could see their backs above the grass. Mr. D. Orange nearly rode over one of the deer.

Macdonald, who was erroneously reported by his American friends to have become Lord of the Isles and Earl of Skye after his return to England, also kept a journal during his American sojourn. He wrote up the same afternoon of following the hounds at Albion, adding other bits of information and misinformation that he came upon during the day.

We rode out with Mr. Flower, Mr. George Flower, Mr. Ronalds and his sister, Mr. Birkett, Dr. Spring, and Mr.

William Orange with some greyhounds to have a deer hunt. Crossing the prairie to the east we put up two, which soon escaped into the woods. We then called on Mr. and Mrs. Daniel Orange, who have a farm on the east side of the prairie, and were introduced to Mrs. Jolly. From Mr. Orange's we crossed through a belt of wood into a small prairie called French Creek Prairie. The grass had been burnt, and we were obliged to return without seeing any deer in it. In the wood we came upon an opossum. It is a small animal, with short legs, having a body about eighteen inches long, gray hair, long snout and tail, and large mouth. It laid down and pretended to be dead. The backwoodsmen have the expression that a person is opossuming when he is shamming. As we again crossed the English Prairie we put up three or four more deer. They bounded over the long grass displaying their white bushy tails and were soon in the woods. We turned southward along the prairie and soon found as many more, which in like manner went off into the woods. As the grass in this wood had not been burnt, the greyhounds did not once get sight of the deer, and we found it fatiguing work riding through it. Our horses were hardy, and displayed more intelligence than I had remarked among horses in England. Here they are little groomed, have to lie out a great deal, and often have to feed themselves. The day was very fine, and the thermometer above temperate in the shade. In the evening I played at chess with Mr. Ronalds.

Varieties of more lavish entertainment were also attempted, not without difficulty. As early as 1818, while Princeton was still a temporary base of operations, Fordham noted the Fourth of July festivities held there in celebration of the day.

Anniversary of Independence. Last night I assisted in raising the flag of liberty in the public square, which this morning waved proudly over the group of young citizens assembled there to celebrate the day with festal games. The young men of the more respectable class gave a ball to all the damsels of the village and the vicinity. It commenced at three o'clock.

Some few of the girls were really handsome, and all were well dressed and appeared to be very happy. English country dances, or sets as they are called, were attempted without success. In reels and cotillions they were quite at home.

In this land of equality it is very difficult to keep improper persons out of a public or even a private party. This evening some of the young men armed themselves with dirks (poignards worn under the clothes) to resist the intrusion of the militia, as the vulgar are contemptuously called. Unluckily one of our party was electioneering, and treated some hunters in the barroom with rum. We supped in the open air at seven, and afterwards continued the dance till ten. After supper several attempts were made by some shabby looking fellows to come in, but they were prevented by the barkeeper. The dancers kept it up most indefatigably in spite of heat almost equal to that of the West Indies. In going away, some of the gentlemen were insulted by the rabble, but the rumour that they were armed with dirks and pistols prevented serious mischief. In the night a large window was smashed to pieces, and the frame driven into the house.

The female part of the company were all well dressed, but their birth and education as different as possible. The daughter of a proud and poor Virginian stood next the heiress of a bricklayer's fortune; an English adventurer danced with the wife of a member of the legislature; the maker of laws with the daughter of a lawless hunter; and a major of militia led out the only female servant in the inn, and who was obliged to leave the party to help, not her mistress but the tavernkeeper's wife, to set out the supper table.

Albion also had balls where, thanks to the stabilizing influence of the English, greater propriety obtained. William Owen rode horseback from Harmonie through foul February weather to attend one in 1825.

A dull morning. I started about ten o'clock on horseback for Albion. Soon after crossing the ferry, it commenced raining and continued with very little intermission till I arrived within one-half mile of Mr. Flower's house. I continually

was in hope that the rain would soon cease and therefore
did not feel inclined to return back, and my Kentucky
boots and cloak kept me tolerably dry. It must not, however,
be denied that a ride over an uncultivated woodland country,
where for many miles not a habitation or improvement is to be
seen, without a single companion, particularly over a deep
muddy road, while the rain descended in torrents, is certainly
a situation not to be greatly desired. The prairie I found
particularly soft and wet. On my arrival, I immediately
changed my clothes and after dining, about 7 o'clock, drove
in Mr. Flower's wagon with Mr. and Mrs. Ronalds to Albion,
Mr. George Flower following on horseback. The night was
now beautiful, but owing to the darkness we were guided by a
boy who walked with a lantern before the horse's head.
When we arrived, we found but few persons, owing to the
wetness of the day. However, after waiting some time, we
entered into the ballroom and found that we formed a considerable party.

I led off with Mrs. Carter in a country dance. Afterwards
in the course of the evening, we danced a Kentucky reel,
but except that, only country dances. I saw no one in the
room at all intoxicated, which they said was often the case.
On the contrary, though several stood usually near the
whiskey, the greatest decorum was observed. About half
past twelve we all went below to supper, which was laid
out on two tables, and about half past one we returned home
as we came. But some stayed until five in the morning. One
man below stairs, I observed tipsy, but he did not belong to
the company. What happened after we left, I can't say. I was
a good deal tired with the day's exercise.

Other kinds of gatherings had their own entertainment value.
John Woods discovered one reason people went to auctions.

I was lately at an auction, of a little livestock and household
furniture belonging to a person leaving this neighbourhood.
The auctioneer was no less a person than a justice of the
peace, and he was an excellent auctioneer. The terms of sale

much the same as in England, except three months' credit on all purchases above three dollars, on giving bond and security. But the most striking contrast in this sale from an English one was, the auctioneer held a bottle of whiskey in his hand and frequently offered a dram to the next bidder. As I made some biddings, I was several times entitled to a sip out of the bottle. And though I much dislike the taste of whiskey, I took a sip for the novelty of the thing. But I found the auctioneer had taken good care to keep his company sober by lowering his whiskey considerably with water.

The meetings of circuit court were also a time when people gathered from great distances. John Woods tells of an early one at Albion.

There was not a great deal of business—only two criminal causes. One for pig-stealing, found guilty, the sentence a fine of fifty dollars and twenty-five lashes, which were immediately inflicted by the sheriff. The other was for stealing peach trees, but was acquitted. Four or five counsellors attended— no particular dress worn by them or the judge. As the heat was great, one of the counsel who had the most causes took off his coat and pleaded without it. Although no wigs or black gowns are worn, there was no more want of quirks and quibbles than in Westminster Hall; nor were they deficient in eloquence, but not so much tied down to forms nor perhaps quite so polite.

And Birkbeck, writing of his experience at Princeton, where conditions were similar, also found the court an object of interest.

I wish I could introduce you to "his honour" the judge, to the gentlemen of the jury, to the learned brethren who fill the parts both of solicitor and counsel, to the assemblage of spectators, all males, for women never attend the courts except on business, and even to the accomplished villains who are here exposed to public indignation far more terrific than the vengeance of the law.

In this early stage of society, where the country is savage and many of the people but just emerging from that condition, much intrepidity of mind and hardihood of body are indispensable requisites in the administration of justice. Brass for the face won't suffice, they must be steel from head to foot.

The judge and the bar are now working their way to the next county seat, through almost trackless woods, over snow and ice, with the thermometer about zero. In last November circuit the judge swam his horse, I think, seven times in one day; how often in the whole circuit is not in the record. What would our English lawyers say to seven such ablutions in one November day?—and then to dry their clothes on their back by turning round and round before a blazing fire preparatory to a night's lodging on a cabin floor wrapped in their blankets, which, by the by, are the only robes used by the profession here.

I have an anecdote of a judge with whom I am well acquainted, and, therefore, I believe it. I give it you as an instance of intrepidity as well as of that ferocious violence which occurs but too frequently; by no means, however, as a specimen of the judicial character. A few years ago before he was advanced to his present dignity, the foreman of a grand jury insulted him outrageously, out of court of course. The man had a large knife in his hand such as hunters always carry about them and well know the use of; but the enraged barrister, with a handwhip, or cowhide as they are called, laid on so keenly that he actually cut his jacket to ribbons in defiance of the knife. And when the beaten and bleeding juryman made his piteous case known to his brethren, they fined him a dozen of wine for his cowardice.

Another anecdote. A notorious offender had escaped from confinement, and mounted on a capital horse paraded the town where the judge resided with a brace of loaded pistols, calling at the stores and grog shops and declaring he would shoot any man who should attempt to molest him. The judge hearing of it, loaded a pistol, walked deliberately up to the man to apprehend him; and on his making show of resistance, shot him immediately. The ball entered the breast and came out behind but did not prove mortal. He fell, was reconducted to gaol, escaped a second time, and was drowned in crossing the Ohio.

My personal knowledge of the gentlemen of the law is not, I fear, a fair criterion of their general character. I have seen many proofs of candour, high principle, and correct judgment. There are lawyers here whom no sum would bribe to undertake a mean business; but I hear of chicanery in some, and have perceived strong symptoms of vice and dissipation in others. The tendency of the profession, here as in England and I suppose everywhere, is to increase the baseness of little, cunning, avaricious minds; and the pestilent example and society of the idle and corrupt have the same baneful influence over inexperienced young men who are exposed to it.

Flower, too, had something to say on the subject.

The first court in a new county excites great interest, and the country population are in, almost to a man. At our first court, a poor Frenchman was convicted of stealing a quart of whisky from a neighboring distillery and sentenced to thirty-nine lashes. He was stripped to the waist, tied to a post, and the lashes laid on without mercy by the sheriff. The sound of the whip and the screams of the poor wretch sent a nervous thrill through the not over-scrupulous country people who came in to see the opening of the court. If an honest vote could have then been taken, I am inclined to think that such institutions as courts of justice would have been banished as dangerous and barbarous by a great majority; and I don't know that the instincts of the untutored backwoodsmen were far from being right.

At that time, a court or an election would draw the people into the small towns from their most secluded haunts for miles around. Their habits on those occasions indicated the existing degree of civilization. The grog shops (pioneer institutions in all young towns) were in full blast. You could scarcely cross the street (even when the court was sitting, perhaps to try some offender for a breach of the laws) without

seeing two or three crowds swaying and cheering at some
rough-and-tumble fight going on in their midst.

v

RELIGION, OF COURSE, was a primary force for bringing people
together. With most gradations on the Protestant spectrum represented, the settlement developed several forms of religious expression, including that backwoods institution the camp meeting.
Flower writes:

In a settlement like ours of a mixed population, various in
nationalities, and individually differing in circumstances as
to wealth and poverty, degrees of intellect and education,
from every county in England, and various districts of
Scotland, Wales, and Ireland, from Germany and France,
and from almost every state of the Union, there doubtless
existed almost every shade of religious opinion. In a new
settlement there may not be found enough of any one sect
to support a minister and build a church; and there is not
often liberality enough amongst religious sects to aid and
support each other. Thus there may be a vast deal of religion laid away and concealed, as it were, no public exhibition
being made of it. In religious sects there is scarcely toleration
enough to allow of a united movement. Each sect, therefore,
is left to struggle on as it can. An itinerant minister would
occasionally ride in and give a sermon in the courthouse, and
pass along. Mr. Jesse B. Browne was clerk of the court at that
time. A fine man was Mr. Jesse B. Browne, six feet seven
inches high, a kind and jovial man too. On one occasion an
itinerant preacher called a hard-shelled Baptist applied to
Mr. Browne for the use of the courthouse, which was readily
granted. The good preacher was invited by Mr. Browne to
meet two or three friends and take a little refreshment in a
private room after the sermon. Corn whisky, the only refec-
tion, was duly honored, each taking his fair share without
flinching. At the end of the sitting, our hard-shell, true to his

name, could sit straight in his chair and walk more steady
out of the door, it is said, than any of his lay companions.
These were not the days of temperance societies. Cold
water was not then inaugurated.

One would like to think that the Baptist minister was the Rev.
James Hoby, a native of Wanborough in England who was sent
out in 1835 to report on the Baptists in America and was aghast
to find no church building at Albion. It is unlikely, though, that the
Rev. Mr. Hoby would have handled the corn whiskey so well. He
wrote that

> the name of the prairie and of the town prepares one to
> find a truly English settlement, and there is much of the man-
> ners and the mind which would adorn any society in the fa-
> therland. But where was the temple of God? It struck me with
> no small degree of surprise that so many of my countrymen
> should have erected for themselves not merely commodious
> but elegant residences, for this part of the country, without
> securing a place for the worship of God! There is a conven-
> ient town hall, or court house, where worship might be
> stately held; but I believe nothing has been attempted ex-
> cept a sort of apology for it by reading a sermon. This seems
> rather to arise from indifference than from the prevalence of
> infidelity.
>
> What a contrast does it present to the conduct of the
> early Pilgrim Fathers, who laid the basis of their country's
> glory in religion and education, and reared the whole struc-
> ture of their civil institutions on the principles taught in
> Scripture!
>
> A request that I would stay and preach on Lord's Day
> was cheerfully complied with, when I took the liberty of
> urging a solemn regard to divine worship lest by laying the
> very foundations of society, in this its elementary state, in a
> neglect of God and his gospel their names should be handed
> down, desecrated, to posterity. May God dispose the hearts
> of some to undertake what can be done for his own glory!
>
> There is a small Baptist church not very far from Albion,
> but I could not hear of any lying in the route which I now

found it necessary to keep. I had secured accommodation for
Sunday night at the house of Col. Mills. I was sorry to find
that my host had been deeply regretting his not having been
made acquainted with my calling as a minister; they would
have been so highly gratified to have assembled a congregation, and have enjoyed a religious service. I smiled at the idea
of a congregation in a spot so remote, and inquired whence
they were to be gathered? where convened? and how sum-
moned? He told me that a blast of his horn would have
quickly brought a considerable number under a grove opposite his house. It was unhappily too late to witness so interesting a scene.

Flower shows that religion was by no means neglected in Albion,
though churches were slow to be built.

Soon after my father arrived, in 1819, he preached regularly
in Albion every Sunday morning. The service was conducted
after the manner of dissenting worship in England—singing, sermon, prayer. Earnest, energetic preaching generally
attracts attendance. It was so in this case. The service was
gratuitously performed from a sense of duty in holding
public worship. No creed, no catechism, no membership; it
was a free church, if it could be allowed to be a church at all
by more strictly organized bodies.

Then came the church, built and brought together chiefly
through the instrumentality of Mr. Daniel Orange, of a
branch of the Baptists called Campbellites or Christian
Church. A Rev. Mr. Baldwin, Episcopalian missionary,
preached several sermons, gathered the Episcopalians together, and organized a church designated as St. John's
Church. Mr. Pickering was an active promoter, and gave very
efficient aid to this organization. But it was not until some
years afterward, when the Rev. Benjamin Hutchins from
Philadelphia came first as missionary, afterward as a permanent resident, that an Episcopal church was built. There was
a handsome subscription raised, a large share borne by Mr.
Hutchins himself; and a church was accordingly built, and

furnished with its pulpit, seats, altar, choir, and bell. But the chime of the English parish church was wanting! And without that charm, episcopacy can never here attain to the same power over the feelings of the people as it does in England. The touching but cheerful peals, simultaneously, from every parish spire in the realm, as the shades of evening close in, are felt by all hearts in every station and condition of life. Their charming melody warms the hearts of its friends, and does more to allay the bitterness of its foes than all the preaching of its clergy and the exaltation of its ceremonies.

Our religious forms in Wanborough and Albion, whether of episcopacy or dissent, although they might suit the religiously English, were not accepted or in any way attended to by the backwoodsmen around. The silence and solitude, the absence from all emotion in which they lived, seemed to demand some excitement. Whenever they came into town, at an election or a court and frequently on any ordinary occasion, the warmth of feeling in which they stood in need, first raised by a little whisky, would show itself in free fights generally. An elegant sermon read from a book, a calm, logical disquisition carrying a chain of reasoning, tracing effect from cause, a hymn sung in moderate tone and without any gesticulation, a short prayer in a subdued voice was all nothing to them. Their religious feeling could only be excited by more powerful influences embodied in a Methodist camp meeting. This was the exhibition of feeling in which they delighted. In the camp meeting their feelings could be displayed in all their force, without restraint, in forms far less objectionable than in groggery brawls or street fights. Well organized and under good discipline, the Methodist Church wisely adapts itself to all classes; and in this it is only exceeded by the Roman Catholic Church, and not by that in its influence over the backwoodsmen of the Northwestern states. Fortunate in appointing preachers suited to the audience, in the camp meeting it avails itself of the influences of nature to aid the words of the preacher. United, the effect is powerful upon all and to a class in a certain stage of civilization quite irresistible. There is no temple constructed by art like the great temple of nature, in beauty, grandeur, and space. It is in the silence of the grove, canopied by the blue heavens or the starry dome, that the feeble voice of man most easily influences the feelings of his fellows. A preacher of moderate abilities with a good voice in the open air, with a health-inspiring breeze, and the influences of nature, can act more decidedly than eloquence, reason, and logic all combined on the feelings of his hearers squeezed between four walls, inhaling the pestilential atmosphere of their own breath.

William Owen expressed polite wonderment at camp meetings when he visited Albion.

We passed the remains of a camp meeting, where the pulpit, benches, and the remains of some log cabins were still visible. We were told that these meetings sometimes last several days, during which time some one or other is speaking all the time, both day and night. In front of the pulpit is an open space, where those who become converted fall down and rage.

And George Flower gave a full description of one.

On a warm summer afternoon, as I was riding from Mt. Carmel, turning a point of wood, came suddenly on a scene that arrested my attention; and, as a stream of people were going in one direction, I joined them and went on. We were soon in front of the Methodist camp. It was in form of a hollow square. On the two sides opposite and on a portion of the third were the log huts, with roof sloping outward, occupied by families from a distance, furnished with bedding and a few simple cooking utensils; these were all, or nearly all, occupied. In the centre of the third side was an elevated platform for the preacher, in the shade of three tall, handsome oak trees, which stood immediately at its back. In front and below was what was called "the anxious pew," a space about fifteen feet square, enclosed by a light post-and-rail fence. The body of the square was covered with ranges of light and even sized logs, smoothed on one side by the axe, affording sitting room for about three hundred people.

There was an interlude in the service, and the seats were nearly vacant; people stood about in little groups, conversing, or welcoming some newly arrived acquaintance. Inside, the camp presented to me a singular scene. In one apartment was a family cooking, and the meal all going on, in company with acquaintances from without. In the next, a little prayer meeting; and all were kneeling at their devotions. In the front of the next division, a lively party of young and old chatting together in high glee. In the next stood a solitary man erect and with rigid mien, and eyes intently fixed on an open Bible held in both his hands. Outside, strangers were continually arriving, some in buggies and some on horseback, fastening their animals to the branches of the trees that in a semicircle stood round the camp.

I withdrew to a little distance to take a general view. Nothing could be prettier. The camp itself, standing as it did in the little prairie, surrounded by beautiful timber, was an interesting object. The various parties of youths and gay maidens with their many-colored scarfs and ribbons streaming in the wind gave to the whole an air of cheerfulness not to be exceeded. At a given signal, all assembled inside the camp and took their seats. The preacher ascended the stand, and began his discourse in a voice scarcely audible. As he raised it to a higher pitch, a sort of groan-like response could be heard from a few in the audience, and now and then an emphatic "amen!" As the preacher raised his voice from bass to tenor, so the responses, in groans, amens, and shouts of glory, increased in number and intensity. The scenes in the anxious pew were getting exciting, and people crowded around. My curiosity induced me to press forward to a closer view. I confess I was startled; but a moment's reflection checked any censure that is apt to arise in the breast of every man who sees doings different from his own. All real feeling is spontaneous; the mode of its display is conventional, a mere matter of taste. There were about fifteen persons then under the highest excitement, chiefly females. One man, a Yankee, a near neighbor of mine, was there rolling and groaning as if in extreme pain, and uttering loud cries for pardon. Among the many shouters and exclaimers, one respectable middle-aged female of pleasing personal appearance attracted my attention among the many extraordinary attitudes, erratic motions, and various voices and sounds in that extraordinary place. With eyes raised upward, arms raised straight about her head, incessantly clapping her hands and shouting glory, leaping continually upward as high as her strength would carry her, with all her fine black hair streaming down her back, and perspiration trickling down her face, she presented rather a fine picture of the frenzy. Two young women recently from Scotland were there, affected quite as strongly but rather differently. Short hysterical laughter, sobs, sighs, and weeping exhibited the depth and sincerity of their feelings.

The preacher lowered his voice; exclamations became fainter. He ceased; and silence was restored. It reminded me of those extraordinary scenes recorded in history of children, women, and men who went about for weeks and months, singing and shouting, the epidemic spreading wherever they went. But the scene in the anxious pew was more pandemonian than paradisical. Fear and flattery, mingled with fevered hope, formed the basis of their violent ejaculations and their many mournful sounds; all seemed to be fearing that the God they worshiped would bestow an eternity of torment for an error or a crime. I was impressed, and somewhat depressed, by what I had seen; for I felt no sympathy and could yield but partial approval. The social meeting of distant friends and acquaintance was the best feature of it all. I could not deny that the whole affair was well suited to the times and to the people.

Yet, because the religious issue had been such a sore point in the criticism of the settlement, Flower could not leave the subject without observing that "it should be remembered that neither Mr. Birkbeck nor myself came here as preachers or teachers of religion."

Religion we left to the people. If we differed from others in their speculation of things unseen and unknown, we tolerated all opinions and as far as was proper promoted the wishes of our neighbors. Doubtless we should have given a site for any building of a public purpose. If for religious purposes, we should never have put any hindrance to the building of a temple, a synagogue, a mosque, a pagoda, a church, or Friends meetinghouse; and this we should do without feeling ourselves committed to a single dogma contained in any one of their creeds.

vi

EVEN IN THE MIDST of laborious work and hardly less laborious play there was still time for quiet study and reflection for those so inclined. Both Flower and Birkbeck did find time to think about their new environment and to apply their European experience to its understanding. Flower, whose contribution was primarily historical, also wrote a pamphlet, *The Western Shepherd,* in which he argued the case for sheep raising on the prairies. It was Birkbeck, however, who could couple observation with scientific knowledge, both for his own pleasure and for the profit of the whole region.

Quite unexpected is a sentence in a letter to an English correspondent, written before Birkbeck's house was even finished, in which he thanks his friend for a telescope and comments that "this climate is favourable for astronomical observations, and it will add to our rational amusements." But not so surprising when we have George Flower's recollection that back in England "if Mr. Birkbeck was absent from the family party in the drawing room— and sometimes he was so, even when his house was full of visitors —he was sure to be found in a small study, a little room peculiarly his own, trying some chemical experiment, or analyzing some earth or new fossil that he picked up in his morning ramble in his chalk quarries." No record seems to remain that the astronomical observations did provide more than "rational amusement," but one striking document comes down to us as a result of Birkbeck's other scientific interests.

Mentioned earlier, his essay "On the Prairies" which he read before the Agricultural Society of Illinois was probably as learned a

treatise as any resident of the region could have produced in 1822.
The essay deals with several aspects of the prairies, including an
analysis of the soil, but the most interesting part is the speculation
on the origin of prairies and the reason they are treeless. Why
these odd geographical features existed was a question intelligent
visitors had been asking since the prairies were first known. Faux
put the question to Birkbeck in 1819 to learn only that he did not
have

any hypothesis on the subject of the immense prairies.
Though but partially planted with timber, he does not think
the soil unfriendly to the growth of it, but deems the cause to
be in the annual fires which run over the surface, checking the
young plants, or destroying the seeds, or rather in a want of
seed; and the decaying, dwarfish appearance of the trees he
attributes to the same fiery cause. That the prairies have been
lakes of water he much doubts.

By 1822, however, Birkbeck's explanation was as simple as it was
reasonable, containing an explanation for the lack of trees that
occurred to him rather than to Americans, again because of his
different perspective.

An agricultural observer who has been accustomed to the
soils of Europe, particularly of Great Britain, where clay,
sand, gravel, calcareous earth, and their admixtures in
every conceivable proportion may be seen within the compass of a few miles or possibly on the same farm, is struck
by the absolute identity of surface which here prevails over
a region comprehending at least twenty millions of acres.
Here the difference of quality depends almost wholly on the
nature of the subsoil and the depth of the vegetable strata.
This is greatest on elevated plains, next on the tops of rounded
swells, and least on steep declivities and hilly uplands; just as
such a deposit, having been nearly of an equal depth in its
formation, would be left by a lake gradually flowing off
through an increasing outlet.
A large proportion of this rich country consists, as I have
before observed, of extensive plains. The surface of these
plains is generally undulating, but not sufficiently so to

break the force of the winds. They are for the most part entirely bare of trees, but clothed with luxuriant herbage.

Those portions of the country which are hilly and broken are generally covered with timber although thinner soiled than the plains, and in this respect less adapted to its growth; but the inequalities of the surface afford mutual shelter. The valleys through which the rivers have their course are also well timbered; and the minor streams are marked by a strip of wood which finds protection from the wind in the narrow and deep hollows with which they intersect the prairies. The woodland tracts appear in very many instances to be extending themselves, being skirted by groves of entirely young timber of extraordinary beauty and vigorous growth.

Those who have traversed the treeless plains and wooded valleys of Europe, and who are aware of the extreme difficulty of raising plantations of timber in exposed situations, will readily conceive that the nakedness of these plains is owing to the want of shelter. But this, which I believe to be the real cause of the existence of our prairies, may not easily satisfy the native American, who has ever considered timber as the earth's natural covering.

Had the cultivation of this continent commenced at the foot of the Rocky Mountains instead of the Eastern coast, when it had reached the Western limits of the open country and was meditating an inroad on the forests of the East as we are now encroaching on the prairies of the West, speculation would have taken the opposite side and the inquiry would have been, "Whence those interminable woods, which obstruct us at every step in our progress to the Atlantic?" A question not more easily solved than the one before us. It is indeed a matter of astonishment that on so vast a tract hardly a spot of earth should be found accessible to the sun's rays and covered with green turf, excepting the bleak glades of the Allegheny Mountains and the alluvial meadows on the seashore.

A recollection of the country I crossed on my journey from the East confirms the opinions I have since formed on this

subject from a view of the prairies; viz. that considerable inequalities of surface are essential to the first growth of timber, but that once established it extends itself by virtue of
shelter of its own creation over exposures where it could not
have made a commencement—that hills and dales are naturally woody, and plains are naturally bare.

8

"I pray you to count the cost

before you make the purchase."

THE LAST MAJOR SUBJECT to engage Birkbeck's pen
before his death was the issue of slavery. To him and most of
the other English settlers it was incredible that any Americans,
boasting of their freedom, should want to preserve the system of
slavery and even extend it legally into the free state of Illinois. Having passed up Virginia and other Southern states because of the
presence of slavery there, Birkbeck and the Flowers had no intention of letting its baneful shadow fall over their community if it lay
in their power to prevent it. Their common aversion and their wise
understanding of the social effects of slavery even on those who
owned no slaves were well expressed by Flower.

A slave, although in human form, is a being despoiled of all
the rights of humanity, purposely kept in ignorance, driven
by the lash or the fear of it to his work, for which his master
gives him no pay. An unfortunate wretch from whom all the
good to which his nature aspires is withheld; steeped in all
that is vicious and depraved. This is a slave; the man made
brute. To this poor degraded being is the slaveholder obliged
to entrust his property, his domestic animals, and his children. We desire not that compound of society found in a
slave state, a degenerate European aristocracy and a full-

blooded African barbarism! Besides, we acknowledge no property in man. With principles and practices so opposite there can be no peace; let us therefore keep apart.

Under every form of government, even the most despotic, where property in man is disavowed there may and do exist a variety of ties, both political and social, not severed by any line of distinct demarkation. They may have family connections and many other interests in common. The rich are frequently brought to poverty, and the poor often become rich. These classes are not naturally hostile to each other, for they have a common interest; friends in peace and companions in war. But in a nation composed of free and slave there is no society. One portion of the people is separated from the other by an impassable gulf. The laws made by one class are known to the other only by their severity. Whatever this may be it is no republic. Give to this tyrannical confederacy some proper name.

In the southern portions of both Indiana and Illinois, slavery existed in fact if not in law as a result of the connivance of judges and juries and such quasi-legal measures as ninety-nine year indentures. W. N. Blane gives us an incident in Vincennes that should never have happened north of the Ohio River but did.

A Missouri planter attended by two slaves, a man and woman, was travelling to St. Louis in a small wheeled carriage called a Dearborn, and had stopped at Vincennes to rest his horses. Now the day before I arrived both his slaves had run away. Trying to travel all night when nearly barefooted, the man had both his feet so severely frostbitten that he could not proceed. Consequently he was overtaken by some people sent after him by his master, and was brought back to Vincennes the very evening after my arrival. When I got up early the next morning, I saw the poor old slave, who had passed the night in the kitchen, with a heavy chain padlocked round both his legs. A man from North Carolina, who had ridden in company with me from White River, where he had been delayed, came into the room at the same time I did; and, although a slaveholder himself, was touched with compassion at seeing the miserable state of this old Negro. Having procured the key, he took off one of the padlocks, and desired the unhappy being to come towards the fire in order to warm his frostbitten legs and feet, which were much swollen and were no doubt very painful. The poor slave was so lame he could hardly move, but managed to come and sit down by the hearth.

The Carolinian then said to him, "You have committed a great crime, as you must be well aware—how came you to do it?" The Negro replied, "Master, I am an old man, upwards of sixty years of age, and I have been all my life in bondage. Several white men told me that as this was a free state, if I could run away I should be free; and you know, master, what a temptation that was! I thought if I could spend my few remaining days in freedom I should die happy." But, replied the Carolinian, "You were a fool to run away; you know you are much better off as a slave than if you were free." "Ah! master," said the poor old Negro, "no one knows where the shoe pinches but he who wears it."

Just at this time, in came the master of the slave, and after swearing a terrible oath that he would punish him, desired him to go and get ready the carriage. The poor old man answered that he was in too great pain even to stand upright. Upon this the brute, saying "I will make you move, you old rascal," sent out for a "cowhide." Now the sort of whip called by this name is the most formidable one I ever saw. It is made of twisted strips of dried cow's skin; and from its weight, its elasticity, and the spiral form in which the thongs are twisted must, when applied to the bare back, inflict the most intolerable torture.

The wife of the tavernkeeper coming in and hearing that the Negro was going to be flogged merely said, "I would rather it had not been on the Sabbath." For my part, I thought it signified very little upon what day of the week such an atrocious act of wickedness was committed; so after trying in vain to obtain a relaxation of the punishment, I called for my horse, determined not to hear the cries of the suffering old man. Yet even when I had ridden far from the town, my imagination still pictured to me the horrors that were then being performed; and I should have thought myself deficient in human kindness if I had not cursed from the bottom of my heart every government that, by tolerating slavery, could sanction a scene like this.

The Constitution of Illinois had, of course, excluded slavery, and had also clearly stated that indentures were invalid unless entered into by persons in a perfect state of freedom. But constitutions could be unmade as well as made. Blane reported in 1822 that

it is the intention of the people of the Illinois to constitute themselves a slaveholding state. So powerful is avarice and so weak is patriotism that many inhabitants to whom I spoke upon the subject acknowledged that it would ultimately be a great curse to the state; but this was indifferent to them, as they intended going away. These wretches think that if their state can be made a slave state many of the wealthy Southern planters will emigrate to it, and that thus the price of land will be increased. As they wish to sell theirs, many will on that account vote for slavery.

This state of affairs had been made possible by a spectacular stroke of misjudgment that occurred back in Territorial days. Near Shawneetown there were large salt deposits which were a valuable natural resource in the salt-starved Ohio Valley. These salines could and did furnish a reliable source of wealth, but it was believed that both for economic and physical reasons no white man could work them. Hence, as Flower says:

The salines were reserved from sale by the United States. The Government leased these salines to individuals, and afterward to the state of Illinois, allowing slaves to be brought into the Territory for the purpose of working them. Under the Territorial law, hundreds and thousands of slaves were introduced into the southern part of the Territory, chiefly from the states of Kentucky and Tennessee.

For all practical purposes, this part of the Territory was as much a slave state as any of the states south of the Ohio River. To roll a barrel of salt once a year, or put salt into a salt cellar, was sufficient excuse for any man to hire a slave, and raise a field of corn. Slaves were not only worked at the saline, they were waiters in taverns, draymen, and used in all manner of work on the north side of the Ohio River. As villages and settlements extended farther, the disease was carried with them. A black man or a black woman was found in many families, in defiance of law, up to the confines of our settlement sixty miles north, and in one instance in it. In some, but not many, cases they were held defiantly; in others, evasively, under some quibble or construction of law; in most cases, under a denial of slavery. "Oh, no! not slaves; old servants attached to the family; don't like to part with them," etc. And in many cases it was so.

Now, in 1822, time was running out on the limitation imposed by the Constitution in Article 4, where it was stated that "No person, bound to labor in any other State, shall be hired to labor in this State, excepting within the tract reserved for the salt-works, near Shawneetown, nor even at that place for a longer term than one year, at any one time. Nor shall it be allowed there after the year 1825." Leaseholders of the salines stood to profit merely by getting the time limit extended, yet in order to appeal widely to enough voters, most of whom were land rich and money poor, they boldly proposed changing the Constitution to make the whole of Illinois a slave state. Thus, the argument ran, everybody would prosper (except the Negroes, of course), land values would soar, and anyone could sell out at a handsome profit to the Southern slave-owners who would rush to buy Illinois land. To people committed to the belief of an automatic rise in land value as a result of increased population, and who expected to get rich from the unearned increment merely by waiting, this must have been a powerful argument. Besides, there was an abundance of cheap land still to be taken up farther west, where one could start all over; as long as that remained closed to slavery, the Illinois holdings would prove to be a bonanza.

Getting the Constitution amended was a complicated process which hinged on a state-wide convention, as Blane explains.

The legislature of Illinois meets only once in two years; and by the Constitution, if any alteration be required all that can be done by the legislature in which the proposition for an alteration is brought forward is to advise the people to enable the next legislature to call a convention of the whole state for the purpose of making the said alteration. In order to give this advice, there must be a majority of two-thirds. I grieve to say that when I was there this majority had been obtained. As, however, the convention cannot be called for two years, there is some little hope that the emigrants from the Northern and New England states, who are all strongly opposed to slavery, may increase so as to make head against the proposition. There is also some little chance that the general government of the United States will, as it ought, interfere. Neither, however, of these chances appeared to me to be very great.

Those who have been the cause of this convention are the men who have come from the slaveholding states. On their success in getting the votes of two-thirds of the legislature, the conventionalists assembled at two or three public dinners at which they drank, among other toasts: "The state of Illinois—give us plenty of Negroes, a little industry, and she will distribute her treasures." "A new constitution, purely republican, which may guarantee to the people of Illinois the peaceable enjoyment of all species of property."

What mortified me the most was to find that many of the English at Albion were in favour of this iniquitous plan. Some few indeed of the more respectable are opposed to it; and Birkbeck and Flower have even declared that should it be carried into effect they will leave the state. It remains to be seen how far they are sincere. There are, on the other hand, certain miscreants who have fled from their own country to avoid, as they tell you, the tyranny of tithes and taxes, and who have yet no hesitation in giving their vote for merciless personal slavery and the consequent entailing of endless misery and degradation upon tens of thousands of their fellow men. It is the conduct of such unprincipled wretches as these that gives a handle to the serviles of Europe to declaim against liberty by showing that there are some men utterly unworthy to enjoy it. It always annoyed me that any person in a free country should uphold slavery; but I felt it doubly mortifying to discover that among such wretches there were Englishmen.

Therefore, those determined to resist the encroachment of slavery had to find a way to block off the convention. When the issue came to a vote in 1824, the matter to be decided was whether or not a convention should be held. Until the very moment the election began, it was Birkbeck's chosen duty to find arguments persuasive enough to convince his fellow citizens to go to the polls and vote no.

ii

HE BEGAN A SERIES OF LETTERS, published in various Illinois newspapers, signed with the name Jonathan Freeman. The Jonathan Freeman letters covered the whole range of arguments against slavery, and the answers they provoked likewise covered the range of arguments for it. These exchanges represent in miniature the great debate that raged through our history all the way down to the Civil War. There is little point in reproducing full details of the debate here; it is only necessary to show how Birkbeck operated his campaign.

He was frankly propagandistic. Gone was the lofty air of detachment that had characterized his part in the paper war over the settlement. Now he appealed to reason, but with equal facility he appealed to passion—even to prejudice. This was a last-ditch fight that had to be won, by whatever means would work.

In the first Jonathan Freeman letter he committed a serious mistake in tactics. Knowing that his appeal must reach the hearts of simple people, he attempted a folksy approach. But the "emperor of the prairies" was anything but a folksy man. He knew the words; what he devastatingly lacked was the tune. His letter was a sitting duck for the accurate marksmanship of John Rifle, as an anonymous reply was signed. Here, rearranged in the form of a dialogue, are a few of Jonathan Freeman's comments, and the compliments John Rifle returned.

JONATHAN FREEMAN

I am a poor man; that is to say I have no money. But I have a house to cover me, and the rest of us, a stable for my horses, and a little barn, on a quarter of good land paid up at the land office, with a middling fine clearing upon it and a good fence. I have about thirty head of cattle, some of them prime, and a good chance of hogs; and by the labors of my boys we make a shift to get along.

JOHN RIFLE

This Freeman lives near the Wabash, and is a neighbor of mine, and from what I know of him, I am certain there is something not right about this letter. I know that he could not have wrote it himself, for two reasons; first, the man has not been sober for three months; and, second, he can't write. Freeman used to be an honest, industrious man, until about a year ago, when he got into the habit of going to Albion, keeping company with the English, and drinking beer. He has got so haunted to the place that there is no breaking him off; and it will be the ruin of him, for beer, you know, has the effect of stupefying and clouding the mind, as we may see by all the English that come over. Some chance ones are peart enough, but in a general way they have what I call a beer-fog over them.

JONATHAN FREEMAN

There is a great stir among the land-jobbers and politicians to get slaves into the country.

JOHN RIFLE

Does he mean the Legislature? If so, the people will not thank him for libelling two-thirds of their representatives as land-jobbers.

JONATHAN FREEMAN

The planters are great men, and will ride about mighty grand, with umbrellas over their heads when I and my boys are working perhaps bareheaded in the hot sun.

JOHN RIFLE

Do the people of Kentucky ride about, mighty grand, with umbrellas over their heads? We have a great many Kentuckians, Tennesseeans, and North Carolinians in this state, and we don't find that they are more grand and proud than other folks. As for working bareheaded in the sun, I did not know that it was usual to do that in this country. They say the poor devils in the old country have to do it; but there is nothing to prevent their covering their heads here; and if they are too lazy to do so, I say let them go bareheaded.

JONATHAN FREEMAN

Negroes are middling light-fingered, and I suspect we should have to lock up our cabins when we left home, and if we were to leave our linen out all night we might chance to miss it in the morning.

JOHN RIFLE

This is as much as to say the blacks are thieves, and therefore we will not admit them among us as slaves, and keep them under control; but we will let them in as free people, and allow them the chance of stealing like gentlemen. I am a little surprised that the objection to light-fingered people should come from that quarter, for I am told that the people of a certain island over the water are so highly gifted in this way that they can scarcely keep their hands out of each other's pockets, and that they are hung for it by dozens; but perhaps they wish to keep the business in their own hands in this country.

In the following letters Birkbeck sensibly dropped the spurious backwoods manner and spoke in his own cultured voice. A mosaic of these letters reveals how he played on fear to influence opinion.

JONATHAN FREEMAN

Look at the Carolinas and Georgia. Consider their constant alarms; the system of nightly patrols, which, horrible as it truly is, is but the beginning of sorrows, something by way of

prevention. As yet the power and the show of fighting has
been all on one side, and so seems to be the suffering. The
white man holds the rifle and brandishes the cowskin, while
the wretched victims, like the souls under the altar, are crying, "How long, oh, Lord, holy and true, dost thou not judge
and avenge our blood?" But is the suffering all on one side?
How fares it with the trembling females when their husbands
and fathers are out on this hateful but necessary duty? Do you
think they sleep, and if they do what are their dreams?

I pray you to count the cost before you make the purchase.
The white man, even the white woman (odious to contemplate), must be ready to apply the lash; and there would be
an incessant war of plunder in which the whites would have
to act on the defensive. If mischief to your property by theft
would be increased a hundredfold, so would danger from
fire, not through negligence only but through design. What
precautions are found necessary in slave states against this
devouring calamity! Then, too, would arise an overwhelming
flood of gross immorality, carrying all decency before it.
But I restrain my pen; the catalogue of calamities would be
endless.

Now a clergyman—or at least someone so signing himself—
entered the debate to quote chapter and verse in defense of
slavery.

THE REV. W. K.

Several gentlemen who are raising a great hue and cry against
the introduction of slavery into this state appear to be influenced strongly by religious considerations and scruples
of conscience. One would conclude from what they say and
write on this subject (if we can believe them sincere) that
they really suppose it contrary to the spirit and precepts of
our holy religion to reduce the black, curled-headed Africans
to a state of bondage to white men, and bring them into the
Western Hemisphere, and compel some of them to serve the
good Christians of Illinois.

It is sufficient for our purpose to quote from the 25th

chapter of Leviticus, the 44th, 45th, and 46th verses: "Both thy bondmen and thy bondmaids which thou shalt have, shall be of the heathen that are round about you, and of them shall ye buy bondmen and bondmaids. Moreover, the children of the strangers that do sojourn among you, of them shall you buy, and of their families, which are with you, which they beget in your land, and they shall be your possession; they shall be your bondmen forever." It is very evident that the African Negroes are to be considered as "strangers" and "heathen" to us Christians, who stand in the place and footsteps of the ancient Jews, God's chosen people; and whatever was lawful for them to do is lawful for us also.

Birkbeck readily answered with his own Scriptural citations—chiefly from Exodus and Leviticus, where conduct toward strangers is considered—and squelched the sanctimonious W. K.

JONATHAN FREEMAN

I have attentively considered the passages you have quoted, and I learn from them that the laws of Moses permitted the Hebrews, according to the custom of those barbarous ages, to buy bondmen and bondmaids of the heathen round about them; but I do not discover that they were permitted to make them slaves. Nothing is said respecting their "curled hair" or sable complexions, or any title we have to stand in the place of the ancient Jews in this particular, or any other. Allow me to remind you that the "black, curled-headed Africans" are men, having the same relation to the Universal Father with yourself, or it may be nearer, for it is written, "he giveth grace to the humble; but he beholdeth the proud afar off."

In other letters Jonathan Freeman addressed a series of queries to the legal profession about the legality of introducing slavery, questions persons without legal training could easily answer, and also wrote on the progressive abolition of slavery taking place elsewhere in the world, including the British colonies.

But tempers were too heated for calm reason to prevail. Now

Jonathan Freeman became the victim of a vicious personal attack by a writer who signed himself "Americanus." This compelled Birkbeck to lay aside anonymity as he tried to smoke his new opponent out into the open.

In publishing my sentiments I perform a duty, as I conceive, to myself, my family, and my adopted country. In subscribing my name to those sentiments, I give my fellow citizens the means of judging of their sincerity by the stake I hold in the general welfare, which is equal to that of "Americanus," whoever he may be. Having been an inhabitant of the territory before it became a state, I am as old a citizen as any in it; therefore, no man has a right to stigmatize me as a foreigner; and no man of honor, under a fictitious signature, would call his neighbor a "foreign incendiary."

He represents me as a Quaker, whether by way of compliment or reproach is immaterial, because it is not a fact; nor do I appear in the garb and character of that sect. But what bearing has this on the question? I object to slavery not as a Quaker but as a man and an American citizen.

And to "Americanus" himself he wrote:

An "exile," too, you are pleased to style me. Unless you chance to be of the few among us who were born in Illinois you are also an exile from the land of your nativity. Whether this be to either of us a matter of disgrace or otherwise will depend on the causes of our expatriation. Come forward, sir, in your own name, and state those causes; let us know your standing, with the occasion and circumstances of your removal. I will do the like; and the public may decide how far you are entitled to reproach *me* as an exile.

Needless to say, the invitation was not accepted.

These letters were but a part of the state-wide defense of the existing anti-slavery Constitution. Others labored as well in the good cause, so that it is impossible to assess the proportional weight of Birkbeck's accomplishment. Nevertheless, the southern portion of the state, containing the bulk of the population, was a crucial area, and here Birkbeck's voice was heard clearly and long. When the vote came, the convention failed to carry and Illinois was saved from becoming a slave state. Yet in Albion alone the contest was embarrassingly close, with 153 votes against the convention and 135 for it.

As the only personal reward he was to receive for his work, Birkbeck was appointed Secretary of State by Governor Coles. But when the legislature next met, such was the animosity against Birkbeck and so strong were the pro-slavery forces that the appointment was not confirmed, and he held office only about two months in all.

iii

THOUGH THE SLAVERY QUESTION had been settled with finality for the state of Illinois, the safety of Negroes in the southern part of the state had been by no means assured. Extra-legal methods of exploiting Negroes had been known before, and they could be used again. On the personal level, events that occurred in the settlement in the persecution of Negroes and those whites who befriended them were as unpleasant as before. "In our neighborhood," wrote Flower, "the recent contest left the feelings sore. A grudge was owed us," and it was more often than not paid off with interest. He tells of the constant harassment and of the costly plan of resettlement he had embarked upon even before the convention question was settled.

Three black men and their families—Gilbert Burris, Neptune Calvin, and Matthew Luther—came from the neighborhood of Carmi, for employment. They appeared to be very decent men, had been brought up in the habits of industry and sobriety by the Shakers, by whom they were emancipated and brought to this state. Their papers were examined, found to be regular, and were recorded. Luther was a miller, and attended the mill in Albion that was built by my father and after his death owned by me. The other two were farmers, and right good corn farmers, too. To these I rented land on the usual terms of ten bushels of corn to the acre. To us it made no difference, black or white; if they did our work we paid them their wages. Whenever they or their little property received injury from wilful theft or violence I gave them protection. I soon found this in some sort to be an offence; and to my surprise, by some Eastern men as well as Southern. We were verdant in those days, and did not know that "black men had no rights that white men need respect."

A black man named Arthur, who had been in my service for more than a year, was suddenly arrested and taken before a magistrate, a New Englander, and claimed as a slave. As he came from Indiana, where he had resided many years, I pleaded that he could not be a slave—the laws of the territory and the state alike forbidding slavery. They claimed to hold him by an indenture law for ninety-nine years. I pleaded the nullity of the law. Our poor magistrate, Moses Michaels, who never dared say boo to a goose, after spending half a day and going over to another magistrate three miles off to consult, did not give the black man up, but put me in unreasonably heavy bonds of two thousand dollars for his appearance at the next county court, to be held at Palmyra on the Great Wabash, nineteen miles and five months of time distant.

Long before the assembling of the court, parties were sent over from Indiana to steal the man away that I might be mulcted in the penalty of the bond, whilst they might run him off and pocket his price when sold as a slave. The interval between the decision of the magistrate and the meeting of the county court was spent in constant watchfulness, mental disturbance, and frequent skirmishes, often imperiling life.

The man, Arthur, appeared duly at court. John McLean of Shawneetown was counsel for plaintiff; Judge McDonald of Vincennes for me, as defendant. The counsel conferred together. McDonald exhibited a decision of the supreme court of Indiana in a similar case. John McLean was too good a lawyer, and too shrewd a man, to allow any case to come into court where the law was dead against him. So the case was never called, and the man returned to my service as a free man. So this case was terminated in Illinois—that is to say, after I had paid my counsel his fifty-dollar fee.

When at Vincennes some months afterward, I was served

with a writ and arrested by the sheriff at the instance of the
claimant of Arthur. I had to choose between going to jail and
giving bond. The latter was easily effected. Before the meeting
of the Indiana court, I received several threatening letters to
deter me from appearing at court. When the time arrived
three friends accompanied me there, all armed. The law was
again in my favor. But an enemy more mighty than the kid-
napper fell upon us. A terrible epidemic resembling the
yellow fever prevailed at this time at Vincennes. We were all
four of us taken down with it, and lay long in a precarious
situation between life and death.

Another case of this kind from Indiana produced another
set of tactics on the part of our opponents. A man of color was
working for me. His pretended claimant, with suitable associates, suddenly surrounded the cabin of the black and had
him bound before the alarm at my house, a short distance
away, was given. In this case the kidnappers gained their
point, taking him before a magistrate of pro-slavery tendencies. He gave the man up to the claimant, who took him into
Indiana, and the man was never heard of afterward. I presented the claimant, a man of note and in official station, to
the grand jury. Whilst stating the case, one of the jurymen
called out with some excitement that the man was quite right
in taking the Negro. In turning to leave the room I saw at
once the case was decided, and so it was. The bill was refused.
The majority of the jury were decidedly pro-slavery.

My presentation to the grand jury gave great umbrage to
all in Indiana who held black men, properly entitled to their
freedom, under their fraudulent indenture law which had
already been decided by their supreme court to be null,
void, and of no effect. Kidnapping of whole families of free
blacks in the south of Indiana was no uncommon thing. The
moral sense of the community received no shock at such outrages. A horse thief was held to stricter accountability than a
man thief.

In the timbered regions of Indiana, on the White River,
lived a set of desperadoes who had the appellation of "White
River Indians." Among these were a family sunk low in bar-

barism and all the grosser vices. The sons of this family, three in number, associated with one or two others more respectable but who would not at that period decline a foray on the pro-slavery side, were sent over to molest us, especially me and my family, even to the taking of life. Yet these wretches found harbor and encouragement among the Southern settlers around us.

Suddenly alarmed by the sound of human voices, the barking of dogs, and the report of firearms, I ran over to my father's house a little before midnight. An Englishman, Thomas Harding, who lived at my father's as farm servant, having occasion to step out of the house was knocked down by the blow of a club on the back of his head by some man who stood concealed in the shadow, close to the wall of the house. My father, alarmed by the noise, went out, saw one man retreating from the courtyard into the woods, and another lying bleeding on the ground, apparently lifeless. He dragged the wounded man into the house and closed the door. At first we thought it an attempt at housebreaking. But finding who the parties were, and their object, we assembled our forces. Many shots were exchanged, and the marauders for a time driven off.

The annoyance from these fellows became so great that we determined to rid ourselves of them at all hazards. Myself, Mr. Hugh Ronalds, Mr. Henry Birkett, together with a constable, mounted and went in pursuit. We overtook them after a hard gallop on a hot summer's day, in the open woods, ten miles distant. We were equal in number, man for man. They with rifles, we with pistols. Whilst the constable was reading his warrant, we rode up, got within the rifle guard, and presented our pistols, each to his man. At this juncture, a very ill-looking fellow, one of the gang, suddenly rode up at full speed. This gave them the advantage of one in number, of which the last comer instantly availed himself by jumping from his horse and leveling his rifle at Mr. Ronalds, whom he doubtless would have shot had not the man I was guarding as suddenly leaped from his horse and knocked up the rifle when in the act of being discharged.

Amid oaths, boastings, refusals to surrender or return, when everyone was meditating murder on the other, our Yankee constable brought forward a quart bottle of whisky, with a deprecatory smile and good-humored voice—"Now, boys, come and take a drink; now come along with us quiet, and we'll treat you like gentlemen." The effect was sudden; the transition of feeling complete. We all laughed, and did as our worthy constable bade us—at least, all our prisoners did. We returned to Albion riding in pairs, with our arms in our hands.

These and similar outrages on ourselves, and assaults on the peaceable blacks settled among us, were of frequent occurrence. Seeing no hope of just treatment to the free colored people that lived on my lands or of relieving myself from the trouble of defending them, I proposed that they should go to Haiti. When they acceded to my proposal, I thought it due to them and myself to acquire more specific information of the island, and of the terms on which they would be received. For this purpose, I employed Mr. Robert Grayham (formerly an English merchant), a gentleman who spoke the French language with fluency. I gave him five hundred dollars to bear his expenses, with a letter to General Boyer, then President of Haiti, representing the case and asking an asylum for my party of blacks, big and little, about thirty in number; also for other free people of color of the United States if they chose to go there. Mr. Grayham returned in good time. He gave me a very pleasing account of his visit to the island, his interview with Inginac, the Secretary, and with Boyer, the President.

When Boyer heard from Mr. Grayham that I had given five hundred dollars to get this information for the poor blacks, he, in the handsomest manner, handed him the amount, requesting him to give it to me, which he did on his return.

The following spring, the colored emigrants prepared to take their departure. Among them were three brothers, men of extraordinary stature, standing six feet four and over. This family of Joneses, able-bodied men and good farmers,

with two or three other colored families, formerly lived
higher up the Wabash and were mustered into the service
of the United States by General Harrison, who formed a
colored company to aid in defending the frontier during
the war in 1812. Provided with a good flatboat, stocked with
sufficient provisions for their inland navigation and sea voyage, well furnished with axes, hoes, and plows, this party of
colored people left the mouth of Bonpas Creek, where Grayville now stands, in March, 1823, under the guidance and
care of Mr. Robert Grayham, the only white man on board.

The testimonials of their freedom were complete, signed
by the clerk of the county, the secretary of state, and by
Governor Coles himself. They floated down the Wabash
and entered the Ohio in safety. As they were floating quietly
and peaceably down the stream, when opposite to Shawneetown they were hailed and invited to land, which Mr. Grayham acceded to, having many acquaintances and being well
known in the town. When about to depart, he was compelled
to remain, with threats of sinking his boat if he made the
attempt to go. He and the people were forcibly detained for
four and twenty hours. They were at length suffered to depart amid much confusion and violent denunciations. Of the
peaceable demeanor and lawful objects of the emigrants there
was no question. By a strange inconsistency, the very people
who profess to dislike the existence of free blacks among
us were the most bitter opponents to their removal.

Upon his arrival at New Orleans, Mr. Grayham, as a
matter of courtesy, waited upon the mayor and informed him
that his boat was manned by free colored people from Illinois
and Indiana who were going, with their families, to Haiti.
This official immediately replied that he would send them
all to jail, and, if they were not sent out of the city in eight
days, he would sell them all for slaves. The remonstrances of
Mr. Grayham against such violent aggression upon the persons of free inhabitants of the United States passing to a
foreign country was to no effect. The men were thrown into
prison. But at the intercession of a humane friend, Mr. Gilbert, the women and children were permitted to remain on

board their own boat; also two men, for whose appearance and good behavior this friend gave a bond. Mr. Grayham, placed in this unpleasant situation, hastily took a passage in a vessel about to sail in three days for St. Domingo. The poor men, deprived of the means of earning anything on the wharves, and more than all they had demanded of them for jail fees, etc., were unable to pay their passage money and would actually have been sold as slaves by the mayor of New Orleans had not Mr. Grayham promptly drawn on me for the necessary funds—three hundred and sixty dollars—to carry them out of the country. Thus were the free inhabitants of the United States, while peaceably pursuing their way to a neighboring country, without fault or crime imputed or alleged against them, threatened with the doom of slavery if they did not submit to the extortion of their money under the title of jail fees, by the chief magistrate of a city of this republic boasting the inalienable and inherent rights of man and vaunting itself as the most enlightened nation of the earth.

The mayor of New Orleans was a refugee from Haiti, which accounts, in some degree, for the unusual violence he displayed on the occasion. But anxieties were not yet at an end. The brig, often becalmed, was long on its passage.

In the meantime, many sinister reports began to be spread about, and afterward more openly circulated, that Mr. Grayham and myself had inveigled the black men, and, under pretence of sending them to a land of liberty, had sold them all for slaves in the South. The return of Mr. Grayham some months afterward with a stock of goods to open a store, in the eyes of many confirmed the report. It was several months (and I confess to some anxiety during the time) before I could confute these slanders by the publication of any letters, either from Mr. Grayham or the colored emigrants. They came, at last, from both sources—from the poor people, rejoicing in their change of country, and thanking me for my assistance in getting them there.

The emigration of this small colony of blacks from Illinois produced movements of greater importance than were involved in their own personal destinies. So well pleased were the rulers of Haiti with the efficient farming, sober habits, and general industry of the Illinois emigrants that they conceived the idea of encouraging the free blacks of the United States to emigrate on a much larger scale. For this purpose, the Haitian Government sent their citizen Granville, a well-informed and well-educated man, on a mission to encourage the emigration of free people of color, and offered fourteen dollars a head as passage money to Haiti.

His mission was successful so far as numbers were concerned. Five thousand or more went, chiefly from the cities of New York and Baltimore. But these city-bred Africans were not farmers like the Illinois men. Barbers, waiters, and a large portion of them found in the lower strata of city life afforded poor materials for any beneficial purpose, and the removal of most of them was a disappointment to themselves and to the Haitian Government.

Thus ends the black chapter of our history.

9

"This was the country we had found."

A S THE PIONEER PERIOD of the English Settlement drew
to a close, several saddening events occurred to sap the enthusiasm and weaken the strength of the two founders. Birkbeck
was distressed by the course his son Richard was taking, Richard
who had married but was unable to carry the burdens imposed on
the head of an independent family by backwoods life. Richard had
long complained that he could read and write like his father, yet it
seemed his lot to dig from sun to sun, and he thought there was no
justice in such a hard life. Unfortunately, momentary escape from
his dreary existence could be had for twenty-five cents, the cost of
a *gallon* of whiskey. Writing to his English brother-in-law late in
1822, Morris Birkbeck said that Richard

has unhappily turned his back, for ever I fear, on everything that renders life worth having. He has sacrificed all—
his family, his friends, his property, his health, and his
character to that execrable vice intemperance. The degradation of mind and body in which this detestable habit finishes
is most lamentable. Poor Richard! he seems to have laid
violent hands on everything but his wretched existence, and
has wandered away towards New Orleans, with what purpose I know not. Afflicting as this is, his absence is a relief
to our feelings. His wife is an object of great commiseration.

Happily there are no children. I gave him a fine farm, with
stock and capital amply sufficient. He made a show of industry for a little time; but that inveterate, cursed habit
soon returned, and everything went to ruin. He grew hateful
to himself and hated everything, and, I suppose, everybody.
What is to be the winding up, heaven only knows!

Richard as readily wandered back from New Orleans, and kept a
school for a time at Albion. Now he attributed all his troubles to
Gilbert Pell, his brother-in-law, a native of New York whose marriage to his sister Elizabeth he had opposed from the first. And
going from bad to worse, he at last left the settlement entirely,
enticed away by the glittering promises of Robert Owen's com-
munistic scheme of a society with much high thinking and little
hard work.

In June, 1825, Birkbeck's troubles came to an end. William Hall,
a settler near Birkbeck's farm, put down in his diary: "On Friday
happened the melancholy catastrophe of Mr. Birkbeck's death,
who was drowned in Fox River on his return from Harmonie,"
adding that the body "was not found till the day following, when it
was brought up with an umbrella firmly grasped in the right hand"
—a grotesque gesture marking Birkbeck an Englishman to the
very last.

William Clark gave further details in a letter to Richard Bush,
Birkbeck's English brother-in-law.

He had been with his son Bradford to Harmonie to visit
Mr. Owen, and was on his return with him home when about
four miles from that place they came to a stream called Fox
River which they had before passed by a ferry, but unfortunately at this time the boat had been mischievously taken
away or sunk, which obliged them either to return or swim
with the horses, an expedient very common in this country.
Morris was ill-mounted, and his son not recovered from an
illness that had deprived him of the use of his legs and at that
time used a crutch. They however ventured, and might have
done very well had the horses performed as they usually do,
but it so happened that Bradford's horse plunged and threw
him in the deep water, and he was just making the opposite
bank by swimming when he perceived his father unhorsed and

struggling in the stream. He directly swam to his assistance, but being encumbered by a greatcoat and weak from illness, after several ineffectual attempts, had just life enough to reach the shore. It would seem strange that Morris, who could swim, should be so lost, but his horse appeared to have sunk outright and rose no more; and by a mark that appeared on his rider's forehead must have been struck by the animal. His umbrella was also found fastened by the string round his fingers, which might contribute to disable him. His body was next day conveyed to Harmonie and buried there with all possible respect, sincerely lamented by all that had the pleasure of his slightest acquaintance.

The troubles he has lately had from the circumstances of his family make this sad event the less to be deplored on his account, his feelings having had a visible effect on his health and spirits. His son and daughter Pell lately left his house to live at New York; Bradford dangerously ill at that unwholesome place Natchez, Charles in the same state at home, with other sources of vexation seemed to press on his mind very heavily lately, and I was pleased when after much persuasion he went to Harmonie to recruit his spirits. He was much pleased with Mr. Owen and his reception there, and was returning home much delighted and his health improved by the journey when this sad calamity happened on the 2nd of this month.

The loss of their worthy parent will probably give a new direction to several others of the family.

It did. His sons Bradford and Charles, untouched by Richard's dissipation but inheritors of their father's adventuresome spirit, also deserted the settlement and went to Mexico to seek their fortune in mining. Prudence Birkbeck had become estranged from her husband, the second-generation Irishman Francis Hanks, and after her father's death also went to Mexico with her three daughters, where she died of cholera. Elizabeth, after a stay in New York, returned to England with her children, ending up at last in Australia. Thus, as Morris Birkbeck's life drew to a close, his family was scattering to far places.

There were personal tragedies in other families too. The same

William Hall, descendant of millers who had possessed mill rights
in Surrey coming down from the Domesday Book of William the
Conqueror, recorded this pathetic event in his diary:

This week has been marked to us by one of the severest afflic-
tions that can befall a parent, the death of a beloved child
accidentally caused by his brother. The distress could only
have been heightened by the act being willful, which is so far
from being the case that I have not even negligence to impute
to my poor Robert. On the fatal morning of the 24th April
I heard the sound of two of my sons passing through the
porch into which my room opens. Soon after, I heard the
report of a rifle. I lay till it was light enough to see to
dress, perhaps twenty minutes. I heard a strange noise, which
I concluded to proceed from the boys driving in the oxen,
which I thought might have broken out. Going into the garden to ascertain the cause, I saw poor Bob lying writhing
and rolling upon the ground, apparently in the most exquisite
torment. I concluded him to be dreadfully wounded. It was
some time before I could get him to speak. At last in answer
to my repeated enquiries where he was hurt he replied, "Oh,
father, I am not wounded; but I have killed Ned, and I wish I
was dead myself." The involuntary exclamation which I
uttered brought out his mother. The scene which ensued cannot be described. Two of our neighbours coming up (for
Bob's cries had alarmed them all to a considerable distance)
assisted me to convey them in and lay them upon the bed. I
went out in search of the body, which was a considerable time
before it could be found, owing to poor Robert not being
collected enough to give a proper description of the place
where it lay. At length it was brought in and the next day
interred in a spot which he had chosen for his own garden.
This fatal accident has caused me by far the greatest affliction I ever knew.

George Flower, drawing on a letter written by Hall, added:

It seems they had found a turkey. Robert dispatched his
brother one way, and lay down himself behind a log to en-

deavor to call up the bird to him with his turkey-call. After a little while he heard a rustling within shot and soon after saw what he concluded to be the turkey, took aim, fired, and leaped up, shouting for Ned, and ran in triumph to pick up his game. Think of his feelings when he found it to be the corpse of his brother!

Not long afterward, a death as shocking and even more senseless occurred in Flower's own family. He writes:

Myself and father were at Pittsburgh, returning from the Eastern cities when the news of the death of my eldest son was communicated to us by Frederick Rapp. It was occasioned by violence, and occurred in the following manner: My eldest son, Richard, then a promising lad, was living at Park House with his grandmother during my own and his grandfather's journey to the East. Late in the evening some backwoodsmen of the lowest description, as they came from Albion probably full of whisky, rode by the house, uttered several whoops and yells, as if in defiance, as they sometimes would do. The noise they made induced the dogs to rush out barking. My son Richard ran out to call off the dogs, which he did. As he turned round to walk into the house, one of the fellows dismounted, and, picking up a large bone, threw it at the poor lad. It struck him with violence on the back of his head. He was assisted to bed, from which he never arose. The skull was crushed and the brain injured. Notwithstanding all medical assistance and care that was given him, he died in a few hours.

To this Prudence Birkbeck, writing to her aunt, added:

You have probably heard of Mr. George Flower's eldest son Richard being killed by some rowdy backwoodsmen, without provocation—the man who fractured the poor lad's skull, in a most shocking manner, was tried last week and *acquitted*, owing to the jury being of his own choice all friends to him. This is one instance of the way in which the laws are put in effect in this state. The jurymen thought that after this fright he would "take religion" and be a right steady fellow, so they acquitted him. Some years back, he almost killed a man in Albion, by stabbing him with his butcher's knife.

Five years later, the traveler S. A. Ferrall picked up the story of Richard's death and used it to discredit the whole settlement. His facts were badly garbled (for instance, George Flower was by no means dead), but there was a measure of truth in the inferences he drew from the murder, and there is no doubt that Flower's fortunes were rapidly declining, as he suggested.

Birkbeck and Flower purchased large tracts of land in this neighbourhood for the purpose of re-selling or letting it to English or other emigrants. These two gentlemen were of the class called in England, "gentlemen farmers," and brought with them from that country very large capitals, a considerable portion of which, in addition to the money laid out on purchase, they expended on improvements. They are both now dead—their property has entirely passed into other hands, and the members of their families who still remain in this country are in comparative indigence.

The most inveterate hostility was manifested by the backwoods people towards these settlers, and the series of outrages and annoyances to which they were exposed contributed not a little to shorten their days. It at length became notorious that neither Birkbeck nor Flower could obtain redress for any grievance whatever, unless by appealing to the superior courts—as both the magistrates and jurors were exclusively of the class of the offenders; and the "Supreme Court of the United States" declared that the verdicts of the juries and the decisions of the magistrates were, in many cases, so much at variance with the evidences that they were disgraceful to the country. A son of the latter gentleman, a lad about fourteen years old, was killed in open day whilst walking in his father's garden by the blow of an axe handle, which was flung at him across the fence. The evidence was clear against the murderer, and yet he was acquitted. Whilst

I was at Vandalia, I saw in a list of lands for sale, amongst other lots to be sold for taxes, one of Mr. Flower's.

ii

BIRKBECK WAS DEAD. Richard Flower, George's father, died in 1829 at the age of 68. And only George Flower of the original planners was left to carry on. Albion had flourished; since 1822 it had been the county seat of Edwards County, when its greater healthiness and superior population had wrested that honor from little Palmyra. Again hard feelings were the offspring of the victory. Mt. Carmel, on the Wabash, had contended for the seat of government, and, not appeased, at last succeeded in splitting off the eastern portion of the county to make Wabash County, of which it then became the county seat.

Losses, however, were compensated by continued immigration. After the slavery question was settled, Flower says that

the tide began to flow again. Individuals and families were frequently arriving, and occasionally a party of thirty and forty. A fresh cause induced this tide of emigration. It arose from the private correspondence of the first poor men who came. Having done well themselves, and by a few years of hard labor acquired more wealth than they ever expected to obtain, they wrote home to friend or relative an account of their success. These letters handed round in the remote villages of England in which many of them lived reached individuals in a class to whom information in a book form was wholly inaccessible. Each letter had its scores of readers, and, passing from hand to hand, traversed its scores of miles. The writer, known at home as a poor man, earning perhaps a scanty subsistence by his daily labor, telling of the wages he received, his bountiful living, of his own farm and the number of his livestock, produced a greater impression in the limited circle of his readers than a printed publication had the power of doing. His fellow laborer who heard these accounts, and feeling that he was no better off than when his fellow laborer left him for America, now exerted every nerve to come and do likewise. Among the many that came, induced by this sort of information, were three brothers, Thomas, Kelsey, and Joseph Crackles, three Lincolnshire men—a fine specimen of English farm laborers, well skilled in every description of farm labor, and particularly in the draining of land. They lived with me for three years after their arrival. They soon got good farms of their own; or, I should rather say, made good farms for themselves. I heard an American neighbor remark on the first farm they bought that nobody could ever raise a crop or get a living from it. It had not been in their possession two years before it became noted for its excellent cultivation and abundant crops. In this way we have given to Illinois a valuable population, men that are a great acquisition to the country. It was observed that these emigrants who came in the second emigration from five to ten years after the first settlement complained more of the hardships of the country than those who came first. These would complain of a leaky roof, or a broken fence, and all such inconveniences. The first comers had no cabins or fences to complain of; with them it was conquer or die. And thus emigrants came dropping in from year to year.

Beginning in 1824 there was a new threat to the continued growth of the English Settlement, this time one that was accepted peacefully—even welcomed—because it was the scheme of a dreamer whose dreams were on a scale larger even than those of Birkbeck and Flower. The German Rappites at Harmonie, on the Indiana side of the Wabash, were ready to sell out and move back to Pennsylvania at a time when Robert Owen, of New Lanark in Scotland, was looking for just such a property on which to locate a pilot community, which he believed would lead to a new era in human social relationships.

From the beginning, Harmonie (as the Rappites spelled it; "New Harmony" after Owen's arrival) had been of great importance to the English Settlement. Most of the English no doubt found the simple German followers of George Rapp quaint, possibly absurd in their singleminded devotion to what the Englishmen considered rank superstition, perhaps foolish in their subservience to the dictatorial pretensions of Father Rapp. But no one could deny that Rapp's policies (even that of discouraging parenthood) paid off in the struggle for survival on the frontier. The Rappite colony had waxed fat; it not only supported itself in comfort but had a generous surplus of both produce and manufactured articles for sale. The industry of Harmonie was even an indirect impediment to the growth of the English Settlement, for, as Birkbeck early discovered, Harmonie could sell grain cheaper than he could raise it himself with expensive English labor. This circumstance scarcely encouraged large-scale farming.

A fair example of how Harmonie struck the English is the account given by William Faux in 1819.

I saw, on the Harmonie lands and fields, of great size, wheat, finer and thicker, planted with two bushels, than in England with three and a half bushels per acre. The fields, however, lie in a vale of prodigious richness.

I reached Harmonie at dusk, and found a large and comfortable brick tavern, the best and cleanest which I have seen in Indiana, and slept in a good, clean bedroom, four beds in a room, one in each corner; but found bad beef, though good bread, and high charges, one dollar, five cents each.

A stranger present asked our landlord of what religion were the community of Harmonie. In broken English, and rather crossly, he replied, "Dat's no matter; they are all a satisfied people." The spell, or secret, by which these people are held in voluntary slavery is not to be known or fathomed by inquiry. We asked if strangers were permitted to go to their church to-morrow. "No," was the answer. This is unprecedented in the civilized world.

Sunday. At Harmonie till ten o'clock, when we were told we must then depart, or stay until after the morning service, which commences at ten o'clock. At the moment the bells began chiming the people, one and all, from every quarter, hurry into their fine church like frighted doves to their windows; the street leading to the temple seems filled in a minute, and in less than ten minutes all this large congregation, 1,000 men, women, and children, all who can walk or ride, are in the church, the males entering in at the

side, the females at the tower, and separately seated. Then
enters the old high priest, Mr. Rapp, of about eighty, straight
and active as his adopted son, Frederick, who walks behind
him. The old man's wife and daughters enter with the crowd,
from his fine house, which looks as if the people who built it
for him thought nothing too good for him. This people are
never seen in idle groups; all is moving industry; no kind of
idling; no time for it. Religious service takes place three times
every day. They must be in the chains of superstition, though
Rapp professes to govern them only by the Bible, and they
certainly seem the perfection of obedience and morality. People who have left them say that Rapp preaches that if they
quit the society they will be damned, for his way is the only
way to heaven. He does much by signs, and by an impressive
manner, stretching out his arm, which he says is the arm of
God, and that they must obey it; and that when he dies, his
spirit will descend unto his son Fred. The people appear
saturnine, and neither very cleanly nor very dirty. They are
dressed much alike, and look rather shabby, just as working
folk in general look. None are genteel. The women are in-
tentionally disfigured and made as ugly as it is possible for
art to make them, having their hair combed straight up behind and before, so that the temples are bared, and a little
skullcap, or black crepe bandage, across the crown and tied
under the chin. This forms their only headdress.

I rode round the town, which will soon be the best and
first in the Western country. At present the dwellings, with
the exception of Rapp's and the stores and taverns, are all
log houses, with a cow house and other conveniences. One is
given to each family, and a fine cow, and nice garden; other
necessaries are shared in common. Their horses, cattle, and
sheep are all in one stable; herds and flocks are folded every
night, in comfortable sheds—particularly an immensely large
flock of merino sheep—and so secured from the wolves. They
have a fine vineyard in the vale and on the hills around,
which are as beautiful as if formed by art to adorn the town.
Not a spot but bears the most luxuriant vines, from which
they make excellent wine. Their orchards, too, are of un-

common size and fertility; and in a large pleasure garden is a curious labyrinth, out of which none but those who formed it or are well acquainted with it can find their way.

Their granary is superb and large, and the barns and farmyards are singularly capacious, as well as their cloth and other manufactories. It is the wise policy of this people to buy nothing which it is possible for them to make or raise, and their industry and ingenuity are irresistible. They have much to sell, at their own price, of almost everything domestic and foreign. They cannot make shoes half so fast as they could sell them. It is not doubted but they are immensely rich, beginning in Pennsylvania with only £4,000, and being now worth £500,000. They keep no accounts, and all business is done and everything possessed in Frederick Rapp's name. They have been in this Harmonie five years only; they bought a huge territory of the richest land, which is all paid for, and keep an immense quantity in high cultivation, and continue to buy out bordering settlers, thus ever enlarging their boundaries.

This was the property Robert Owen decided to buy, in a negotiation begun for him by Richard Flower in 1824. As George Flower said, the existence of the snug and comfortable Harmonie when contrasted with the dirt and discomfort of a log hut had already caused the backwoodsmen to open their minds to new possibilities of life. Now Robert Owen, taking over this model establishment and renaming it New Harmony, came to speak of the better life in a language the people could understand as they could not understand Rapp's German. Arriving with plans and diagrams—even with a model of the castellated city that was supposed to rise beside the Wabash—Owen was indefatigable in lecturing about the glowing future he foresaw, wherever and whenever he could collect an audience.

The full scope of his plan, much changed and much debated as the new settlement got under way, called for a communitarian society in which most goods were shared in common. Ultimately declaring the "Mental Independence of Man" on July 4th, 1826, Owen envisioned complete equality of the sexes, the abolition of marriage, the rearing of children in day nurseries with their education carried out by Pestalozzian methods, religion replaced by

serious ethical discourse, and a happy intellectual society supported on only a few hours' work a day by each person. Few of the
great reforms were carried through with any completeness—for
to his credit it must be said that Owen was always ready to listen
to the other man's opinion, and he attracted to himself a body of
notably opinionated followers—and the community rapidly developed into a debating society continuously in session. Yet to
most of his followers who came from the immediate backwoods,
theory must have been secondary to the fact that the substantial
town build by Rapp was already there, a welcome refuge from an
inhospitable wilderness. Let others argue social theory, they knew
the good life when they saw it. But to people like Flower and the
other educated Englishmen, Owen was one of their own; they too
had theorized on the nature of society, they too had staked their
theories to the experiment of making a settlement. They welcomed him with open arms even when they disagreed with him
about particulars.

Robert Owen's son, William, accompanied by Capt. Donald
Macdonald, arrived in advance of the proprietor of the new
colony. After investigating the potentials of the purchase they
promptly paid their respects to the leading families of the English Settlement. From the journals both kept we gain some further
views of the settlement during the winter of 1824–25. William
Owen gives the following impressions.

Albion presents the appearance of a small American town—
2 or 3 brick buildings, including the public buildings, and
perhaps 20 log houses. Saw Mr. Flower's cotton gin, which
consists of a number of circular saws which draw the cotton
through openings too small to admit the cotton seeds. It is
turned by cattle walking on an inclined plane. Dined with
Mr. G. Flower and afterwards walked with Miss Ronalds to
her home and stayed there playing chess with Mr. Ronalds
and talking till near eleven. There is very little comfort here.
Everything is done in an inferior manner. No one dresses
tidily; but dirty coats, shoes, etc. Mr. Ronalds tans and works
very hard but to little purpose.

Miss Ronalds, Capt. McD. and I walked to Albion, with
Mr. G. Flower. We called on a working blacksmith, J. D.
Johnston, Esq., justice of the peace and deputy sheriff of the

county. We proceeded then to Mr. Warrington's school, in a small room in a stone building, where we found him instructing about 15 boys and girls. He showed us some good specimens of writing and told us he made the children take places. We then called on Mr. Beckett, but his wife being in deshabille would not appear, though Miss Ronalds asked if she could not be seen. Afterwards we called on Mrs. Carter, with whom I wished to barter a deer's horn, but could get nothing for it. Mr. Carter was not at home, being now on a visit to some Kickapoos, which are supposed to be now about 40 or 50 miles off. They are now hunting, intending going down in the spring to attack the Osages, who killed a number of their tribe some time ago.

We then walked through a fine wood about 2 miles to Wanborough—Mr. Birkbeck's settlement—and called on Mr. Brown, a shoemaker, with whom we and Mr. G. Flower engaged to dine on Tuesday next. From thence we returned through the Boltinghouse Prairie, about 2 miles, home. We found the heat quite oppressive; very pleasant sitting in the open air in the shade. We got in about ½ past 4, dined with Mr. G. Flower. We had scarcely finished when we were informed my father had just arrived with a Harmonite called Joe Healey. They had left Harmonie about ½ past 9, and my father had guided himself by a map of the Illinois, which he had with him. About ½ a mile from here he took the Albion road instead of the one which leads directly to Mr. G. Flower's house, but he had been set right by Mr. Cave, who met him just in time and who knew him by his resemblance to me. In the evening we had supper and a musical party at Mr. Flower's, attended, besides his family and ourselves, by Mr. and Mrs. Carter, Mr. and Mrs. Lewis, who all sang, and by Messrs. Cave, Spring, and Ronalds, who played the violin, flute, and violoncello. All the pieces sung and played in chorus were hymn tunes. The two principal performers, we were told, were absent—Judge B. and Mrs. Pickering. The former is leader and the latter presides at the pianoforte, which was left out this evening altogether.

Saturday, 25th Dec. Christmas day. A most beautiful

day, not a cloud to be seen for two days. Thermometer at
10 o'clock 56, afternoon 62 in shade, after sunset 52. Mr.
Flower, Mr. Owen, and I rode to Mrs. Ronalds' and sat
down in the shade as being the pleasantest place we could
find. Mrs. Ronalds is a quiet, pleasant lady and has two children, Kate and Hugh, 4 and 2 years old. We then rode on
to the prairie and rode twice through the prairie fire, which,
owing to there being no wind, moved very slowly. It certainly
would be terrific enough to see a fire like this coming up to
your log cabin. They then fight it, as it is termed, endeavoring
to overcome it by striking it with clapboards, which are about
2 or 2½ feet long and are used to cover log houses. The fire
we saw was at least ½ mile long, and we were told that
it had been known to proceed so rapidly as to overtake a
man on horseback, even though he were galloping at full
speed to escape from it. It is usually stopped by a road or a
fence.

We rode slowly over Boltinghouse Prairie and viewed
several beautiful sites for communities; indeed we all agreed
that Duke Hamilton Park was not at all degraded by being
compared with it; yet we were told by everyone that no one
could form any idea of its beauty in the spring when gazing
on it in its present faded and dried-up appearance, surrounded by and studded with black leafless trees. My father
told us that he had been riding about in the woods every day
since we left him, dining on cold meat and Harmonie wine,
in old trees which were lying on the ground, and enjoying
this life very much. The capabilities of Harmonie seem to
please him more and more. He settled nothing with Mr. Rapp,
but expects him on Monday with his daughter here. Though
moving very slowly we found the heat of the sun quite re-
laxing, and the thought occurred to me how insupportable
the heat must be when the thermometer stands 40 degrees
higher, which we were told is sometimes the case. I was told
by one man that he had seen the thermometer at 106—I think
at 109—but this very rare indeed.

After leaving the prairie, Miss R., Mr. O., and I rode to
Albion and met on the road a large party going to dine at

Daniel Orange's. We saw then for the first time Mrs. Beckett. She is rather a pretty woman. From Albion we proceeded to Wanborough and called on Mr. Birkbeck, when we saw Mrs. Pell—a very pretty but dejected looking woman—and Mrs. Hanks, both Mr. Birkbeck's daughters. We returned home about two miles over the prairie. We dined at 5 at Mr. Flower's, whither his children had been invited to eat Christmas dinner, of which roast beef and plum pudding formed a conspicuous part.

Sunday, 26th Dec. My father and the rest of the party went to chapel, where Mr. Ronalds read a sermon to them. At one I walked to town, called on Mr. Pickering, and at two went to a meeting where Mr. Owen intended speaking, which had been notified the day before. As the room was too small for those present, we adjourned to the open air, and after the benches had been removed and filled, members stood or occupied fallen trees. Mr. Owen spoke for about two and a half hours to about 200 persons, who were very quiet and apparently interested. I observed a great many ladies, both old and young, many with infants in their arms, and almost all English emigrants, as almost all the settlers of Albion and neighborhood are from Britain. My father explained his principles and showed how they must naturally produce union and good feeling, and banish anger and irritation from society. He told them that this and only this was true religion, and that we might be sure that when even this was wanting, whatever might be the individual belief, there was no true religion. He then read the rules and regulations of a community and showed his drawings. All parties seemed much pleased. Although the day after Christmas, we found ourselves quite warm and comfortably seated in the open air, till the sun went down, about which time the meeting broke up. In the evening my father showed the drawings to Mr. Pickering.

Captain Macdonald narrated the same events in his journal, adding a somewhat fuller account of Owen's speech and its reception. On Christmas Day, he wrote,

Mr. Flower having prevailed on Mr. Owen to have a meeting
to explain his plans, a notice was written advertising it for
the next day at ½ past one in Albion. I rode with Mr. George
Flower, and left it in Albion. Thence we rode into the East
Prairie, about two miles distant, called at the distillery & gave
notice, and then went to Mr. Woods' farm. Mr. Woods is a
farmer from Nottinghamshire. His family live with him. His
eldest son is married to the daughter of Mr. Flower's housekeeper. They belonged in England to a society of freethink-
ers. We had some conversation relative to the advantages of
associating in community, which they said that they had
wished for a long time. The father said that in England the
people could not so soon understand the advantages of such
a plan because they had never, like his family, had the experience of beginning the world in a new country; and the
son remarked that he wished to live in such a society—as he
was convinced it would be the happiest life that could be led
by mankind. In the evening Mr. Owen had a long argument
with Mr. Flower and Mr. Ronalds relative to the consistency
of his principles, their connexion with a religious belief, & the
distinctions between right & wrong, virtue & vice.

Sunday morning we went to meeting held in a room in
Albion, where about 2 dozen persons were present. The day
was remarkably clear, calm, and temperate. A little before
2 o'clock so many persons collected that it was judged necessary to have Mr. Owen's meeting in the open air. Benches
were brought out of the houses, & when these were filled
numbers sat on the logs of trees which lay on the grass. The
meeting consisted of about 200 persons, the great majority of
whom were English settlers. Many who are Methodists did
not attend. There were very few Americans present. The
company formed into a ring & Mr. Owen stood in the center
and spoke to them for about 2½ hours. All were extremely
attentive and both interested and pleased. Husbands brought
their wives & daughters, and many infant children were to be
seen in their mothers' arms, as they could not be left alone at
home.

Mr. Owen commenced by congratulating himself at being

surrounded by so many speaking his own language & brought
up as he had been, & so far from his own home. He then
stated the principles of human nature—that man's character
consists of & is formed first by the Power that creates him &
2ndly by the circumstances in which he is placed after birth.
Thence he traced the effect of charity, kindness, & benevo-
lence, and the absence of the angry passions. He told them
that such alone was pure religion, and that they might be
certain it did not exist wherever anger, ill will, and uncharitable conduct was found. He called their attention to the
necessity of placing themselves in the best and excluding the
worst circumstances, commented on the advantages of union,
and spoke of those principles alone being able to produce it.
He shewed his plans & read the rules & regulations for a
community as drawn out & adopted by the British & Foreign
Philanthropic Society formed in London four years ago.
About sunset the meeting broke up quietly & in high good
humour. Several persons spoke of his views & plans as being
highly satisfactory.

Owen's plans were so promising that a number of settlers rushed
to join the new venture. William Owen mentions that on Tuesday

Messrs. Lewis and Carter called as a deputation from a party
of a dozen or more who had signed a paper offering to join a
community. They said they had got the names in a great
hurry. They could get very many more in a short time. Some
of the names were Messrs. Lewis, Carter, Orange, Spring,
Young, Birkbeck, Beckett, etc. Mr. Owen agreed to meet as
many as chose to attend on Thursday at 1 o'clock at Albion.

And on Thursday the meeting was held.

We went to Mr. F.'s brick tavern and after waiting for some
time my father opened the meeting by showing his drawings.
There were upwards of 100 persons present, who were very
quiet and orderly. During the meeting a tipsy man came in,
but no one seemed to notice him, and he departed.

My father said the meeting had been called to endeavor to discover any means of bettering the condition of the inhabitants of Albion. He told them he knew no way by which they could be enabled to do it themselves, or any means by which it could be accomplished so long as they remained in their present situations. He said if he completed the purchase of Harmonie, he thought he could promise them comfortable lodging, the most wholesome food, the most useful clothing, and a good education for their children; but that to accomplish this it would be necessary to exert something of the same labor and diligence as was at present necessary for their support, for some years, and to allow themselves to be guided by one who had long been conversant with the principles and practices necessary to such an undertaking. He added that as belief was in no respect under the control of the individual it was necessary that each one should be allowed perfect liberty of conscience. He told them also that it had occurred to him only this morning that, perhaps, if he purchased Harmonie, the community might rent the houses and land from him and cultivate the land in common. Mr. Brown thought they could not do it by themselves. Mr. Clark wished to know what would become of their present property. Mr. Owen thought if the soil was wet it might be laid down in grass; if dry, in cotton or farmed for the private benefit of the individuals of the society. Mr. Warrington asked why a community might not be established nearer so that the present houses should remain of value. Mr. O. said if anyone could form a community near them he would give it all the assistance in his power. The meeting lasted about an hour and a half and we then, in compliance with a previous invitation from the ladies of Albion, went to Judge Wattle's where, after waiting about an hour, supper was served up.

We were waited on by Mrs. Wattle, Carter, Lewis, Jolly and Miss Ross, who seemed already to have commenced the community system. Soon after 6 we took leave, greatly to their disappointment, as they said they had counted on our company until 12 o'clock; but my father was tired, and as we proposed leaving Albion tomorrow we wished to spend the evening with Mr. Flower. On returning home, we found tea laid out for us at Mr. G. Flower's and Mr. Warrington awaiting our arrival. We talked to him about the management of children, and this led us to the attributes and properties of God. Mr. W. agreed that man's actions were the result of necessity, but he was puzzled because in that case he must throw the blame of all the misery in the world on his Creator. When returned home we prepared for next day's journey and went to bed.

It is difficult to say how many from the English Settlement decided that New Harmony was the more attractive place to live. Certainly there were dissenters from Owen's views. William Owen returned to Albion in February and mentions that he dined with Mr. Flower (probably George's father, who was still living), and that Mr. Flower contended "that selfishness would govern a community as it has governed individuals heretofore"—as indeed proved to be the case at New Harmony. George Flower merely says that "these discussions produced some effect, and some of our citizens went to Harmony in the hope of realizing some portion of the happier future predicted by Mr. Owen. Some came back and are prosperous citizens in the vicinity of Albion; some remained and are prosperous citizens of Harmony." And he made the important observation that "although Mr. Owen failed to make his community, the doctrines he taught and the opinions he promulgated spread far and wide. Accepted by some with fervor, opposed and denounced by more, they nevertheless were in a fragmentary way accepted by a vast many."

By their nature, Owen's theories encouraged difference of opinion, and splinter groups began forming from the first. One such was organized in Albion. William Hall wrote in 1825 of going to New Harmony to hear Owen lecture; by summer of that year he and five others "constituted ourselves into a society to be styled the Wanborough Joint Stock Society," which apparently was based on their own version of Owen's theories, for in subsequent diary entries they are busily engaged in evaluating each other's possessions to determine how much stock each shall receive. What came of this tiny communitarian venture is not clear—probably nothing more than a lot of complicated bookkeeping. But this illustrates at least how Owen's ideas influenced even those unwilling to give up their Illinois holdings and move to his settlement.

iii

MANY LEAVENING INFLUENCES had been at work to bring the
English Settlement into closer conformity with other American
communities and to make it less and less exotic, though traces of
its English heritage are visible in Albion to this day. Such changes
would not have displeased Birkbeck, and they did not displease
Flower. From the first they had counted themselves Americans,
and they expected their English followers to adjust themselves to
American conditions. Yet, the peculiarities of geography, the kind
of agriculture carried on in the vicinity of Albion, the speech of the
people, some characteristics of the architecture all continued to remind visitors of England and to provoke comment. As late as 1830,
they still came to inspect the English Settlement, expecting to find
a bit of transplanted Surrey, and to judge the degree of success or
failure of the settlement. In that year, for example, James Stuart
showed up and left a rather typical report.

We then passed through some fine woodland before we
reached Wanborough and the settlement of Messrs. Birkbeck
and Flower on the English Prairie, on which the town of
Albion, now the capital of the county of Edwards, with a
population of 4,000 or 5,000 persons, is situated. The first
view of the settlement is by no means favourable. The road is
good; the soil seems of excellent quality, and the whole appearance of the country is agreeable; but there are obvious
traces of the fences having been in better order, and of more
of the land having formerly been in cultivation. This was Mr.
Birkbeck's part of the English Prairie. Mr. Birkbeck was
drowned in the Wabash River some years ago, and none of
his sons were in a situation to succeed him here. Since his
death the property has not been managed as he would have
managed it. Mr. Pell, one of his sons-in-law, is here but, as I
was afterwards told, has no turn for proceeding with the
improvements. It is, however, sufficiently apparent that Mr.
Birkbeck was possessed of a very comfortable settlement here,
and that his residence and the accommodation afforded were
in substance such as he represented them in his publications.

In proceeding from his land towards Albion, I was passing a nice looking English villa, at the distance of perhaps a hundred yards to the northward, when I found a young man at the plough close to me in the field in front of the house. I learned from him, on making inquiry, that the place had belonged to Mr. Pritchard, a gentleman from England of the Quaker persuasion; that he was now dead, leaving a widow, a daughter, and two sons, of whom this young man was one. At his request, I went to the house, which is extremely neat, and the view from it quite as delightful as an inland view can be. In short, it is a bijou of a place.

Albion is upon Mr. Flower's part of the prairie, and was built by him. It was only begun twelve years ago, and contains a town house, a smithy, three stores, one broad street with lanes to the prairie and woods, all handsomely laid out and perhaps more in the substantial English style than I have seen elsewhere in the Western country. Mechanics of every necessary description are now resident at Albion. I should rather suspect that too large a sum has been expended upon the town.

The hotel here, kept by Mrs. Oveat, is excellent. She attended to everything I wanted herself, and showed every sort of attention that a traveller requires. In going through the village, I accidentally met in one of the stores Mr. Charles Stephens, son of the late respected Mr. Richard Stephens, well known in Edinburgh and over Scotland for his skill in the draining of land, and as a judicious adviser in laying out pleasure grounds. Mr. Charles Stephens is now in a very comfortable situation here.

After a rest at the hotel, I mounted one of the barouche horses and set off to get a look of Mr. Flower's prairie. His house is at the distance of somewhat more than a mile from Albion, and the approach to it is singularly beautiful.

Not far from the town there is a charming cottage belonging to Mr. Pickering, an English gentleman married to one of Mr. Flower's sisters, who has lately been at great pains in bringing from England varieties of the best sheep.

Beyond this cottage the approach passes through as beauti-

ful a piece of wood as I have ever seen—majestic oaks with
fine underwood on varied ground.

Mrs. Flower happened to be in the way when I was passing
near the house, and was so obliging, on my asking the way
into the prairie, as to insist on my seeing Mr. Flower, who
was engaged in some agricultural operation, overseeing
sheepshearing in the neighbourhood.

The situation of the houses on Mr. Flower's prairie is very
much that which a large landed proprietor in England would
select for his residence in the heart of an extensive wooded
park, and there is a neatly erected porter's lodge at the gate.
There are two houses on Mr. Flower's prairie almost adjoining each other; the one occupied by Mrs. Flower, a fine old
lady, the mother of Mr. Flower, whose father died here
lately, and the other occupied by Mr. Flower himself and his
family.

I had the pleasure of accompanying Mr. Flower in a ride
through the prairie, and saw him—for he puts his hand to the
work himself—assist in laying a trap with part of a dead
horse for the wolves, which had lately been troublesome.

Both Mr. and Mrs. Flower seem to me perfectly disposed to
conform to the customs of the country in everything, and are
very fond of the situation. They have a fine family. Mrs.
Flower was very recently the mother of twins. It is, however,
impossible to deny that persons brought up in England in
luxury and affluence, as Mr. Flower's family were, must have
frequent cause for self-denial here. It is only by reasoning on
the advantages and disadvantages of their present situation
for themselves and the future prospects of their family that
they can reconcile themselves to the privations to which persons formerly in their circumstances in England must necessarily submit in the Western country of America.

George Flower, thinking back over the accomplishments of the
settlement, could point to ways in which the English had been a
leavening influence on their neighbors also. Like his kinsman
Elias Pym Fordham, he knew that the romantic notions of the
benevolent wilderness did not hold up in practice. Fordham, for

all that he liked to slip off on a spree with the backwoodsmen, wrote:

I am inclined to think that man's virtues are like the fruits of the earth, only excellent when subjected to culture. The force of this simile you will never feel till you ride in these woods over wild strawberries which dye your horse's fetlocks like blood yet are insipid in flavour; till you have seen wagonloads of grapes choked by the bramble and the poisonous vine; till you find peaches tasteless as a turnip; and roses throwing their leaves of every shade upon the winds, with scarcely a scent upon them. 'Tis the hand of man that makes the wilderness shine. His footsteps must be found in the scene that is supremely and lastingly beautiful.

It was culture, and especially the desire for culture, that the English could promote. Their agency was the school. Recalling those first country schools, Flower wrote:

A little after school has begun, two tall, stout chaps enter, men grown, take their seats, and begin conning their lessons from their schoolbooks as the children are doing. Who are they? They are two of that class brought up in the solitude of the wilderness without a chance of learning a letter. They are now endeavoring to regain their lost time at the first schoolhouse within their reach, with equal diligence but more painful effort than is given by their young compeers. Masters in our first country schools have often told me that they have had some scholars older than themselves.

The erecting of a little log schoolhouse in a frontier settlement is to me a far more interesting object than a Girard College, with all its costly and elaborate domes and columns. They are the seedbeds of knowledge, giving permanence to the growth of our organized and complex system of society. When the new country school has been in operation a single week its influence is felt both on parents and children. Occasionally will be seen a boy ten or twelve years old leaning against a doorpost, intently gazing in upon the scholars at their lessons. After a time he slowly and moodily goes away.

He does not look like the other children; his dress is less tidy, his hair uncombed, and perhaps his face and hands unwashed. Neither has he the bright and self-confident look of the scholars. He belongs, perhaps, to some farmer's family residing outside the radius of the one-mile school circle, or what is more likely to some backwoods hunter within the circle. The solitary boy feels his exclusion from some benefit enjoyed by all the other children giving to them a bond of fellowship. This feeling soon ripens into an intense desire to go to school, or to quit the neighborhood and go deeper into the wilderness, far away from an odious comparison. A crisis has now arrived in the fate of this backwoods family. All other influences of encroaching civilization it has withstood, but the influence of the school can no longer be resisted. To see all the children of his neighbors advancing in their own self-respect and in the respect of others whilst his own family are left on the dead level of ignorance on which only a few days before they all rested together creates a feeling he cannot stand. He can no longer say I am as good as you. He feels that he is a notch below them; and, if he decides to remain, he must send his children to school and join the ranks of civilization.

Thus, with the invasion of civilization in the backwoods, the pioneer days of the settlement came to a natural conclusion. Even the lamentable gulf between the Birkbeck and Flower families shrank with the passage of time. It was said that Birkbeck had gone to Harmonie to get Owen to effect a reconciliation when he was drowned returning. However that may be, Flower tells that

Sometime after the death of Mr. Birkbeck, a circumstance occurred which brought me once more into personal intercourse with the members of his family then living in Wanborough, his two daughters, Mrs. Pell and Mrs. Hanks, neither of whom I had seen since our parting at Princeton, eight years before. Mr. and Mrs. Hanks had for some time lived apart. Mrs. Hanks and her children lived with her sister, Mrs. Pell, to whom she was ardently attached, and by whom she was much beloved. Mr. Hanks and myself had always been on friendly terms. From the peculiar position of my own and his father-in-law's family, we had never conversed on his family affairs. Mr. Hanks now thought it his duty to take his children under his own care. He called on me to ask the loan of my carriage to bring his children and their little effects from Mr. Pell's to his own house. This led to further conversation then, and to more the next day. I questioned the wisdom of his intention in taking his daughters from the custody of their mother and bringing them to a house without a housekeeper or female domestic, and in a country where a governess was scarcely to be procured.

He listened to my suggestions, and, at his request, I went to see Mrs. Hanks on the subject. Mr. Pell met me at the hall door with some surprise, for I had never been there before. I briefly explained the object of my visit. He invited me in, and opened the door of the parlor, which I entered. There stood my two former friends, Eliza and Prudence, pale and motionless. Prudence soon became tremulous; her nervous temperament scarcely allowed her to stand, but she could not move. Her sister, with slight motion, invited me to a seat, which I for a few moments could not take. All the past was passing through our minds; we were scarcely conscious of existence. I asked Mrs. Hanks if she would like to retain her children, and received her almost inaudible assent and thanks. Mr. Pell came in, to our relief; we all made an effort, and spoke aloud, as if to dissipate the impression of some unhappy dream that had long oppressed us.

Mr. Pell sat down to table to draw up an agreement, all of us sitting, participating in what was being written. I soon returned with Mr. Hanks' signature. Dinner was now ready. I was pressed to stay. I sat at the right hand of Mrs. Pell, Mrs. Hanks opposite, Mr. Pell at the bottom, and three or four children near him. Mrs. Hanks never completely recovered her self-possession. Mrs. Pell, calm, conversable, and cheerful. The conversation became general. Yet it was evident that there were different parties at the table, feeling a different existence, and living in different worlds. Three of us saw all the happy days of the past and the darker hours

of separation and regret to which the husband could get
but faint glimpses. The children knew no other world
than they were enjoying and the play to which they soon
returned. At leaving, Mr. Pell requested a moment's stay
at the hall door. "Mr. Flower, there has been an estrangement between our families. May we hope that it is now at
an end, and that all may be forgotten." As in the evening
of a dark and dreary day, the clouds lighted up with a
bright streak of sunlight in the western horizon, showing
that the storms are past, giving promise of a fair and tranquil
morrow. So one gleam of sincere but melancholy friendship
closed our dark day.

iv

ON BALANCE, shall the English Settlement be written down a success or failure? Certainly it brought no riches to its founders. Un-
selfishly, both of them sank their fortunes in the enterprise. George
Flower says that his first bill at Harmonie for food and supplies
amounted to $11,000, and that "between the years 1818 and 1824,
the Harmonites received from our settlement one hundred and
fifty thousand dollars in hard cash"—nearly all of it his and Birkbeck's. And this was not all, for uncounted wagon-loads of supplies
came from Shawneetown also—all paid for by the founders. Both
Birkbeck and Flower were financially ruined by the settlement.

Birkbeck, of course, did not live to see the conclusion of the
debacle. Flower, having tried unsuccessfully to mortgage his land
in England, at last was forced to leave the settlement he had
founded, and was reduced to inn-keeping at Mt. Vernon, Indiana,
where, because of his failing health, the brunt of the work fell on
his uncomplaining wife. On January 15, 1862, at the home of their
daughter in Grayville, Mrs. Flower died at dawn and her husband
the evening of the same day. They were buried at Grayville in a
single grave.

As George Flower well knew, the settlement was a signal success in ways more important than the financial. He wrote, with
justifiable pride:

This was the country we had found, made known, and recommended to others. The almost uniform success of those who

came has justified our choice and vindicated our judgment. Our after mission was to point out its situation and the way to it; to defend it from the misrepresentations and barefaced lies unscrupulously uttered by its enemies; to spread before the European public from time to time our progress and success; to aid many who had expended all their means; to assist, both by pecuniary means and long periods of time and labor, any great object of public advantage, whether of roads, schools, buildings, or laws. And this we did from the first to the last.

There had been dark days, of course—especially when the propagandists for Eastern regions had been most slanderous, and during the slavery controversy. When he came to write his history, Flower could be philosophical about these temporary reverses, accepting them as the lot of those who dare to strike out into the unknown.

There are certain classes of men who appear destined to receive sometime in their life, and oftentimes during their whole career, a large share of opposition, detraction, and misrepresentation. The inventors of new machines whose labor-saving power benefits the whole family of man receive cruel opposition in their first attempts to perfect their inventions and bring them to the notice of the public. Scorn, contempt, and ridicule are poured upon them during their lives, and after dying in their fruitless struggles, someone steps in and reaps the reward of their labor, and disingenuously claims the honor of the invention. Fitch and Fulton, of the steamboat, and Whitney, inventor of the cotton gin, are familiar instances of this class in America. Discoverers of new countries, whose penetration and perseverance have carried their attempts to a successful issue, and whose toils have changed and improved the condition of the world, are subject to the same fate. Witness Columbus pursuing his great idea, with slender and apparently inadequate means, through scorn, neglect, and opposition, to a successful issue; after short éclat, in a dungeon and in chains. The first founders of settlements in new or uninhabited countries seldom fail of receiving a large share of opposition, detraction, and pecuniary loss.

Yet he was puzzled why such things should be.

For facts so conspicuous the reasons seem rather obscure. Is it some great law of compensation that runs through all things, balancing advantage with disadvantage? pleasure with pain? As the old poet has it,

> *Every* white *must have its* black
> *And every sweet its sour.*

Or is it to be found in the universal but unextinguishable propensity in every human breast, the love of giving pain— ethics, morals, and religion notwithstanding?

There is a mysterious antagonism in the order of nature running through all life, vegetable and animal. Every plant as well as animal has its own peculiar enemy, persecutor, and destroyer. But man is the chief enemy of man. Let no man think to pass through this life without his share of annoyances, and as in duty bound I had mine. If he belongs to either of the classes I have mentioned, he is an imperfect calculator who does not sum up a considerable share to his own account.

As an old man looking back, he could see that his temperament and habits were not those to encourage popularity in the egalitarian West. But for all that, it had not been a bad life.

It is true, I neglected somewhat that shield of popularity which men of any standing in our new Western country might not at that day with impunity neglect. I rode into our little town most days to attend to any business, or speak with those to whom I had anything to say. I did not linger much, or enter grog shops, for I used neither whisky nor tobacco, their chief articles of sale. I did not sympathise in these matters with the population around me, and this position an enemy could turn to my disadvantage at any time. A man to be popular in our new Western towns, and with the country people around, should be acquainted with everybody, shake hands with everybody, and wear an old coat, with at least one good hole in it. A little whisky and a few squirts of tobacco juice are indispensable. From much of the former you may be excused if you treat liberally to others. If there is one fool bigger than another, defer to him, make much of him. If there is one fellow a little more greasy and dirty than another, be sure to hug him. Do all this and you have done much toward being a popular man. At least you could scarcely have a jury case carried against you. I did not do all this, and was therefore at a disadvantage against active enemies who did, and who were leagued against me to drive me and my family from the settlement. This period was the only exception to an unusually happy life of thirty years' duration. And thirty years is a large slice of a man's life.

And his final thought on the experiences he and Birkbeck had shared can stand as a monument to all pioneers, everywhere.

There are fortunately some compensations in store for those whom the world regards as visionary characters. Their actions have been unselfish. An unselfish life leaves few regrets and no repinings. The first explorer or founder of a settlement in a new and distant country follows the instincts of his nature and the promptings of his early being. In early manhood the dreamy imaginings of his youth prompt to action. He takes journeys and voyages. He has intercourse with a variety of members of the great human family living under institutions, language, climate, and a host of other circumstances all different from his own. From a local and stationary being he becomes a cosmopolite. He has intercourse with all classes, from the gifted, the intellectual, the educated, of every grade of mind and morals, to the lowest specimens of humanity, the dregs of civilization. His local habits become changed, many of his prejudices are swept away, opinions altered or modified, and his mental vision extended.

He pierces through civilization, and stands in uninhabited

regions. There he sees what none who come after him and fall
into the routine of civilized life can ever see—nature in the
plenitude of its perfection, its varied beauties undisturbed
and undistorted by art; the forest in its native grandeur,
unscathed by the axe; the prairie, with its verdure and acres
of brilliant flowers; the beauties of the prospect varying at
every step, and limited in extent only by his power of vision.
All these scenes, with their accompanying influences, exhibited under the varying aspects of light and shade, day and
night, calm and storm, have surrounded him. His being has
received the impress of them all in solitude and silence. Refreshed, strengthened, and purified, he feels, for a time at
least, superior to the irritations and annoyances of an imperfect civilization.

NOTES ON SOURCES

MANY BOOKS which touch in one way or another on the English Settlement appear in Solon J. Buck's indispensable bibliography, *Travel and Description, 1765–1865* (Springfield, 1914), which also lists hundreds of book reviews. Two articles by Jane Rodman printed in the *Indiana Magazine of History* (XLIII, 329–62; XLIV, 37–68) are a good recent secondary account based on the chief primary sources. Edwin E. Sparks, *The English Settlement in the Illinois* (London, 1907) reprints Birkbeck's *Extracts from a Supplementary Letter from the Illinois;* Richard Flower's *Letters from Lexington and the Illinois,* and his *Letters from the Illinois.* The volumes edited by R. G. Thwaites, *Early Western Travels,* contain complete reprints of Faux's *Memorable Days* (XI–XII), Richard Flower's *Letters from Lexington and the Illinois* (X), Richard Flower's *Letters from the Illinois* (X), Thomas Hulme's *Journal* (X), Adlard Welby's *A Visit to North America* (XII), and John Woods' *Two Years' Residence* (X). The first two volumes of the *Centennial History of Illinois*—Solon J. Buck's *Illinois in 1818* and T. C. Pease's *Frontier State*—are standard. Worthy of mention also is *Yesteryears in Edwards County, Illinois* (2 vols.), by Edgar L. Dukes.

The sources for this book, with dates of the particular editions used, are these:

BIRKBECK, MORRIS. *An Address to the Farmers of Great Britain; with an Essay on the Prairies of the Western Country . . . to Which Is Annexed the Constitution of the State of Illinois.* London, 1822.

BIRKBECK, MORRIS. *Letters from Illinois*. Philadelphia, 1818.

————. *Notes on a Journey in America, from the Coast of Virginia to the Territory of Illinois, with Proposals for the Establishment of a Colony of English*. Philadelphia, 1817.

[BLANE, WILLIAM N.] *An Excursion Through the United States and Canada During the Years 1822–1823 by an English Gentleman*. London, 1824.

COBBETT, WILLIAM. *A Year's Residence in the United States of America*. (Second edition, Part I.) London, 1819.

FAUX, W[ILLIAM]. *Memorable Days in America: Being a Journal of a Tour to the United States Principally Undertaken to Ascertain, by Positive Evidence, the Condition and Probable Prospects of British Emigrants; Including Accounts of Mr. Birkbeck's Settlement in the Illinois*. London, 1823.

FEARON, HENRY BRADSHAW. *Sketches of America: A Narrative of a Journey of Five Thousand Miles Through the Eastern and Western States of America . . . with Remarks on Mr. Birkbeck's "Notes" and "Letters."* London, 1818.

FERRALL, S[IMON] A[NSLEY]. *A Ramble of Six Thousand Miles Through the United States of America*. London, 1832.

FLOWER, GEORGE. *History of the English Settlement in Edwards County, Illinois, Founded in 1817 and 1818, by Morris Birkbeck and George Flower*. Chicago, 1882. (A second edition appeared in 1909.)

FLOWER, RICHARD. *Letters from the Illinois, 1820–1821, Containing an Account of the English Settlement at Albion and Its Vicinity, and a Refutation of Various Misrepresentations, Those More Particularly of Mr. Cobbett, with a Letter from M. Birkbeck, and a Preface and Notes by Benjamin Flower*. London, 1822.

————. *Letters from Lexington and the Illinois, Containing a Brief Account of the English Settlement in the Latter Territory, and a Refutation of the Misrepresentations of Mr. Cobbett*. London, 1819.

FORDHAM, ELIAS PYM. *Personal Narrative of Travels in Virginia, Maryland, Pennsylvania, Ohio, Indiana, Kentucky; and of a Residence in the Illinois Territory: 1817–1818*. Edited by Frederic Austin Ogg. Cleveland, 1906.

GRECE, CHARLES F. *Facts and Observations Respecting Canada and the United States of America, Affording a Comparative View of the Inducements to Emigration Presented in Those Countries*. London, 1819.

HALL, HON. JUDGE [JAMES]. *Letters from the West, Containing Sketches of Scenery, Manners, and Customs, and Anecdotes Connected with the First Settlements of the Western Sections of the United States.* London, 1828.

HALL, WILLIAM. "From England to Illinois in 1821: The Journal of William Hall," edited by Jay Monaghan, *Journal of the Illinois State Historical Society,* XXXIX (1946), 21–67, 208–53.

HARRIS, WILLIAM TELL. *Remarks Made During a Tour Through the United States of America in the Years 1817, 1818, and 1819.* London, 1821.

HOBY, J[AMES]. *The Baptists in America; A Narrative of the Deputation from the Baptist Union in England to the United States and Canada,* by the Rev. F. A. Cox and the Rev. J. Hoby. Second edition revised. London, 1836.

HODGSON, ADAM. *Remarks During a Journey Through North America in the Years 1819, 1820, and 1821, in a Series of Letters.* New York, 1823.

HOWITT, E[MANUEL]. *Selections from Letters Written During a Tour Through the United States in the Summer and Autumn of 1819.* . . . Nottingham [1820].

HULME, THOMAS. *Journal Made During a Tour in the Western Countries of America.* In Cobbett, *A Year's Residence.*

LORAIN, JOHN. *Hints to Emigrants, or a Comparative Estimate of the Advantages of Pennsylvania and of the Western Territory.* Philadelphia, 1819.

MACDONALD, DONALD. "The Diaries of Donald Macdonald," with introduction by Caroline Dale Snedeker, *Indiana Historical Society Publications,* XIV, no. 2. Indianapolis, 1942.

MELISH, JOHN. *Information and Advice to Emigrants to the United States and from the Eastern to the Western States.* Philadelphia, 1819.

The Monthly Review, XCVII (February, 1822), 200–207. (Anonymous, untitled review of several books of Western travels.)

OWEN, WILLIAM. "Diary of William Owen," edited by Joel W. Hiatt, *Indiana Historical Society Publications,* IV, no. 1. Indianapolis, 1906.

The Quarterly Review, XIX (April, 1818), 54–78. (Anonymous, untitled review of Birkbeck's and other volumes of Western travels.)

STUART, JAMES. *Three Years in North America.* Third edition. Edinburgh, 1833.

THOMSON, GLADYS SCOTT. *A Pioneer Family: The Birkbecks in Illinois.* London, 1953.

WELBY, ADLARD. *A Visit to North America and the English Settlement in Illinois. . . .* London, 1821.

WOODS, JOHN. *Two Years' Residence in the Settlement on the English Prairie, in the Illinois Country, United States.* London, 1822.

[WRIGHT, FRANCES.] *Views of Society and Manners in America, in a Series of Letters from That Country to a Friend in England During the Years 1818, 1819, and 1820.* London, 1821.

Page numbers in the left column are those on which each reprinted passage begins. Except as indicated otherwise, references to George Flower's *History of the English Settlement* are to the first edition of 1882.

3   Frances Wright, *Views of Society and Manners in America,* pp. 261–62.

4   Adlard Welby, *A Visit to North America and the English Settlement in Illinois,* pp. 109–10.

4   W. N. Blane, *An Excursion Through the United States and Canada,* p. 149.

5   Adam Hodgson, *Remarks During a Journey Through North America,* p. 25.

6   William Faux, *Memorable Days in America,* p. 298.

6   George Flower, *History of the English Settlement* (2nd ed.), p. 142.

8   G. Flower, *History,* pp. 27–28.

8   G. Flower, *History,* pp. 30–36.

12   G. Flower, *History* (2nd ed.), p. 35.

12   G. Flower, *History* (2nd ed.), p. 40.

13   G. Flower, *History* (2nd ed.), p. 41.

14   G. Flower, *History* (2nd ed.), p. 22.

15   The account of the Western journey is drawn from Morris Birkbeck, *Notes on a Journey,* pp. 3–145, and G. Flower, *History,* pp. 47–74.

54   Some indication of the history of the area prior to the arrival of the English appears in the anonymous *Combined History of Edwards, Lawrence and Wabash Counties, Illinois* (Philadelphia, 1883), pp. 58–60. Other settlers who were already there when the English arrived are mentioned throughout Flower's *History of the English Settlement.*

55   W. T. Harris, *Remarks Made During a Tour,* p. 139.

56 Birkbeck, *Notes,* p. 147.

56 Birkbeck, *Notes,* pp. 175–78.

58 Birkbeck, *Notes,* pp. 184–89.

61 G. Flower, *History,* pp. 77–80.

63 G. Flower, *History,* pp. 83–87.

66 G. Flower, *History,* pp. 93–94.

68 *Quarterly Review,* XIX (April, 1818), 73.

68 Birkbeck, *Letters from Illinois,* pp. 50–57.

71 Birkbeck, *Letters,* pp. 147–49.

73 *Monthly Review,* XCVII (February, 1822), 201.

73 F. Wright, *Views of Society,* pp. 263–64.

74 Birkbeck, *Letters,* pp. 116–18.

76 G. Flower, *History,* pp. 99–102.

78 G. Flower, *History,* pp. 102–25.

88 G. S. Thomson, *A Pioneer Family,* p. 44.

89 H. B. Fearon, *Narrative of a Journey,* pp. 263–64.

89 Fearon, *Narrative,* pp. 265–66.

89 E. P. Fordham, *Personal Narrative,* p. 217.

90 Thomas Hulme, *Journal,* in Cobbett's *A Year's Residence,* pp. 471–75.

93 Birkbeck, *Letters,* pp. 42–44.

94 Birkbeck, *Letters,* pp. 127–30.

97 Richard Flower, *Letters from Lexington and the Illinois,* pp. iii–iv.

98 G. Flower, *History,* p. 130.

98 G. Flower, *History,* pp. 100, 120. Elizabeth Birkbeck wrote in 1819 that her brother Bradford had been "employed in laying out five acre lots within half a mile of our house which Papa sells for 20 dollars, upon a written agreement that it shall be fenced round and a house built upon it within eighteen months. Many of Papa's labourers have bought these lots and are now industriously building their cabins and laying out their gardens." (Thomson, *A Pioneer Family,* p. 55.)

98 Welby, *A Visit,* pp. 113–21.

100 Welby, *A Visit,* pp. 123–24.

101 Blane, *An Excursion,* pp. 160–61.

101 William Cobbett, *A Year's Residence,* p. 530.

102 S. A. Ferrall, *A Ramble of Six Thousand Miles,* pp. 111–12.

102 Faux, *Memorable Days,* pp. 250–53.

104 Faux, *Memorable Days,* pp. 269–70.

104 G. Flower, *History,* p. 105.

105 Faux, *Memorable Days,* pp. 284–85.

106 William Owen, "Diary," *Indiana Historical Society Publications,* IV (1906), 79.

107 Faux, *Memorable Days*, pp. 290–98. Faux's book was roundly
     attacked. The *North American Review*, XIX (July, 1824), 92–
     125, objected to his use of the English language but—an Eastern
     publication—was not greatly bothered by his strictures on the
     Western settlement. A famous review appeared also in the
     Quarterly Review, XXIX (July, 1823), 338–70. This review was
     suppressed in the American reprint of that magazine—pirated
     anyway, of course—on the ground that it was libelous: Faux's
     harsh words about George Washington appeared in the review of
     his book.

111 Faux, *Memorable Days*, p. 434.

111 G. Flower, *History*, pp. 112–15.

113 G. Flower, *History*, pp. 125–26.

114 R. Flower, *Letters from the Illinois*, pp. 14–16.

115 R. Flower, *Letters from the Illinois*, p. 14.

115 R. Flower, *Letters from the Illinois*, p. 24.

116 William Hall, "From England to Illinois in 1821," *Journal of the
     Illinois State Historical Society*, XXXIX (March, 1946), 215–16.

117 W. T. Harris, *Remarks Made During a Tour*, pp. 137–39.

118 G. Flower, *History*, pp. 127–28.

118 Fordham, *Personal Narrative*, p. 233.

119 G. Flower, *History*, p. 128.

119 J. Hoby, *The Baptists in America*, p. 308.

119 G. Flower, *History*, pp. 128–30.

120 John Woods, *Two Years' Residence*, pp. 166–77.

125 Fordham, *Personal Narrative*, p. 218.

125 Faux, *Memorable Days*, pp. 270–71.

126 G. Flower, *History*, pp. 131–33.

127 R. Flower, *Letters from the Illinois*, pp. 16–18.

128 Faux, *Memorable Days*, pp. 271–72, 279.

129 Thomson, *A Pioneer Family*, p. 60.

129 Welby, *A Visit to North America*, pp. 115–17.

130 Faux, *Memorable Days*, p. 282.

131 Faux, *Memorable Days*, pp. 269, 287–88.

132 Welby, *A Visit to North America*, pp. 110–12. Judge Hall also
     had some hard things to say about Western taverns, but he
     placed the blame somewhat differently. "I have never travelled in
     England. All my knowledge of that country is derived from her
     authors, who fail not to include cleanliness in the monopoly of
     virtues which they arrogate to their nation; but this I do know,
     and there are thousands who can bear me out in the assertion,
     that if the English really possess this virtue, they leave it behind
     them when they abjure the realm. The worst taverns in Illinois
     have been kept by Englishmen; and there has never been in this

state an inn so badly kept, so filthy, and so extravagant as has been kept in Albion by the emigrants from that country." (*Letters from the West,* pp. 384–85.)

133 G. Flower, *History,* pp. 130–31, 133–34, 135.

135 Faux, *Memorable Days,* pp. 268–69.

135 Welby, *A Visit to North America,* pp. 112–13.

136 Faux, *Memorable Days,* pp. 270, 279–81.

137 Faux, *Memorable Days,* p. 270.

138 Faux, *Memorable Days,* p. 271.

138 R. Flower, *Letters from the Illinois,* pp. 22–24.

139 Faux, *Memorable Days,* p. 289.

140 Fordham, *Personal Narrative,* p. 178.

140 The letter by "J. C." appears in the preface to *Selections from Letters Written During a Tour Through the United States,* by Emanuel Howitt, pp. x–xiv. Howitt never got to the English Settlement, though this oversight did not keep him from knowing what was wrong with it. His book is a catch-all of odd bits and pieces, including a discussion of the "sufferings of emigrants" and an argument for the theory that the Indians descended from one of the ten lost tribes of Israel.

142 G. Flower, *History,* pp. 135–36.

142 G. Flower, *History,* pp. 135, 136, 137, 159–60. He also remarks that "you never see in Albion 'Mr. & Co.' It is Joel Churchill, George Harris, Matthew Smith, and so on. Every tub stands on its own bottom. Americans, so self-reliant in all other things, seem to want the support of numbers in trade. Mr. Hook would hardly venture his name alone as storekeeper in a new American town. His card would certainly be—Hook, Fish & Co. Mr. Foot would feel diffident of asking an extension of time and amount of the wholesale house. But who would think of refusing any request from that well-known house of 'Foot, Fryingpan & Fiddle'?" (*History,* pp. 329–30.)

144 R. Flower, *Letters from the Illinois,* p. 28.

144 G. Flower, *History,* pp. 160–61.

146 R. Flower, *Letters from the Illinois,* pp. 25–26.

146 G. Flower, *History,* p. 162.

146 G. Flower, *History,* pp. 183–91.

152 R. Flower, *Letters from the Illinois,* p. 18. George Flower mentions the names of some of the English donors of books, and remarks that the books rapidly got dispersed, requiring legal action to bring them back together. (*History,* 2nd ed., p. 251.) Despite its ups and downs, this was apparently the first library in Illinois, an honor that has usually gone to the one at Edwardsville. Birkbeck also possessed several hundred books. After his death these were bought by William Maclure at New Harmony.

(Flower, *History*, 2nd ed., p. 196.) These probably went, with
the rest of Maclure's books, to the Academy of Natural Sciences
of Philadelphia.

152   Birkbeck, *Notes on a Journey*, p. 171.
152   Birkbeck, *Letters from Illinois*, p. 119.
152   Blane, *An Excursion*, p. 159.
153   Blane, *An Excursion*, pp. 159–60.
153   Blane, *An Excursion*, pp. 161–62.

155   G. Flower, *History*, pp. 168–69.
156   *Quarterly Review*, XIX (April, 1818), 67–68.
157   *Quarterly Review*, XIX (April, 1818), 70.
157   *Quarterly Review*, XIX (April, 1818), 65.
158   G. Flower, *History*, pp. 320–21.
160   Hodgson, *Remarks During a Journey*, pp. 27–28.
161   C. F. Grece, *Facts and Observations*, pp. v–vii.
162   Grece, *Facts and Observations*, pp. 1–3.
163   Grece, *Facts and Observations*, pp. 4–5.
163   Grece, *Facts and Observations*, pp. 7–9.
164   Grece, *Facts and Observations*, pp. 10–11.
165   John Lorain, *Hints to Emigrants*, p. 39.
165   Lorain, *Hints to Emigrants*, pp. 114–15.
166   Lorain, *Hints to Emigrants*, pp. 13–15.
167   Welby, *A Visit to North America*, pp. 95–96.
167   H. B. Fearon, *Sketches of America*, p. 264.
168   James Hall, *Letters from the West*, p. 355.
168   Birkbeck, in R. Flower's *Letters from the Illinois*, pp. 51–52.
      Despite the hard feelings between the two families, this is one
      instance of their ability to work together—at least in the im-
      personality of cold print—against the common enemies of Albion
      and Wanborough.
169   R. Flower, *Letters from the Illinois*, p. 32.
170   Faux, *Memorable Days*, pp. 285–286.
170   William Cobbett, *A Year's Residence*, pp. 521–22, 534–36, 529.
173   Cobbett, *A Year's Residence*, pp. 548–50, 571–73, 557.
176   Birkbeck, in John Melish's *Advice to Emigrants*, pp. 62–64.
178   Melish, *Advice to Emigrants*, pp. 48–52.
180   Birkbeck, *Address to the Farmers*, pp. 5–10, 13–15.
182   Blane, *An Excursion*, pp. 162–63.
183   J. Hall, *Letters from the West*, pp. 346–48, 380–81, 348–49.

186   Thomson, *A Pioneer Family*, p. 54.
186   Ferdinand Ernst, *Bemerkungen auf einer Reise durch des Innere
      der Vereinigten Staaten. . . .* (Hildesheim, 1820). The section

dealing with Illinois was translated by E. P. Baker and printed in the *Transactions* of the Illinois State Historical Society, VIII (1904), 150–65, under the title "Travels in Illinois in 1819." All that touches specifically on the English Settlement appears on p. 150 of this translation.

186 Karl Postl (pseud. Charles Sealsfield) wrote *Die Vereinigten Staaten von Nordamerika,* translated as *The Americans as They Are* (London, 1828). He mentions that he passed through Birkbeck's land.

187 Henry Schoolcraft, *Travels in the Central Portion of the Mississippi Valley* (New York, 1825), p. 163.

187 G. Flower, *History* (2nd ed.), p. 246.

187 James Stuart, *Three Years in North America,* p. 388.

187 G. Flower, *History,* pp. 322–26.

190 Blane, *An Excursion,* pp. 153–54, 156–57.

193 Hoby, *The Baptists in America,* pp. 317–18.

193 Welby, *A Visit to North America,* pp. 98–106.

198 Blane, *An Excursion,* pp. 239–42.

200 Fordham, *Personal Narrative,* pp. 234–35.

201 Blane, *An Excursion,* pp. 186–88, 190, 189.

202 Thomson, *A Pioneer Family,* p. 55.

203 G. Flower, *History,* pp. 297–302.

206 Fordham, *Personal Narrative,* pp. 181–82.

207 Fordham, *Personal Narrative,* p. 224.

208 G. Flower, *History,* pp. 293–94.

209 Birkbeck, *Letters from Illinois,* pp. 137–40.

210 G. Flower, *History,* pp. 309–10.

212 Faux, *Memorable Days,* pp. 277–78.

212 G. Flower, *History,* pp. 138–41.

215 J. Hall, *Letters from the West,* p. 359.

215 Woods, *Two Years' Residence,* pp. 243–45.

216 Birkbeck, *Notes on a Journey,* pp. 120–22.

218 Blane, *An Excursion,* pp. 163–64, 166–70.

222 Birkbeck, *Notes on a Journey,* pp. 78–80.

223 Woods, *Two Years' Residence,* pp. 265–69.

225 Faux, *Memorable Days,* p. 275.

226 Faux, *Memorable Days,* p. 282.

226 Hulme, *Journal,* in Cobbett's *A Year's Residence,* pp. 475–76.

227 Birkbeck, "On the Prairies," in *Address to the Farmers,* p. 27.

227 Faux, *Memorable Days,* p. 283.

227 Thomson, *A Pioneer Family,* p. 64.

227 Faux, *Memorable Days,* p. 262.

227 Woods, *Two Years' Residence,* p. 181.

228 Woods, *Two Years' Residence,* pp. 192–93.

229 Woods, *Two Years' Residence*, pp. 212–13.
230 Woods, *Two Years' Residence*, pp. 213–14.
230 Woods, *Two Years' Residence*, pp. 231–33.
232 Birkbeck, *Letters from Illinois*, pp. 62–63.
232 Blane, *An Excursion*, p. 239.
233 Birkbeck, *Letters from Illinois*, p. 63.
233 Woods, *Two Years' Residence*, pp. 256–57.
234 Blane, *An Excursion*, p. 175.
234 G. Flower, *History*, p. 289.
235 Faux, *Memorable Days*, pp. 278–79.
235 R. Flower, *Letters from Lexington and the Illinois*, pp. 25–27.
236 Woods, *Two Years' Residence*, p. 296.
237 Owen, "Diary," *Indiana Historical Society Publications*, IV (1906), 80–81.
237 Donald Macdonald, "Diaries," *Indiana Historical Society Publications*, XIV (1942), 254–55.
238 Fordham, *Personal Narrative*, pp. 219–20.
239 Owen, "Diary," pp. 118–19.
240 Woods, *Two Years' Residence*, pp. 296–97.
241 Woods, *Two Years' Residence*, p. 308.
241 Birkbeck, *Letters from Illinois*, pp. 88–91.
243 G. Flower, *History*, pp. 141–42.
244 G. Flower, *History*, pp. 167–71.
245 Hoby, *Baptists in America*, pp. 308–10.
246 G. Flower, *History*, pp. 171–74.
248 Owen, "Diary," p. 86.
248 G. Flower, *History*, pp. 174–77.
250 G. Flower, *History*, p. 178.
251 G. Flower, *History*, p. 182.
251 Birkbeck, in R. Flower's *Letters from the Illinois*, p. 53.
251 G. Flower, *History* (2nd ed.), p. 23.
252 Faux, *Memorable Days*, pp. 302–3.
252 Birkbeck, "On the Prairies," in *Address to the Farmers*, pp. 22–25.

255 G. Flower, *History*, pp. 258–59. Faux says that Mrs. George Flower, "while in Virginia, kissed a beautiful black babe before the owner, a lady, who felt great disgust and indignation at the act. 'Oh, take it away!' " (*Memorable Days*, p. 276.)
256 Blane, *An Excursion*, pp. 149–52.
258 Blane, *An Excursion*, p. 170.
258 G. Flower, *History* (2nd ed.), pp. 155–56.
260 Blane, *An Excursion*, pp. 171–72.
262 G. Flower, *History* (2nd ed.), pp. 163–67.
263 G. Flower, *History* (2nd ed.), pp. 169–70.
264 G. Flower, *History* (2nd ed.), pp. 170–71.

265 G. Flower, *History* (2nd ed.), pp. 172–73.

266 G. Flower, *History* (2nd ed.), p. 188.

266 G. Flower, *History* (2nd ed.), p. 189.

267 G. Flower, *History*, pp. 260–67, 269–73.

275 Thomson, *A Pioneer Family*, p. 82.

276 W. Hall, "From England to Illinois," *Journal of the Illinois State Historical Society*, XXXIX (March, 1946), 243.

276 Thomson, *A Pioneer Family*, pp. 102–4.

278 W. Hall, "From England to Illinois," pp. 208–9.

278 G. Flower, *History* (2nd ed.), pp. 120–21.

279 G. Flower, *History*, pp. 277–78. Faux relates that Birkbeck said that the rowdies "had threatened him with assassination; but showing and convincing them that he would shoot them if they attempted to enter his house without permission, they had abandoned their design." (*Memorable Days*, p. 284.)

279 Thomson, *A Pioneer Family*, pp. 106–7.

280 S. A. Ferrall, *A Ramble of Six Thousand Miles*, pp. 109–11.

281 G. Flower, *History*, pp. 287–88.

283 Faux, *Memorable Days*, pp. 264–67.

286 Owen, "Diary," pp. 80–85.

290 Macdonald, "Diaries," pp. 256–57.

291 Owen, "Diary," pp. 88–89.

291 Owen, "Diary," pp. 89–90, 91.

293 Owen, "Diary," p. 120.

293 G. Flower, *History* (2nd ed.), p. 217.

293 G. Flower, *History* (2nd ed.), p. 218.

293 W. Hall, "From England to Illinois," p. 244.

294 Stuart, *Three Years in North America*, pp. 380–81, 383, 385–86.

297 Fordham, *Personal Narrative*, p. 225.

297 G. Flower, *History* (2nd ed.), pp. 260–62.

298 G. Flower, *History*, pp. 115–18.

300 G. Flower, *History*, p. 278.

300 G. Flower, *History*, p. 181.

301 G. Flower, *History*, pp. 273–74.

302 G. Flower, *History*, pp. 274–75.

302 G. Flower, *History*, pp. 275–76.

303 G. Flower, *History*, pp. 356–57.